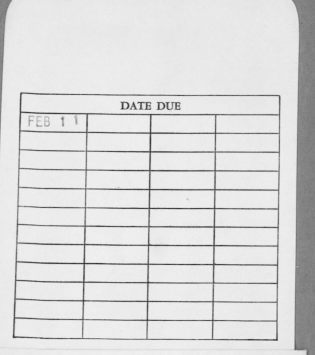

PSYCHOLOGY

for

CONTEMPORARY LIVING

PSYCHOLOGY

for

CONTEMPORARY LIVING

Dr. Charlotte Buhler

Translated from the German by Hella Freud Bernays

Hawthorn Books, Inc. · Publishers · New York

To

my children

Ingeborg and Alf-Jörgen Åas
Rolf and Mary Buhler

and

my grandchildren

Audün and Erlend
Ingrid, Craig, Brooke, and Alice

PSYCHOLOGY FOR CONTEMPORARY LIVING

First American Edition: 1968

Design: Gene Gordon

CONTENTS

PART I: THE INDIVIDUAL

   Life is primarily active. The newborn infant is already an
individual. From the beginning of life there is a mingling of
inherited and acquired characteristics. Determining heredity in
retrospect is easier than predicting. The crucial importance of
environment for personality development. Basic facts of growth
and aging. Basic facts about biological maturation. Maturation,
experience, and development. Maturation in later life. The influence of sexuality. Time as a factor in development. Everything that happens is psychophysical. Health and illness.

   What is motivation? Healthy and sick motivation. New
theories about basic motivations. Existentialism. Humanistic
psychology. Basic tendencies and life goals. Freud's theory of
motivation. A psychosomatic case. Various views concerning the
causes of mental illness. Definition of neurosis and of mental
disposition. The new ego psychology.

PART II: SOCIETY

PART III: PRACTICE

FOREWORD

The purpose of *Psychology for Contemporary Living* is to point out how much understanding and help readers can gain by applying modern psychology to their personal lives.

Parents and teachers in many different cultures are struggling to reach a better understanding of the younger generation and to find more adequate methods of handling them. Currently there is widespread dissatisfaction with traditional methods of child rearing and with educational procedures, and there is much experimentation with new ideas and techniques. In all of these the psychology of development, of motivation, and of cultural impacts plays a major role, and people are eager for more information about such matters.

From day to day we see distinctly that everyone is concerned with reaching a deeper understanding of himself and of questions of human existence. At no previous time have the meaning and value of human life been so deeply questioned by so many.

In response to these inquiries, I have discussed in the book such theorems as psychoanalysis, the psychology of self-realization, existentialism, and logotherapy, and I have also suggested a philosophy of life. My purpose is to help people find their way through some of the modern hypotheses about human life.

I feel that we live in a time of enormous cultural change and of an unprecedented intermingling of people from different cultural backgrounds. For this reason it has seemed advisable to present some comparative data of different approaches to social life and of different social structures and cultural patterns.

Nevertheless, the book is less an academic exposition than it is a pursuit of educational, clinical, and humanistic objectives. In presenting these, I have tried to assemble all important viewpoints, concepts, and data.

The book was originally written in German; its original version has been translated into Dutch, Swedish, Finnish, Italian, Spanish, Portuguese, and Hebrew. The American edition represents a somewhat modified version of the book. In view of the different interests of American readers, some of the European data were replaced by American research findings, and some chapters have been omitted or reduced to the most essential and succinct information.

Not trusting my own information and judgment alone, I have asked for critical comments as well as some original contributions from colleagues. Contributions of material were made by the following: Althea Horner, clinical psychologist, private practice, Arcadia, Calif., on personalistic psychology; George Bach, clinical psychologist, private practice, Institute of Group Psychotherapy, Beverly Hills, Calif., on details of Kurt Lewin's personality theory; Ruth Leeds, graduate student, Department of Sociology, Columbia University, New York, N.Y., for the chapter "The Individual and Society"; William L. Kimball, graduate student, Department of Anthropology, University of California at Los Angeles, for the chapter "Cultures"; Rogers H. Wright, clinical psychologist, private practice, Long Beach, Calif., a diagnostic case; Franz Alexander, Director, Department of Psychiatry, and Director, Psychiatric and Psychosomatic Research Institute, Mount Sinai Hospital, Los Angeles, additional remarks on one of his cases; Hedda Bolgar, Chief Clinical Psychologist and Director of the Clinical Psychology Training Program, Mount Sinai Hospital, Los Angeles, a psychotherapy case; Zelda Wolpe, clinical psychologist, private practice, Brentwood, Calif., a psychodrama case with children.

Critical comments on various chapters were obtained from Gordon Allport of Harvard University; Wilhelm Arnold, University of Würzberg; George Bach, Institute of Group Psychotherapy, Beverly Hills; Ludwig von Bertalanffy, University of Alberta, Edmonton, Alberta, Canada; Hedda Bolgar, Mount Sinai Hospital, Los Angeles; Frederick Hacker, Hacker's Psychiatric Clinic, Beverly Hills; Robert Heiss, University of Freiburg; Hildegard Hetzer, University of Giessen; Fay and Maurice Karpf, private practice, Beverly Hills; Paul Lazarsfeld, Columbia University; Ruth Leeds, Columbia University; Welty Lefever, University of Southern California at Los Angeles; Harvey Locke, University of Southern California at Los Angeles; Arthur Maier, Handelshochschule, Mannheim; Lotte Danzinger-Schenk, University of Innsbruck, Austria; John Seward, University of California at Los Angeles; Councill Taylor, University of California at Los Angeles; Hans Thomae, University of Bonn; Margaret Thomes, University of California at Los Angeles; Robert Williamson, Haverford College, Haverford, Pa.; Pauline Young, Modesto, Calif.

Biographies and photographs were contributed by Dr. Anna Sethne Holter, Bodö, Norway, and by Mrs. Larri Welty, Los Angeles, Calif.

General advice and comments were given by Dr. Felix Guggenheim, Dr. and Mrs. Robert Jungk, and Dr. Ilse Pichottka.

As always, my husband, Karl Bühler, supported me with his understanding and advice.

CHARLOTTE BUHLER

PREFACE

We Need Psychology Today

Throughout history, peoples and cultures come and go. Looking back, we can see how mankind, ever changing and developing, has step by step taken possession of the earth. Today man has even pressed forward into outer space.

This process of man's increasing mastery over the world is imposing. But in man's mastery of himself, there has been no corresponding progress. In spite of the achievements of civilization, improvement in our customs and ways of life, and increasing knowledge in science and technology, industry, trade, and communications, we are, to a great extent, the same human beings we used to be. Man continues to be pursued by his anxieties, driven by his passions and desires, plagued by his fears, torn by his conflicts, and bowed down by worry and a sense of guilt. We still destroy one another by war and by crimes. We are still unable to guide our destinies constructively or to build through thoughtful planning and cooperative effort. And we are still without an answer to the eternal question: What is the meaning of human existence?

From time immemorial, man has tried to create spiritual and mental tools for himself. He has turned to superstition, religion, philosophy, and science in his attempt to understand God and himself and to find his way about in his external world and in his innermost being. He wants to lead a good and meaningful life.

Time and again this hope has been shattered. Many of us lived through the bitterest and most recent of these disappointments—World War II and the partial breakdown of Western culture. Today, we stand aghast at the overwhelming upheavals that are afflicting masses of people all over the globe.

What can we do? What ought we to do?

Apparently, we are in no position to do anything. The only meaningful thing we can do is attain better understanding of what is going on in the world. We must try to acquire a point of view and guidelines for our behavior—in other words, we must have a philosophy of life.

First, we must understand what is happening. Newspapers, periodicals, books, radio, and television provide us with what we need to know of politics, history, economics, and culture in general. But to understand what goes on inside us—our inner processes—there is today only one meaningful, reliable, and serviceable method, and that is psychology. We must turn to psychology as the only reliable basis for self-knowledge and self-direction.

This book aims at opening up a pathway to psychological understanding and self-understanding. It seeks to provide a comprehensive picture of the scope of modern psychology. If it provides the reader with knowledge and insights leading to a better understanding and mastery of life and the world, its purpose will have been served.

What Psychology Is and What It Includes

Psychology is the science of the mind; it deals with mental, or psychic, life.

We are all familiar with this mental or psychic life, which is directly accessible to us. We experience it in the steady flow of our feelings, thoughts, memories, hopes, and perceptions.

On a deeper level—and one of greater consequence to us—we experience more disturbing things, such as problems, conflicts, hidden wishes, feelings of anxiety, guilt, and grief.

And when we look still deeper, we are confronted by life's riddles that block our eternal search for the meaning of existence.

All this and more is included in our mental or psychic life, the depths of which poets and thinkers throughout the ages have sought to fathom.

Modern scientific psychology first confined itself to a search for the inner processes accessible to us through direct observation. Today, these are known as mental or psychic functions. Soon, however, psychology began to expand in many other directions, until it embraced all phases of life on which man has influence and which have an effect on man's innermost being.

Thus we have functional psychology, experimental psychology, developmental psychology, the psychology of personality, social psychology, industrial psychology, educational psychology, geriatric psychology, and military psychology.

At the same time, psychology also expanded in depth. From confrontations and cooperation with modern psychiatry and philosophy, there developed clinical psychology, and existential and humanistic psychology.

Here some explanation may be in order. Psychiatry is a medical discipline that originally concerned itself primarily with disturbances in mental life. More recently, psychiatry has developed an increasing interest in the comparisons between healthy and unhealthy mental life. This applies to modern research regarding "types," and, to a still greater degree, to modern research in depth psychology.

Both branches of research were further pursued by psychologists who studied normal development and personality. Today the medically trained, psychologically oriented *psychiatrist* and the *clinical psychologist,* trained in the study of healthy as well as unhealthy mental life, work hand in hand on diagnosis, counseling, and treatment of human problems. Both disciplines use the methods and points of view of depth psychology.

Finally, existentialism, as will be explained in more detail later, is a modern philosophy that examines the problems of human existence. Today these problems are also included in the field of psychology and have become the special concern of the clinical psychologist.

The expansion of psychology in breadth and depth gives us reason to hope that this science, like no other before it, can help us understand ourselves and our problems. Hopefully, it will point the way to meaningful and satisfying conduct.

This book is divided into three sections: the first deals with the psychology of the individual; the second, with the psychology of social relationships and groups; the third, with the practical applications of psychology. The importance of psychology for an understanding of community life and practical life is now considered as important as the problems of the individual, which in earlier days commanded the total attention of psychologists.

Even in its dealings with the individual, psychology has undergone a complete change. Today the psychological interpretation of human life, human development, and mental health or disease is in the forefront. The formerly predominant teachings on mental or psychic functions and activities as a set of problems to be considered in isolation have been relegated to the background.

This change does not mean, however, that the earlier period in the history of psychology has turned out to be proved unnecessary or even mistaken. Quite the contrary. Without the tremendous amassing of factual information that we owe to functional psychology, there would be no possibility of expanding our present research as we are now doing. Functional psychology remains basic to the structure of modern psychology. For if we did not understand the functioning of our sense organs, our perceptive apparatus, our thought processes, our motor systems, and our emotional life, we could make no assertions about man as a functioning, developing creature capable of mastering his environment.

Functional psychology has also been influenced by developments in other fields. Our understanding of human behavior, particularly of motivation and group interaction, has had a significant effect on modern functional psychology. Much of the new understanding derives from the tremendous advances in anthropology and from the experimental study of group processes. It also owes much to an emphasis on the practical role of psychology, especially in teaching. In research on perception, for example, entirely new facts came to light when the effect of motivation—that is, the goal that these perceptions serve—was taken into consideration.

What is still undeveloped territory is the utilization of psychological knowledge and insights in formulating a philosophy of life. But applied psychology today extends to almost all phases of private and public life.

PART I

THE INDIVIDUAL

CHAPTER I

THE BIOLOGICAL ROOTS
OF PSYCHOLOGY

Life Is Primarily Active

The most important thing that can be said about life is that, even from its very earliest existence as an embryo, it is *active.* We call this stage *primary activity,* for with it begins the movement that signifies life even before any stimulation has had its effect. Although for nine months it is a part of the mother's womb—surrounded by it and connected to it by the umbilical cord—and although it is still incapable of breathing independently or of nourishing itself, the tiny new individual already has a life of its own. This is felt by the mother after a few months: "I can feel it moving," she says happily of her five-month-old fetus.

The Newborn Infant Is Already an Individual

From the very beginning, this tiny new organism is subject to what is later to be one of the principal laws of the life process: namely, that on the one hand life follows certain general rules. On the other hand each organism is always an individual.

All newborn babies, for example, are active. Yet different *degrees of activity* can immediately be noted, and it has been observed that these characteristics are inborn and not subject to change. Hand in hand with these degrees of activity goes an inborn tempo. Five of these tempos, from the slowest to the fastest, have been distinguished.

However, this does not necessarily mean that all children who drive their mothers to distraction by their slowness in dressing themselves or eating have a low degree of activity. Most of these little dawdlers are just rebellious or bored. Careful professional study is required to determine a child's actual tempo.

One hears repeatedly that all newborn infants look alike. And, as a matter of fact, maternity wards use name bracelets to prevent mix-ups. Yet, despite such superficial resemblance and the similarity of behavior— the first cry, the first reactions to food, light, and sound, to temperature and pressure—each newborn baby makes an individual response to his environment. And if one observes carefully, one often discerns individually distinct facial expressions.

From the Beginning of Life There Is a Mingling of the Inherited and the Acquired

The question to what extent an individual's development is determined by what he has inherited and to what extent by environmental influences has persistently engaged man's thinking. Radical and extreme views concerning the role of heredity have brought dire results within the recent past. Today, scientific findings exclude every extreme point of view about the roles of heredity and environment.

Recent findings from educational experiments and the overwhelmingly favorable results of adoption demonstrate the benefits of a favorable environment.

In view of its great significance and the widespread interest in the role of heredity, it will be given a detailed treatment later. Here we shall merely take up briefly some of the latest scientific findings.

Two recent findings are especially important in this connection. First, there are the results of research on the behavior of the genes, those tiny, ultramicroscopic structures that are the transmitters of heredity. From the very beginning of the science of heredity in 1900 (when Gregor Mendel's famous experiments in the years 1854 to 1866 were rediscovered), genes were held to be immutable and incapable of being influenced. It now turns out—and this is without doubt one of the most sensational findings of modern biochemistry—that in the very earliest stages of development, genes are capable of being influenced in their functioning.

Equally startling is a second finding: biochemical and neurological discoveries prove that from the first instant of life, that is, *immediately after the egg has been fertilized,* environmental influences begin to affect the embryo.

By "affect" we do not mean that this tiny new being is formed only by the environment, as certain sociologists of extreme views would have it, but that from the moment of fertilization an "inborn structure" takes shape, brought about by the complicated mosaics of the genes. This activity, however, immediately calls for a countereffect from the *environment* in which it finds itself. This countereffect in turn immediately influences the inborn genetic structure. In other words, from the beginning there is what we shall call an *interaction*. In this continuous interaction between heredity and environment, the baby grows, first inside the mother, then in the world outside the mother.

These new findings make each of us give thought to our own development. They are of the greatest importance for all parents and for those who hope to become parents.

Determining Heredity in Retrospect Is Easier Than Predicting It

These new findings are not to be interpreted as meaning that there is no such thing as heredity. Of course, heredity exists, but the variability of inherited traits is much greater than was formerly assumed. The number of traits that can be determined absolutely as hereditary is limited. Consequently, the predictability of an individual's development is limited.

It is often more possible to determine that a quality, talent, or illness *was* inherited than to predict that it *will be* inherited, for in the commingling of genes the combinations of hereditary tendencies cannot be predicted nor can the change brought about by environmental influences be predicted.

Parents, therefore, are sometimes disappointed that none of their children has musical talent. If they have several children, they might expect this talent to show up in at least one or two of them. But it cannot be predicted. For example, Kirsten Flagstad, the opera singer, comes from a family in which two generations had already possessed absolute pitch and musical talent. On the other hand, Arturo Toscanini, the famous conductor, was the only musically gifted member of his entire family.

Of interest also is the Fishberg family. Isaac Fishberg was a professional musician in New York until he was ninety years old. At the age of 102 he still played the flute so well that he could participate in chamber-music concerts with his sons, who were also musicians. All of his twelve children, half of his thirty-seven grandchildren, and many of his sixty great-grandchildren are highly talented and, in part, professional musicians —a parallel to the well-known genealogical table of the forebears and descendants of Johann Sebastian Bach.

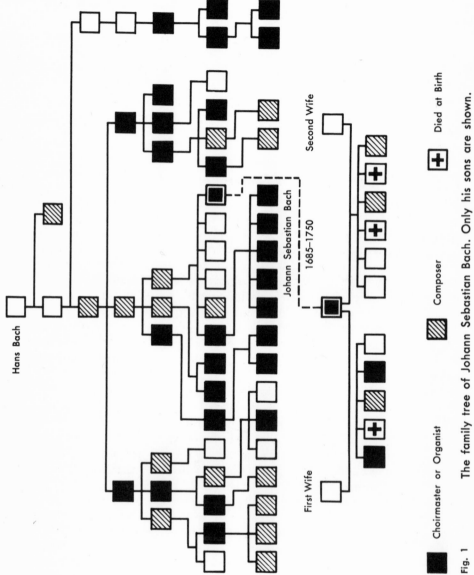

Hans Bach

Johann Sebastian Bach
1685–1750

First Wife

Second Wife

Choirmaster or Organist

Composer

Died at Birth

Fig. 1   The family tree of Johann Sebastian Bach. Only his sons are shown.

Conversely, the nine members of the Engel family, under the leadership of the father, a music teacher, have learned to play fifty musical instruments and the family orchestra presents a wide repertory before international audiences—and there is no record of any outstanding musical talent that might have been inherited.

If one were to try to set up general rules as to the traits that are more or less frequently inherited, the result would be something like this:

Certain *physical traits* appear to be the most readily inherited. Examples are a tendency toward longevity or short-livedness, toward greater or lesser speed of growth, and toward a certain physical type. Probably also inherited is the tendency to beget twins or triplets, or a disposition to certain organic weaknesses, defects, or diseases, particularly mental illnesses that have a physical basis. Speed of reactions, physical and technical skill, peculiarities of movements, degree of activity, keenness of mind, sensitivity, intelligence, and specific talents may also be considered hereditary.

The Crucial Importance of Environment for Personality Development

It is important to establish that, from the very beginning, environment has as much influence on the personality as heredity.

"From the very beginning" includes even the pregnancy period. As the result of a number of experiments, we know today that from the very instant of conception the growth, health, and entire physical-mental make-up of the embryo is vastly influenced by the conditions existing during pregnancy. An accident to the mother, an infectious disease, or a long-lasting serious mental disturbance or depression can have an adverse physical or mental influence on the child. For every mother-to-be, therefore, a careful regimen is essential. Much of the fate of the developing human being depends on her health. Of even greater importance is the mother's total behavior during the first years of a child's life.

The newborn infant brings with it into the world a certain degree of activity and passivity, sensitivity to stimuli, as well as other characteristics. Yet from the start, a mother who is loving and sensitive can exert a favorable influence by working in the right way against certain weaknesses. Let us take as an example a baby that is not very active, one that behaves passively when it is a suckling and does not exert itself to get its food. From the very first hour of this infant's life the patience and understanding of the mother or nurse determine whether it will get enough nourishment and whether it can even be made to suck more energetically.

In this way, many an inadequate development can be guided into proper channels, and tendencies unfavorable for development can be lessened or even made ineffective. But when the mother's behavior is wrong, quite the opposite can come about and unfavorable tendencies are strengthened.

The environmental influences become more and more important as the organism grows. To understand this fully, we must become thoroughly familiar with the basic facts of growth and maturation.

Basic Facts of Growth and Aging

Growth and biological maturation are among the most important basic facts of life. Whether plant, animal, or man, living organisms grow and develop. Obvious as these processes appear to be, they are, in certain respects, among the most difficult to understand scientifically. The forces and tendencies that play a part in these processes have given rise to a number of diverse assumptions and theories.

Growth consists of a continuous increase in the *size* and *weight* of a child. This increase takes place differently in different individuals—more or less regularly, more or less speedily. Normally, it stops at about the age of twenty years. With rare exceptions, twenty-five is the latest age up to which a person continues to grow.

Every mother knows that a steady increase in the weight of her baby is of the utmost importance to the child's healthy development. In civilized countries many mothers weigh their babies after every meal for the first year. Losses in weight, which sometimes occur as the result of illness or the wrong diet, are taken seriously by the conscientious mother and the pediatrician. For, in the first year, a proper gain in weight is one of the basic requirements for normal development.

Many parents believe that as the child grows older the matter of a gain in weight need not be given the same attention it received during the first year. But they should remember that modern medicine has established a close connection between body weight and mental health. In childhood, as well as in later life, significant overweight or underweight is often an indication not only of physical ill health, but of mental disturbance.

Less indicative is increase in height, which often varies with the family. Some parents worry because their son is too short, or their daughter too tall. Generally, however, such characteristics have no symptomatic importance.

There is an enormous variation in growth and general development. The schematic diagram of six adolescent boys provides a striking picture of the differences encountered between the ages of thirteen and fifteen.

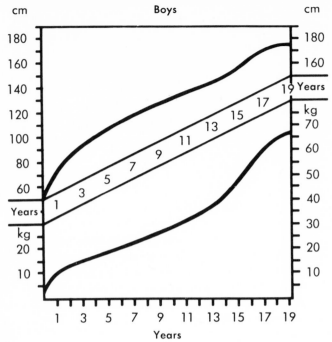

Boys

Fig. 2

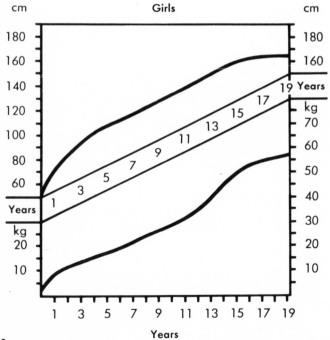

Girls

Fig. 3

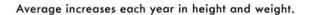

Average increases each year in height and weight.

Although the small stature and late development of two boys in the picture are not symptoms of illness or abnormality, the adolescent can suffer because of his apparently retarded appearance.

Soon after puberty, growth in height ends—but this does not mean the end of growth in general. On the contrary, there are growth processes throughout the life of the organism. The most important of these is cell renewal. Even so, we speak of growth in the narrow sense as that period in which the building up of the body exceeds the body's decline. Growth is considered to be stationary in the middle period of life, when both processes—the building up and the decline—are in equilibrium.

Accordingly, one can speak of a life curve, which rises to the age of twenty-three, remains on a plateau to around fifty, then declines.

Today, however, with improved hygiene and medical knowledge, not only has the life span been lengthened, but the decline has been delayed.

No one knows precisely how *aging* actually comes about. One of the most widely held theories is that every organism becomes exhausted from *stresses* to which it is increasingly less capable of adapting. This process is called an exhaustion of *adaptive energy*.

Nor is it definitely known how the functioning of the sex glands affects aging. Recent studies show that degenerative bone changes in women, called osteoporosis, which usually occur after the menopause, can be pre-

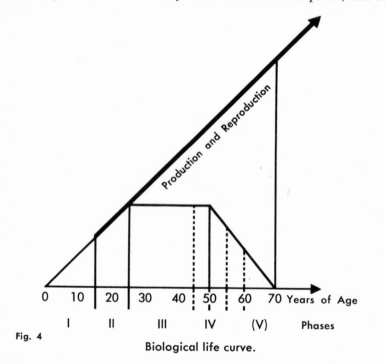

Fig. 4

Biological life curve.

vented by the oral intake of female sex hormones. We do know that the *reproductive* capacity of the human organism begins with sexual maturity, which comes between the ages of eleven and sixteen. For females it ends at menopause, between the ages of forty-five and fifty-five; for males, usually at a later age, but one that varies considerably.

In this century the *average life span* has been enormously increased. In 1900 it was only about fifty years; it has now moved closer to seventy years. With increasing age, apart from the exhaustion of the organism, diseases play an increasing role as *causes of death*. Heart and circulatory diseases and cancer are the most frequent causes of premature death.

Premature death in other age groups has, for the most part, other causes. There are many causes for infant deaths. In other age categories *accidents* play a major role. This is so for all age groups, but especially for people under twenty-four and over sixty-five.

One thing is clear: health and illness, as well as life expectancy, greatly affect our attitude toward life.

Basic Facts about Biological Maturation

Much more difficult to survey than the facts of growth are those of biological maturation, which, because of their great significance for life, deserve careful attention.

By *maturation* is meant certain changes that occur throughout our lives in our bodily structures and functions and in our behavior. These changes represent a *one-way succession*—or *sequence,* to use the technical term. In true maturation, the succession of phases is not reversible. Each phase can come about only after the achievement of the preceding one.

For example, among the most important of these phases is maturation of *bodily movements,* such as grasping. If you touch the palm of a newborn infant with your finger, the tiny hand will close around your finger. This is what is called the *grasping reflex*, and it is one of the countless bodily reflexes that are inborn in human beings.

Besides reflexes, the newborn infant gives us the opportunity to recognize many nonstructured and aimless movements. These are termed *mass movements*—unspecific reactions to all sorts of internal and external stimuli. Among these mass movements there are arm movements, but they are undirected; they have no goal.

Only from the age of about three months does the baby stretch out his arms toward an object he sees at a distance; at about four months he grasps an object held close to him; and at about five months he will stretch out his arm in the direction of the object at some distance and pull it toward him.

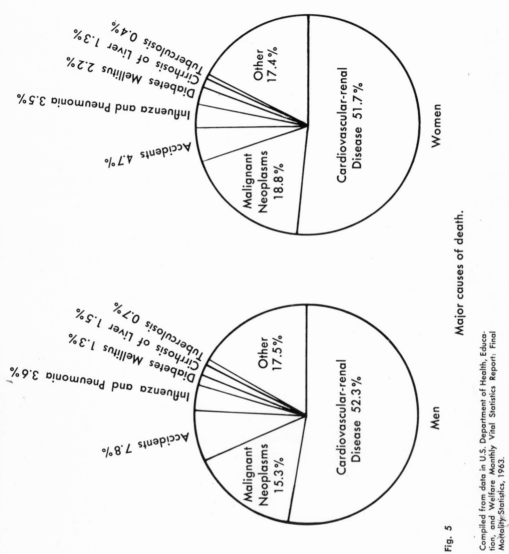

Fig. 5   Major causes of death.

Compiled from data in U.S. Department of Health, Education, and Welfare Monthly Vital Statistics Report: Final Mortality Statistics, 1963.

The sequence of these accomplishments depends on maturation, because each new working-together of different organs, with their increasingly complicated activity, presupposes the development of simpler accomplishments. The increasing *coordination* and *complexity* of the activities testify to the progress in maturation.

There are great and individual differences in the ages at which these progressive steps in grasping can be expected. But the sequence as such is not subject to change. It is determined by the possibilities for development. These are, as it were, firmly built into the organism. This is why we can speak of *laws of structure,* or *structural laws.*

The actual appearance of each new accomplishment in turn, however, presupposes appropriate environmental influences with respect to time and to individual *uniqueness* and *normality.* Here we are referring to functioning. Therefore, it can be said that in functioning we see evidence of the various conditions of life as well as the structural conditions. For example, if an infant were kept in an absolutely empty room and never given a single object to look at, to touch, or to grasp as a "stimulus," then, though its organism would mature (law of structure), its ability to coordinate (its functioning) would be adversely affected.

Maturation, Experience, and Development

In mountain villages of Albania infants are often tied into a narrow wooden cradle standing in a dark corner of a mud hut. Because of swaddlings around their entire body, the babies are kept from any free movements whatsoever throughout their first year of life. Only when a child is being bathed or occasionally shown to a visitor is it taken out of its corner or its crib.

How does such an infant behave when freed from its swaddling clothes, brought into the light, and offered a toy? At first the baby is totally inactive. It has to be touched and encouraged to reach for the toy. A five-month-old touches an object or reaches out for it in the way a normal three-month-old would. At seven months the grasping movement is still poorly coordinated; at ten months the child does reach out both hands for a rattle, but is unable to grasp it. Later, a continued paralysis of activity and defective technical skill results in all these children.

Anyone who wants to understand his own development, and particularly parents who want to bring up their children successfully, can draw from these observations the fundamental conclusion that development depends on the opportunities for development provided in earliest childhood.

Today, science has a superabundance of findings that allow us to recog-

Fig. 6A   Fig. 6B

16 weeks

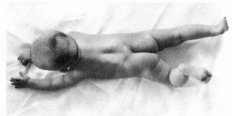 

Fig. 7A   Fig. 7B

28 weeks

 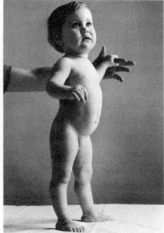

Fig. 8A   Fig. 8B

40 weeks

Four stages of development during the first year of life (from Gesell, *The First Five Years of Life*, 1940).

Fig. 9

52 weeks

nize this rule in greater detail. Important, for example, is the fact that accomplishment in certain fields depends on the stimuli provided.

One example relatively independent of given circumstances is the development of walking. All human infants walk at the age of about one to one and a half years at the latest if there are no organic or mental impediments. The children of Hopi Indians, who swaddle their children in wooden cradles as the Albanians do, begin to walk at the same time as Indian children who have been brought up differently or as the children of other races and groups.

Other behavior, however—the mastery of material, the knowledge of the world of objects, an understanding of people, and the development of the inner world—require appropriate stimuli. That is, in order to develop adequately and normally, children must have support through teaching, guidance, and loving contact.

In other words, the developmental progress of human beings, more than that of other living creatures, is almost never a result of maturation alone, but also of *experience*. For this reason, a distinction is made between *maturation* and *development*.

Developmental progress is partly maturation, which the organism contributes. But for full developmental progress there must also be the effect of the environment, which transforms the maturation into experience.

Maturation in Later Life—the Influence of Sexuality

One of the most important influences on maturation and development all through life is *sexuality*.

By "sexuality" we mean both the human being's inborn capacity to reproduce and the behavior and needs that serve sexual relations. These belong to a specific group of inborn ways of behavior called *instincts*.

Instinct designates the reactions that regularly follow upon relatively unchanging stimuli in such a way that they cause a chain reaction. In the case of human beings, however, one cannot speak of instincts in the strict sense in which the expression is used with respect to animal behavior. For, in the case of man, the instincts do not function as identifiable units. There exist only rudimentary remnants of inborn ways of reacting.

One has to be on one's guard with words like "instinct." The layman has a way of using the word "instinctive" lightly, just as he is also likely to talk of "intuitive." These simple words, however, cover very complicated processes.

The sucking of the newborn infant, for example, is a purely instinctive form of behavior, consisting of a chain of reflexes: opening the mouth, movements of the tongue, swallowing. The reaction may be apparent in an embryo of three months; in the newborn it appears in response to all sorts of stimuli, as if the little creature did not want to neglect any opportunity for taking in nourishment.

The reflexes and the inborn ways of behavior assigned to the complicated human sexual apparatus are subject to extremely varied changes and disturbances. Nevertheless, we can speak of a maturation in the development of sexuality insofar as a succession of phases is concerned. These phases are: the time before the capacity to reproduce; puberty, or maturation of the capacity to reproduce; mature reproductive ability; the climacteric, or period of loss of the capacity to reproduce; the period after the loss of the capacity to reproduce.

One might assume that the development of *sexual drive* would parallel the building up and the decline of the reproductive capacity. Because, however, the sexual needs of humans appear vastly separated from the activity of the reproductive system, there is no natural rhythm and no specific expectation with respect to the appearance of these complicated needs.

In the sexual drive there is also, to be sure, a sequence of behavior traits, but the way they manifest themselves in time and character depends on diverse influences. In other words, in the human sexual drive, psychological factors play a greater role than biological ones.

Time as a Factor in Development

As animal experiments have shown, the factor of *time* is of enormous importance in maturation. This means that certain stimuli or other influences from the outside world have to be offered at a very definite *point in time* to make possible an advance that can come about only at that particular time.

For example, newly hatched chicks kept in a dark place remain throughout their entire lives less skillful in pecking than barnyard chicks, because this behavior has to be learned in the early days of life.

Konrad Lorenz's experiments with wild geese showed that behavior up to a certain point in time acquires a definitive "imprint," to use the technical term. Young geese "adopt" as a parent the first living creature they see. They follow it, and beg food from it. Normally, this creature is itself a wild goose; but if—as in the experiments—it should be a human being, the young geese are still stamped with it, that is, attached to it.

Of great importance for conclusions with respect to humans is an experiment in which young mice were repeatedly put into a cage where there was a particularly strong mouse that had been trained for fighting. This mouse would attack the others and promptly defeat them. The younger the mice were when they suffered defeat in this way, the more hesitant and fearful they were when they became adult. Older mice, however, who had had combat experiences early in life, were not intimidated to the same degree.

The author can report similar facts from her own psychotherapeutic experience. Repeatedly, extreme aggression or a fearsome withdrawal in combat situations could be traced to very early "training." Thus, for example, one patient had a mother who encouraged him, even as a two-year-old, to hit out when another child got in his way. Another patient had been influenced by a mother who carried her pacifism to the extent that she forbade her four-year-old ever to let himself get involved in a fight; she dinned into him that he was to run off as soon as anyone attacked him.

Aggression and fear, of course, have roots other than these, but it is important to be aware of the significant role of early admonitions and prohibitions.

Many a reader may find this notion alarming and will ask himself how he is supposed to know just what influences are the right ones for his children and in what sequence they should be brought to bear. Still other readers may react with skepticism.

From the practical point of view, this is how matters stand: in influencing a child, the parents are dealing with things that are known, or which become known, through usage or tradition or from contact with the environment. Here is an example.

"My mother was against pacifiers," Mrs. Smith says to her neighbor. "She often told me not to let my children have a pacifier, because that's nothing but a bad habit."

"Yes," Mrs. Miller replies, "but my doctor tells me that today there's quite a different opinion about it. He says that children who don't have enough opportunity to suck will later tend to suck their thumbs much more or much longer, or, if they are kept from sucking their thumbs, they feel this as a deprivation, and it has unfavorable results."

"Well, if it does have such unfavorable results, that should have been evident in *my* case," said Mrs. Smith.

To which Mrs. Miller answers, "Well, you do say very often that you're nervous. Perhaps that has something to do with it."

But Mrs. Smith has the last word: "Oh, I don't believe that. Those are just modern theories."

Naturally, the question of Mrs. Smith's nervousness isn't so simple. But it is possible that the prohibition against pacifiers may have been one of the early *frustrations,* or deprivations, that led to the experience of being disappointed.

It may be that Mrs. Smith continues to be unimpressed by Mrs. Miller's remarks. The new idea she has just heard, however, may cause her to stop and think, and perhaps she will ask her doctor or other young mothers, and in this way will learn something about the importance of the environment for the early sucking activity of her baby.

It is good to be able to report that in the Western world public health has developed so far that, through teaching in the schools, books and magazines, doctors, nurses, social workers, and, last but not least, neighbors and acquaintances, a mother can be informed about all the important influences that can affect her child for good or ill.

Most important of all, from the first moment of being, are certain *psychic* influences, mother love above all, and the proper admonitions and encouragements that correspond to the particular age of the child. But in later life as well we experience time and again the need for certain things at a certain time, or else it will be "too late." "Too late" for what? For the emergence of certain progress in inner development.

Love, marriage, the begetting of children, and success in one's work thus belong to those fundamental experiences that at certain points in time appear to be more necessary than anything else. Most of them are psychical in nature. Sexuality is an important exception.

To be sure, the sexual needs of human beings, as has already been said, are conditioned in their development by many circumstances, but timely influences contribute essentially to their healthy unfolding. This applies particularly to development in puberty, which can be hastened, delayed, or guided by environmental influences into channels that are healthy or unhealthy.

It cannot be overemphasized that for healthy development the *experiences of the first years are of the utmost importance.*

Sigmund Freud was the first to state this fact, in the framework of his psychoanalytical researches. It became the focus of stormy discussions about Freud's theories. It was rejected by many as an exaggeration but accepted trustingly by others.

Today we are in a position to substitute facts for belief or disbelief in this field. Such knowledge rests on recent biological experiments with animals. On the basis of a comprehensive survey of the entire literature in this field the conclusions are inescapable that, first, habits acquired early are particularly long-lasting, and second, the adult throughout his life remains influenced by what he saw and learned as a child. Findings based on more than a hundred carefully controlled experiments are worth a great deal more than a personal opinion based on emotion.

Everything That Happens Is Psychophysical

The expression "psychophysical" is used for those happenings that are at once psychical and physical.

In many actions it is perfectly clear that both body and mind are involved. For example, when a person glances at an object, his eyes, his optic nerve, and his brain, on the one hand, and his attention and capacity to perceive, on the other hand, are involved in the action.

In other occurrences this is not so easy to recognize. If it appears strange that even automatic processes such as breathing or digestion always have a psychological aspect as well, only think of ancient folk sayings that something "touches the heart," "takes one's breath away," or "makes me sick at my stomach." So-called *psychosomatic* research (*soma* is Greek for "body") has proved these and many other connections. By doing so it has shown the significance of a person's entire psychic state for all his bodily processes.

Today we know that even in those diseases in which no one formerly even thought of psychic influences—for example, peptic ulcers, gout, and rheumatism—the mental or psychic state plays a role. Perhaps the cause may be a continuous inner tension, worry, or anxiety, or a hostile attitude and feelings of hate.

How can such psychophysical connections be explained from the biological point of view? There are, in the main, two theories that attempt to explain the psychophysical occurrence. One of them credits *interaction* between psychophysical processes, and the other sees the psychophysical happening as a *total happening*. Among those who hold to the interaction theory, many believe that the psychical factor takes precedence; others ascribe the leading role to the organic factor.

Seen from the clinical point of view, sometimes the one and sometimes the other appears to be the case. Thus, for example, a sick person is more likely to feel low in spirits than someone in perfect health. On the other hand, someone who is depressed because he leads a life without love can feel worn out and tend to suffer from headaches when there is no physical basis for such complaints.

These complicated connections are often confusing for the layman, and can be difficult for even a professional to understand. The one fact to be kept in mind is that everything which happens inside us has a psychic and a physical side.

Health and Illness

There is a direct application of this principle—the double-sidedness of our being—that we must be aware of when we consider health and illness.

Not so long ago, *health* and *illness* stood for very clear and simple concepts. Illness was supposed to be an obviously physical ailment. Occasionally someone even today will say, "The doctor says my husband is perfectly well. His illness is just imagination." To be sure, it has become more and more rare to hear something like this, because modern physicians now know that illnesses may be psychological without being purely imaginary.

The fact of the possible double nature of an illness makes the diagnosis and treatment a vastly more complicated problem than it was formerly. A few examples will illustrate the sometimes hidden causes of illness.

Little Emily has been going to school since fall. When her mother wakes her up in the morning, the child often complains of feeling sick at her stomach. Sometimes she vomits. The mother cannot understand why Emily suffers so frequently from "a spoiled stomach."

She takes the child to the doctor. After a thorough examination he comes to the conclusion that Emily is probably fearful of something at school. He is a modern young pediatrician, and by friendly questioning of the little girl about her teacher and the other children he finally draws from her the confession that she is afraid of being called to recite in class. So the pediatrician suggests to the mother that she talk to the teacher and ask her not to call on Emily for a while, until the child has grown more accustomed to the school.

But the problem cannot always be solved so simply as this. Sometimes a psychologist has to be called in for professional advice.

In this case the situation was quite the opposite of Emily's.

Jo Anne, age twelve, complains of fatigue and headaches. Her mother, a hard-working, robust factory worker, has no patience with such "shenanigans," as she calls them. "Go out into the fresh air and play with the other children, instead of always sticking your nose in a book," she scolds. Fortunately, Jo Anne has a teacher who takes a great interest in her pupils and who is also a good observer. So she sends the tired, pale youngster to the school doctor. He diagnoses a definite case of anemia and prescribes the proper medication as well as more sleep. He also sends a note to the mother to let her know that her daughter's weakness is not "shenanigans."

Another case concerns the wife of a psychiatrist:

For years Mrs. Meyer has suffered from fatigue. Her husband, in whom she has complete confidence, sees the cause of her trouble in the psychical repercussions of the fear and strenuous exertion connected with her escape from a country under military occupation. He sends her to one of his colleagues for psychoanalytic treatment, but even prolonged treatment does not succeed in giving her a zest for life. Finally the couple conclude that the wife should have a complete physical examination. This is done—with the astounding result that an insidious case of tuberculosis is diagnosed. A year of bedrest and medical treatment in a sanatorium transforms Mrs. Meyer once again into a healthy individual.

And here is a case of an opposite nature:

For years Mrs. Gross had gone to a hospital clinic for medication for pains in the heart region and heart congestion. Finally, a psychiatrically trained doctor discovered, in a lengthy interview with her, that her trouble had an exclusively psychical basis—the woman was very unhappily married.

As we now know, a healthy development presupposes not only a healthy body, but a healthy mind or psyche. Our life has its roots in the conditions that prevail in our organism, but these are, from the beginning and throughout our entire lives, interwoven with the conditions of our psychic life.

CHAPTER 2

MOTIVATION

What Is Motivation?

An everyday incident will serve to introduce the topic of this chapter:

Herb came home and told his wife that he had finally given notice at his job. Marie was beside herself with agitation.

"But why in the world did you do that?" she asked.

Herb replied that she knew perfectly well that he had contemplated this move for a long time. As long as he remained in the organization, he had no chance for advancement. He was frustrated because he knew he was equal to greater challenges. He felt no anxiety about his resignation; he had confidence that he would soon find a better position.

Marie would have none of this. A tirade ensued: he was always impulsive and must have allowed his temper to get the best of him; he certainly was not thinking of his family's welfare; if he had been, he surely would have waited until after Christmas.

Herb answered it was precisely because of his family's welfare that he was eager to have a position with a greater future. But Marie would not listen and so the argument went on—distressing and ineffectual, as such arguments usually are.

Every day there are thousands of such more or less violent conflicts. The above debate, analyzed psychologically, reveals a complicated structure of arguments, of which the couple was actually unaware. The basic disagreement centered on the validity of Herb's reasons for his decisive action—in short, *motivation*.

Marie's *life goal* was her family's welfare. She saw this well-being as best preserved by the *security* of her husband's job. Herb, on the other hand, looked beyond the momentary security to the future betterment of his position and his income. His desire for *creative expansion* made him willing to jeopardize his present security. His life goal was the total realization of his potentialities.

Marie's need for security allowed her to adapt satisfactorily to conditions as they were. She believed that *adaptability* should be as important a motivation to her husband and blamed him because he was more concerned with the future. In other words, she felt that his behavior was determined by his personal need for achievement and that he disregarded the fact that she was satisfied with what they had. Herb, for his part, declared that the motivation for his action was well thought out. He felt that he had certainly not succumbed to a momentary whim.

Without delving deeper into the situation, we do not, of course, know who was right. Nor are we in a position to judge whether Herb's *interpretation* of the problem was correct. When personal feelings are involved, a situation often is given an incorrect explanation or interpretation. In other words, one's perception is often distorted by one's own motivation.

Knowing a person's motivation helps us to understand his behavior, and it is solely through this understanding that an individual can be guided, educated, and treated.

Healthy and Sick Motivation

After his astounding discovery of *psychoanalysis,* Sigmund Freud developed a theory of motivation. As a physician, he was primarily interested in the investigation of mental illness. He was a systematic thinker, however, and very soon turned to the construction of a psychology that would embrace healthy as well as sick human personality and development.

Freud believed that, from a theoretical understanding of the mental processes of the mentally ill, it is possible to draw conclusions about motivation in healthy people. Although this procedure has great advantages, its limitations have become increasingly obvious. Among the advantages is the fact that mental illness became comprehensible for the first time. This is particularly true of the psychoses—the serious mental illnesses in which the patient is out of touch with reality. Freud was the first to find a hidden meaning and connection in these psychoses.

The error of Freud's conclusion lay in the fact that he developed his theory of healthy motivation and healthy development from his knowledge of pathological motivation and development. His conclusions were attacked as questionable by many psychologists who considered healthy mental life to be fundamentally different from sick mental life. A scientific definition of this fundamental difference remained unexplained for a long time, and only now is becoming clear.

Several of the first dissenters among Freud's students—Alfred Adler, Carl G. Jung, Otto Rank—had already criticized the predominance that Freud assigned to the sexual factor in life. They pointed out two factors—Adler emphasized the *striving for perfection,* Jung and Rank the *creative urge* in man—that increasingly proved to be better suited in distinguishing the healthy from the sick. These factors take into consideration a *constructive orientation toward the future* that is important to the healthy, but is lost on the neurotic, who is in continuous inner conflict with his unhappy past.

This concept is illustrated by the argument between Herb and Marie. They are discussing his job problems from the standpoint of the family's future. If in the course of their discussions, Marie and Herb were to get to talking about the past, that too would probably be primarily expressed with a view to the future. Perhaps they would ask themselves whether he had made mistakes that hurt his prospects in the present job, or other questions of this sort. But if they are healthy people, they would not lose themselves in fretting about what is past. Furthermore, if Marie was worried because her husband does not pay enough attention to present security, her worry would not normally hinder her from having a hopeful outlook toward the future. Such a hopeful orientation is a sign of good mental health. It is quite a different story with neurotics.

A psychology that does not give sufficient recognition to the important difference between the orientation toward the future of the healthy person and the orientation toward the past of the neurotic is not in a position to furnish a foundation for an understanding of normal life.

The principal reason why the neurotic remains entangled in his inner problems and is incapable of seeing life and, especially, his own future, with a sense of inner freedom is that, in the depths of his being, he is *an unsatisfied person.* We might say that he lives in *discord* with himself and that this absence of inner peace makes him *unfree.*

The healthy person, on the other hand, even when dealing with serious problems that are difficult for him to solve, is not so enmeshed in them that he loses his *inner freedom.* This inner freedom means that he is inwardly able to cut himself loose at any given moment from his problems—unhindered by strong emotion and despite conflicts that may be difficult to solve. It means being able to keep his life as well as his inner self in proper perspective. This inner freedom is, of course, not a magic wand that enables us to see everything and to evaluate it in its proper light. The healthy person, like the neurotic, will make mistakes. But his mistakes are the result of human limitations and lack of foresight, not the result of an outlook that is distorted by confused emotions.

Just how are we to explain this difference? Freud recognized (and herein lies his most fundamental and important accomplishment) that the emotional disturbance in the neurotic almost always goes back to *early childhood*—that it has its origin in an early deep disturbance of the individual's emotional equilibrium.

Freud further concluded—and in this we are no longer able to follow him—that these disturbances of the emotional equilibrium are always generated by unsatisfied needs or drives. He then stated that the inner equilibrium of the mentally healthy person is explained by the fact that he has been able to solve the problem of *need satisfaction*. Finally, Freud arrived at the conclusion (which forms the cornerstone of his theory) that the *goal of life is preservation of the inner equilibrium, obtained by solving the problem of need satisfaction.*

This maintenance of equilibrium is a continual, ever-renewed task. In the normal person, according to Freud's theory, it takes place and is completed primarily in the present; in the neurotic person, on the other hand, it continually leads back into the unmastered and unfinished past.

New Theories about Basic Motivations

We have here formulated the meaning of Freud's theory in terms that correspond somewhat better to our modern scientific concepts. At present this theory is contradicted by two new theoretical approaches—*humanistic psychology* and *existentialism*.

Although the two are very different in many respects, they both agree with Freud in one respect and disagree with him in another. Both theories are unable to see a life goal in terms of need-satisfaction and in the establishment of an inner equilibrium. Both theories have quite a different concept of life. They hold in common the basic idea that what really matters to a person, and what indeed should matter, is to live "right," that is, according to an order inherent within him.

According to the proponents of humanistic psychology if a man lives "right," then, in principle, he is psychologically sound, satisfied, and good. Satisfaction and being good, in this theory, do not constitute the conflict that they represented for Freud. Freud held that man, in order to be good, must give up to a great extent the satisfaction of needs and that mental illness results in those who are unsuccessful in this.

In this view of Freud's, which emerged from his study of neuroses, we are dealing with facts that we should never lose sight of. For, without a doubt, everyone always has unsatisfied needs, the satisfaction of which can, in certain circumstances, be psychically essential for life.

Later we shall review the case of Bob, a child who did not get any warmth or affection from his parents and on whom difficult demands were made. For such a child it is almost impossible to find the "right" life. How can he be satisfied? And how can he escape mental illness? How hard such a person must struggle in order to be "good"!

We must recognize that many conditions of life make it almost impossible for a person to combine mental health, contentment, and goodness. It is to these people that modern psychotherapy strives to bring successful solutions to their life problems. In this Freud was a pathfinder of genius. Yet, in actual cases, the humanistic psychologists have often demonstrated that man can fulfill his life by living it in inner freedom and in accordance with rules inherent in his being.

Existentialism

Existentialism is the most abstract of the three theories that have been mentioned. This theory, which has only recently been applied in psychotherapy and psychiatry, is intrinsically more a philosophy than a psychology of motivation.

The name "existentialism" stands for a theory of existence. This school, which is particularly widespread in Europe and has recently gained momentum in America, has its origins in the works of Kierkegaard and Nietzsche. In this century the theory was developed and expanded primarily by Martin Heidegger. It was then taken up by writers with a philosophical orientation, such as Jean-Paul Sartre and Gabriel Marcel, and by psychologists and psychiatrists.

In contradiction to psychoanalysis, existentialism sets up, instead of a theory of needs or drives, a theory concerning the *meaning of existence.* That is, existential analysis concerns itself with "authentic" human existence.

In this realization of the essence of one's own existence, the individual must become aware that his main task is being human. The main characteristic of human existence is that it is "transcendent," that it reaches out beyond itself and becomes effective outside one's own life. In this it is called upon to realize *values.*

"Become what you are," Nietzsche said.

In this sense, the case of Ellen West, as described by Ludwig Binschwanger, has become well known. Ellen West was a severely disturbed woman; her subsequent suicide was recognized as the inevitable outcome of the meaning of her existence, that is, the suicide had been for a long time anticipated, discussed and, in a certain sense, prepared for.

The cases described by Viktor E. Frankl are more in the sphere of practical everyday life. He is particularly concerned with developing the motivation appropriate to the specific person, to bring *values* to realization. Only the realization of values makes life meaningful. In this value realization through the "will to meaningfulness," the individual is expected to develop and to apply his "optimum potentialities."

The question of how this is accomplished in practice, it must be admitted, remains as much a problem with Frankl as it does with many humanistic psychologists who, to a certain degree, represent a similar point of view.

Humanistic Psychology

The expression "humanistic psychology" arose by chance with the founding of a new society and a periodical with that title. This group has a basic idea in common with the existentialists: that human motivation must be understood from the point of view of *what the human being as a human being wants*. What are the things of which he is specifically capable as a human being and which are important for him to do? These are the basic questions that both existentialists and humanistic psychologists pose.

Existentialists and humanistic psychologists arrive at somewhat different answers, but ones that have much in common. Both recognize that the human being is continually occupied with *making something of himself and with being effective over and beyond the moment*. When he does this, he creates values.

The humanistic psychologists emphasize that this creative activity occurs in a process that the individual experiences as *self-realization* or as a striving toward *fulfillment*. This fulfillment includes the creation of cultural values as well as one's own development.

In this process, the human being tries at the same time to maintain his inner equilibrium. This, however, is a secondary goal, not, as in psychoanalysis, the main goal.

The various exponents of these tendencies emphasize somewhat different points as the most important.

Erich Fromm was probably the first to introduce into modern psychology the word "humanistic," which had its origin in the Renaissance. At that time it was used to designate the admirer and the student of the antique. It was Fromm who referred to our "humanistic" conscience in contrast to our "authoritarian" one. In Fromm's language and in the most recent clinical psychology, "humanistic" refers to the truly human, that which, in the best sense, is peculiar to the human being.

The "authoritarian" conscience represents the precept of authority accepted by us and incorporated by us. This found its clearest conceptualization in Freud's "superego."

Fromm's "humanistic" conscience, by contrast, represents our innermost knowledge of whether we are behaving "right" in the light of the human capabilities that dwell within us. When we obey this conscience, we are living meaningfully and are developing our best abilities.

Karen Horney may historically have the distinction of being the first, at the beginning of the 1930's, to develop the main principles of this new orientation. She considers the striving for *self-realization*—a concept derived from Carl Gustav Jung—as the basic tendency of the human being who develops normally. By "self-realization" she means the realization of an individual's best potentialities. She holds that by the development of these potentialities he gives expression to his innermost self and furthers not only himself but others as well. In this way he participates in *cultural creativeness.*

She sees the mentally sick development of the neurotic as rooted in inner insecurity, in a deep anxiety that is the result of a lack of love and generally unfavorable environmental factors.

The credit goes to Gordon Allport for having been one of the first to once more move to the foreground the meaning of the *self* and of *values* in human life. These concepts had been pushed aside as apparently unscientific by the first-generation psychologists. In his thought-provoking book *Personality,* he opens the way to a modern method of observing the self and values. He assigned an important place to the categories of value attitudes set up by Eduard Spranger, specified as theoretical, economic, aesthetic, social, political, and religious values.

The study of motivation in healthy persons was central to the studies of Abraham Maslow and the author.

Abraham Maslow, today one of the principal advocates of the self-realization theory, made a special effort to provide many concrete examples of healthy persons, happy in being creative, who, in their often strenuous work, experience self-realization. As a follower of Kurt Goldstein, he emphasizes that this sort of exertion is experienced by the healthy person as pleasurable. Kurt Goldstein and the author, too, repeatedly pointed out that the healthy person is by no means, as Freud postulated, always directed toward relaxation; rather, just as much pleasure can be experienced in healthy exertion. To this system of thinking belong the important observations of Karl Bühler. He emphasized that especially in children's play and in other activities experienced as successful there is pleasure in the activity itself, which he called the *"function pleasure."* During the pleasurable functioning, too, a certain tension is maintained.

In a rather large number of people whose biographies he studied, Maslow demonstrated how motivation that is directed toward growth differs from defective motivation. The terms he uses are *growth* motivation and *defense* motivation. He worked out a list of indications of a self-realizing personality. For example, these personalities are more directed toward creative activity than are others. They are more occupied with the problems occasioned by their work than by their own personal problems. They are ready to accept themselves and others; they can face reality as it is.

The author's investigations of human *life goals,* begun in the early 1930's, also used biographical material. She regarded the concept of self-realization, which she had taken into consideration, as being too one-sided since it can be applied only to the life-goal of certain types of personalities. And even for these she considered it applicable only with limitations. These limitations concern consideration for others. Karen Horney's assumption that, if everyone were to achieve self-realization to the fullest extent it would work out for the best for everyone, also seemed to her contestable. The world is not paradise. In order to give others their opportunity, the individual must, in many respects, forego his own self-realization.

An everyday example of this observation is provided by those marriages that are maintained because there are children, even though the marriage partners no longer promise each other the happiness of self-realization in conjugal love.

But aside from the limitations set by reality on the individual's self-realization, there are personality types for whom self-realization is not a goal at all. The example of Herb and Marie shows the tendency toward self-realization in Herb but not in Marie.

What does a woman like Marie expect from life? She criticizes her husband's decision to give up present security for far-reaching plans. This does not appeal to her; it is not what she wants. She prefers more modest circumstances, circumstances she can depend on. Why?

It is possible that a woman like Marie is suffering from inner insecurity because her childhood environment gave her little love and security. However, it is also possible that Marie belongs to the group of persons, by no means rare, who easily and gladly adapt to modest circumstances so long as the conditions of their personal life make them happy or at least satisfy them. Their life with their family and their care of the family are more important to such people than the wealth, fame, influential position, or opportunity to express themselves of those who want to achieve self-realization.

While one can see in the latter type, of which Herb is an example, a tendency toward *creative expansion,* in persons like Marie the tendency toward *self-limiting adaptation* is predominant. The author considers both these tendencies to be basic life tendencies. There are in addition two others, termed by the author as tendencies to *satisfaction of needs* and tendencies to *maintenance of inner order.*

The person who is primarily creative goes out into the world to "conquer" it. He is the one who sees the fulfillment of his life in amassing wealth, in creating relationships, and holding authoritative positions, or in the production of goods and services, which, if possible, he hopes to transmit to posterity. He prefers these to other life values.

The self-limiting, adaptive individual, on the other hand, is satisfied with successfully fitting into a specific environment—the family, society, culture, nature, the world in general.

There is a third type—the person who is primarily bent on satisfactions brought by enjoyment, love, happiness, and well-being. A fourth group is composed of those for whom peace of mind is most important. They value inner and outer harmony, a good conscience, or what might be called a well-organized inner household.

The author calls the end goal of these various strivings *fulfillment.* It is a closing-off experience, arising out the consciousness of a life that has on the whole been successful. Fulfillment embraces a mass of experiences, happy and painful. It is an inner wealth achieved in the course of decades that has been amassed from the life that has been lived. If this life has been successful, it provided, in a relatively well-proportioned way, expansion and adaptation, satisfaction and inner order. Fulfillment presupposes that all four areas of striving are furthered, even though the particular individual may prefer one or the other and even though life may deny complete fulfillment.

Basic Tendencies and Life Goals

It is assumed that the four principal tendencies take effect from the very beginning of life. At various times in life one or another of them plays a greater role.

The baby and the young child are obviously primarily need satisfying. Only when the child reaches school age does he gradually become more *adaptable* than need satisfying. The young person and the adult are primarily *creatively expansive*. As a person ages, he wants to survey his life thoughtfully and to establish an *inner order*. In later life, pains and aches and the failing of powers tend to transport him back to the *need satisfaction* of early childhood.

In the transition from early to late childhood, Freud assumes a change from instinct satisfaction, as he calls it, to an adaptation to reality and society. But he sees the newborn baby as purely an instinctive being.

In contrast to this, the author is of the opinion that in the normal individual all four basic tendencies are continually in effect from the beginning of his life to its end, even though there are different emphases depending on development and individuality.

This point of view can be proved by facts; for example, the fact that every living organism (and this of course includes the human being), from the stage of the fertilized egg cell, adapts itself and undergoes changes by way of this adaptation, is generally recognized, as was shown in Chapter 1.

Tiny beginnings and pre-stages of creative expansion are apparent in the spontaneous activity that begins in the mother's womb in the form of bodily movements and a few sense perceptions. The inner organization is at first preserved at this pre-stage of conscious life probably more or less exclusively through automatic regulations in the organism. Even at this very early stage, the infant turns actively toward objects and seeks to expand the boundaries and sensations of his world.

Soon after birth, the original and, in their roots and beginnings, unconscious processes apparently progress into *consciousness*. However, the precise period at which consciousness begins is still controversial. Deferring the discussion of development, we will concern ourselves here with what is called *motivational structure*. From the very beginning and all through life, motivations form a complicated structure that functions as a *multiplicity of drives*.

Freud called the multiplicity of drives, in which he saw an interplay of forces, the *dynamics of motivation*. Even though his concepts of energy are today no longer applicable in the sense in which he conceived them, his expression "dynamics of motivation" is still generally retained.

Let us look at these dynamics in the example of a nine-month-old baby.

Little Annie is sitting in her crib with a drum in front of her and holding a stick, which she rubs along the drum. Her mother comes by, sits down by the crib for a minute or so, and shows the child how to hit the drum with the stick. Annie watches with wonderment, looks up, and smiles. Then she takes hold of the stick and begins to drum by herself, at first shyly and quietly, then louder and more strongly, now smiling up at her mother, now admiring the new toy.

Fig. 10

Fig. 11

This little girl is interested in examining her new drum. At first she rubs it with the drumstick. Then after she is shown how to hit the drum, she glows with happiness at her success and the praise she gets.

Fig. 12

Examined carefully, just what is the motivational structure here? This child at play is at that moment apparently fully satisfied in her *needs* and can therefore devote herself to the discovery of the new toy. This is an *expansively creative action.* When the mother shows the child how it can be done even better, the child *adapts herself* and learns the new game. The success with the drum and praise from the mother make the child happy. At that moment she is obviously quite in *harmony with herself* and with the world.

Here, of course, the child's striving does not yet go beyond the present moment into the future, nor is she concerned with the past. Both of these, however, have their effect on her.

In view of the child's general satisfaction, her past must have been relatively favorable to be capable of such harmonious enjoyment of play with her mother. And the future is already endowed with certain potentialities, which are more or less inherent in the whole setting.

If we were to make a similar examination of the dynamics of motivation at a specific instant in the life of an older child or adult, the picture would naturally be much more complicated because of the increased multiplicity of simultaneous drives, caused by both a greater reservoir of effects from the past and the increased influence of the anticipated future on the present.

However, before adolescence we can hardly speak of self-determination or a specific outcome of life as a goal. Even then, as demonstrated by biographical studies and interviews, the individual self-determination is only *temporary, experimental,* and *indefinite.* Only at about the age of thirty does it become *final* and *definite.*

Victor, a fifty-year-old law professor at a small university, is a man whose life has not been very eventful. But, aside from the disappointments that no one is spared, his life can be considered good. Victor has a happy marriage; his wife, Elly, is ten years younger than he and is as devoted to him as he is to her. All sorts of disagreements about the bringing up of their two childen, about how to spend their income, about Victor's lack of interest in social affairs, cannot harm their good relationship. But because of these disagreements, Elly finally persuades Victor to go with her to a marriage counselor.

Let us first pick out, in the development of Victor's self-determination, those phases that are tentative and those that are final.

Victor's father was a tailor who had worked his way up from abject poverty and had built up a small establishment. His three sons had to work along with him. When he was only twelve, Victor was already an errand boy for his father; while attending high school and working part-time, his life was busy and strenuous.

Victor, a talented boy, was the oldest child. His father, with whom he got along well, used to tell him how much he himself had wanted to go on with his studies but that the poverty of his family and their lack of understanding had made this impossible. The father also said he hoped that Victor would make the old dream come true, although, of course, he would in no way push the boy into studying. In other words, the sensible and understanding father left his son free to do what he wanted to do.

Both Victor and his father were agreed that the second son, Louis, was much better suited to take over the tailoring establishment. Louis was interested in business matters and did not possess Victor's talents.

The decision to continue his studies and the choice of a career presented difficult problems for Victor. He knew that he could count on very little financial assistance and on no guidance at all from his environment. Besides, his parents felt that it was a wise plan to bring up their children to be independent at a young age. Later, Victor once told his wife that he had had too much responsibility at too early an age and had to make too many of his own decisions. The result was that he became indecisive. He was often in a quandary as to whether he had made the right choice and had handled things the right way.

He began his law studies with much doubt and hesitation. For a long time he could not make up his mind whether to become a lawyer, a government official, or a college professor. After several years of indecision, he decided to enter academic life. Today he knows—and has known for some time—that he chose what was right for him.

Victor experienced similar uncertainty when he faced the problem of getting married. His parents' home had not provided him with the opportunity to acquire experience in social matters. In school he was well liked, but girls had not been particularly interested in this serious and withdrawn boy. Besides, he was not particularly charming, and he did not know how to attract girls. At an age when all of his friends had already had some success in sexual matters, he was still inexperienced. Not until he was in his middle twenties did he become involved with a young colleague.

She, however, was not the girl he wished to marry. For a long time the problem of whom to marry remained unsolved; his several attempts at a relationship did not work out in the long run.

When Victor was thirty-four, he met Elly, one of his students, and knew immediately that this was the girl he unconsciously had been waiting for. He made the decision to win her as his wife.

Despite her youth, Elly had already lived through a stormy marriage. For her, too, the solution that now presented itself seemed the right one.

But just what do we mean by "right"? What does it imply?

Victor himself used the word "right" at a counseling session when, during the discussion of their marital differences, he spoke of his life. "Essentially," he said, "I think I have done everything right, despite the many doubts I usually have before I come to my decisions—all except my decision to get married. That seemed to me to be right from the start."

"What do you mean by 'right'?" I asked.

"Oh," he said, "right means, somehow, the way it ought to be. I mean, like the right solution to a problem, to a riddle—perhaps the various constitutent parts of life's riddle," he added with a smile.

"But if you solved it correctly, then why are you here?"

"That's a good question," he replied. "Well . . . Perhaps I have to explain further just what I mean. I'm of the opinion that I chose the career that is right for me and the wife that is right for me. Both suit me, and give me the chance for development."

"Would the expression 'self-realization' fit what you want to say?"

"Yes, indeed. That's a very good expression. That's precisely what I mean. Despite everything, we really could have a good life. As a matter of fact, we do have it. But then we argue about the children or about the way Elly keeps house, or about my not liking to go out to social affairs the way she wants me to.

"She's right, of course. I am not sociable enough, and probably I'm old-fashioned in many ways—it seems silly to me that we should be coming to you with this sort of thing. But when Elly said that these perpetual quarrels put her out of sorts, and that a marriage counselor might perhaps give us some guidelines, I said to myself that when I was a child I could never indulge in the luxury of asking my parents for advice—we children always had to solve all our problems ourselves—and perhaps it's good to ask somebody something once, although I must say I always feel very proud that I was able to handle everything myself."

After we had talked for a while about the disagreements in their marrige, there emerged for the first time the really important point—Victor's criticism of himself for his lack of success in his career.

"I'm fifty now," he said. "I'm teaching at a small college and my income is very small. I don't have much of a reputation, and I often reproach myself for not having got further ahead. At school my teachers were always full of praise for my performances, but later, at the university, I saw that I didn't really belong among the most talented. It wasn't easy to admit that to myself. I was full of ambition—I'm not a good loser—and yet I'm not ready to make those extra efforts that, perhaps, might enable me to get further along."

"Do you think that making those efforts would have been the right thing for you?"

"Yes and no—I don't know exactly. My wife often says that if I had cultivated more personal contacts I would have got further ahead. Perhaps . . . but it just isn't in me . . . my wife doesn't understand that. You know," he continued after a pause, "when one arrives at my age, one begins to brood over everything that one has missed in life. It's probably too late to try to get a better position, but should I try, anyway? Do I owe it to myself and to my wife?"

What Victor is saying is that he has arrived at a stage where, looking backward, he evaluates his life. He draws a *balance,* asking himself whether, in the sense of fulfilling his life, he has made enough of himself and of his life—enough, that is, in view of the potentialities he had available.

On the one hand, Victor is obviously a man who is directed toward creative expansion. On the other hand, the fact that he has been more or less content with his unimportant professorship shows that he passively adapts himself to his circumstances. Perhaps, too, he finds comfort in having lighter demands made on him than those a high degree of performance would impose. This would mean that his tendencies toward creative expansion are balanced by need-satisfying and adaptive tendencies. Perhaps it is only his wife's ambition, perhaps it is a remnant of the ambition aroused by his father, or perhaps it is, indeed, a bad conscience caused by neglected potentialities that does not allow his self-criticism to abate.

In the critical *self-assessment* that occurs during the climacteric, all former self-evaluations, from earliest childhood on, are assembled and united into one enormous self-accusation or, as the case may be, into self-praise.

Man accompanies his actions and thinking with self-evaluations. He begins with monologues like the following, in which little Peter, not yet two years old, meditatively discusses with himself: "Is he bad boy? Is he good boy?—No, he's bad boy." That, for the moment, is his decision—a self-report that is satisfying to this young rebel. These self-evaluations reach their summit and their decisive significance between the ages of fifty and sixty, when a sort of *life balance* is struck. Then the question is posed: How far have I succeeded in bringing my life to its fulfillment? To what extent can I still make up for what is lacking? How much of what I originally hoped for and dreamed of must I forego?

This sort of self-evaluation results partly from what one feels are one's potentialities and partly from wishful dreams or ideals. We must now get acquainted with the motivating forces of these factors.

Potentialities and Values

By "potentialities" we mean the aptitudes and opportunities that are at the disposal of an individual. His aptitudes are governed by his disposition, his ability to learn and reason, and his talents; but, through depth of feeling, breadth of outlook, and strength of drives a person is capable of developing his own opportunities. Further possibilities may be provided by his environment, by his social and economic position, by cultural and national conditions. Finally, possibilities are determined by his age, the life that has gone before, the particular times, and so on.

Potentialities are thus, on one hand, the given conditions in the individual himself and, on the other, the opportunities and the possibilities provided by circumstances.

As a result of the multiplicity of these factors, it is difficult, if not impossible, to predict the development of an individual except within narrow limits.

Modern tests and interviews, of course, provide a great deal of valuable knowledge about a person. In general, the experienced counselor or psychotherapist, after a little while, will be able to understand a person with whom he works. But even so, certain things remain open questions.

If, for example, an experienced counselor were asked whether Victor will change his condition of life drastically in the future, he would answer "probably not." He would take into consideration Victor's age and his life circumstances, which, by and large, are quite comfortable. Because of this, he would deduce that, despite the possibilities that Victor's talents, education, and training have opened up for him, he is less directed toward expansion than toward adaptability and a quiet enjoyment of life. By all these factors his potentialities are decided.

Why, then, does Victor still believe that he must reproach himself? His self-reproaches are primarily the result of his inadequate self-knowledge; he is thinking of his talents and his extensive education, not of his tendency to avoid great exertion.

Yet we must note that Victor's self-reproaches are connected with still another factor: his values. Values are preferences we give to certain things in the world, both material and ideal. They may be property or qualities, successes, performances, or any number of things.

There are *factual* and *normative* preferences. The factual preferences are things that we wish for ourselves, such as love, happiness, or wealth. The normative preferences are things that we admit are deserving of value, whether or not we wish them for ourselves. Of these values (for example, truth, goodness, justice, or love of truth and beauty), we say that they have a "should character"—meaning that everyone ought to want them.

Very early in life, a child learns to believe in certain values. A girl may believe she will be happy if she gets a doll, or that her mother will love her if she is good. In some cases such a belief arises out of the child's own wishes; in others, especially when we are dealing with values that have a "should character," the value is taught to the child by the environment. However, there are also roots for *ideals* (as values that have a "should character" are called) within the individual himself.

It is astounding how early in life children set goals for themselves that represent specific values.

Long before seven-year-old Allen tells his loving aunt that he wants to be an airplane pilot, he has unconsciously made certain resolutions that will be decisive in his later life. When he was only four he had resolved that he would always work with tools. As a small boy he had made repairs around the house with his children's tools. Later he became a skilled engineer.

Still more important, however, is another ideal that arose in Allen. This was never to make a mistake, *never to deserve a reprimand*. Of course, the child did not say this to himself in so many words. But he recalls to this day, as a twenty-six-year-old, the exact circumstances that led him to this decision.

One evening when he went to the dinner table with unwashed hands, his mother sent him away with a scolding. Allen found it unbearable to be reprimanded. He wanted to be absolutely above and beyond criticism. Holding back his tears, he went to his room and thought about how he could manage to do everything absolutely right in the future.

Notable in this is not so much the fact that Allen is still a perfectionist. Rather, we must take note of this fact: the problems and anxieties that arose from his perfectionism became so great that they eventually compelled him to seek psychotherapeutic help.

In Victor's case we learned how, as a boy, he had discussed his future with his father. He had determined to go on with his studies so that, in a sense, the wish-dream whose fulfillment had been denied to the father might at last become a reality for both.

Freud called the taking over of an ideal *identification*. Without a doubt, identifications, which are the assuming of characteristics of another person as one's own, contribute decisively to an individual's development.

However, a great many other things besides identification contribute to building up an *identity*. By this is meant a person's feeling and knowledge that "That's me; that's what I am." An individual's own tendencies as well as the development of his potentialities contribute to his identity.

A person's values are included in what he finally is.

Victor, as we saw, had made the values of his beloved father his very own. He himself became what his father had wanted to become. His father was proud of him.

The conflict that Victor later experienced, wherein he feels that by avoiding difficulties he is not doing justice to his potentialities, did not originate in his childhood but is of more recent origin. It has to do with the problem of how Victor wants to establish his identity more or less definitively. Will he retire into his present comfortable way of life, or will he make an effort toward further expansion?

In Allen's case the complications are of a different sort. By the age of four Allen appears, in his values, to have identified completely with all that his parents approve of. But actually, perfectionism cannot possibly be very important to a child.

Since Sigmund Freud, behavior such as that of four-year-old Allen is interpreted thus: apparently he believes that he can be certain of his parents' love only if he yields extensively to their demands. For this reason he sacrifices the pursuit of his childish needs to strive for perfection.

But why would a child like Allen think that he had to make such a tremendous sacrifice if, as he declares as an adult, he was perfectly sure of his parents' love? It would seem that he had an unusually self-limiting need to adapt. As a result, obedience to rules to a degree that is not required has become the main goal of Allen's life.

Freud's Theory of Motivation

Up to this point we have concerned ourselves with theories of motivation in which the personality is seen as an undivided whole. We thus speak of *totality theories*. Motivation always has its origin in the whole person and has but a *single goal*. That goal is self-actualization or self-realization.

In Freud's theory of motivation, however, the personality is split into three systems: the *id,* the *ego,* and the *superego.* These represent three relatively independent types of drives and inner worlds.

The *id* is the drive that seeks pleasure. Freud assumes the newborn infant to be entirely dominated by the id. As long as the id dominates an individual, he is not conscious of his actions and his drives.

Consciousness awakens only with the *ego,* which owes its birth to the individual's confrontation with reality. As long as the individual functions as an id, he lives as the captive of his drives or wishes. He does not become aware of reality. He becomes aware of reality only later, when he is frustrated in the satisfaction of his needs or when satisfaction is denied. At this moment the problem arises whether the individual can and will accept the frustrating reality or whether he will continue to insist on the satisfaction of his wishes. This is the first *conflict* in the infant's life.

Soon a second conflict joins the first. This is the conflict between one's own drives and the wishes and the regulations of others, especially of parents. It is a conflict between the id and the *superego,* which corresponds in part to what is generally called the conscience. According to Freud, the superego represents the regulations of society that have been "internalized" in the individual—that is, the norms, regulations, and prohibitions that were transmitted to the child by the parents and that the child has made his own.

The conflict arises from the fact that the child has to sacrifice the satisfaction of his own desires—his id—to the wishes of others—represented by the superego. Often he cannot or does not want to do this. If then, despite his resistance, he is compelled to deny his desires, he can do so only by *repressing* or pushing them back into his unconscious. From such painful repressions neuroses arise.

The extraordinary significance that *repression* of unpleasant or hard-to-bear experiences has in human beings was put into its proper light for the first time by Freud. It does not matter whether one agrees with Freud in everything or regretfully concludes that this great genius failed to ultimately encompass all perspectives of human existence. Nevertheless Freud's theories have brought about a complete change in our understanding of ourselves.

It is the writer's belief that, among our contemporaries, we can refer to *pre-Freudians* and *post-Freudians.* Post-Freudians are those who have accepted the idea of *self-deception* resulting from repressions. Pre-Freudians are those who still refuse to acknowledge this fact. Even today there are pre-Freudians. Here is an example:

Two mothers come to me for counseling. The one assures me perfectly seriously that she has never felt anything but the deepest, most unselfish love for her children and that she always and completely devotes herself to her family. The other says, somewhat ruefully: "You know, quite often I catch myself feeling that my children, whom I love so much and who mean so much to me, seem a terrible burden. And sometimes I wish that at long last I could be free and have a chance to do something for myself . . . Perhaps you'll say I'm a bad mother." Here is an example of a pre-Freudian mother, who deceives herself about herself, and a post-Freudian, who sees herself in a clear light.

It is true that those who have really understood human nature have always known that too great virtue is suspect, even when it seems to be associated with great honesty. They suspected that there were always other, less "virtuous" motives at work as well.

But only since Freud have we got a real insight into how complex the structure of motivation is. Sometimes it is a highly involved conflict of the most diverse motivations. Through Freud we learned, for instance, that the "unselfish" mother in our example may perhaps be seeking a compensation for a lack of conjugal love or for sexual frigidity. Or it may be that in her sacrifice for her children she sees her only value—a value that she does not grant herself as a person. Or it may be that feeling herself to be a martyr provides her with an unrealistic satisfaction. Normally, of course, everybody needs for himself at least as much as he gives to others. Freud made clear that people who believe that they find their full satisfaction in giving are deceiving themselves as to the nature of their motives.

In addition to his discovery of the role of the unconscious and of the related role of repression of unpleasant experiences, Freud recognized two other things of fundamental importance.

One is the concept of the *dynamics* of all processes. This means that psychic processes are not merely reactions to stimuli; rather these reactions are built into *processes* that are conditioned by an interplay of forces. Precisely what causes the play of forces is not yet wholly explained.

Also accepted by probably the majority of theoretical and practical psychologists is Freud's recognition of the fundamental role the *experiences of earliest childhood* play in the development of personality. The cases that we shall present all provide proof of this.

The three discoveries concerning the role of the unconscious and of repression, the dynamics of psychic life, and the importance of childhood experiences are closely connected with one another. Freud, together with Joseph Breuer, made these discoveries in the course of treating a hysterical woman patient, Anna O. As Freud himself says, they were made "by chance" and to the great "surprise" of both physicians.

Anna O. was cured of her illness by being induced to remember her forgotten *traumatic* experiences and to talk about them. The word "traumatic" stems from the Greek word *trauma*, meaning "wounds." Traumatic experiences are those that are deeply disturbing and are harmful in their psychic aftereffects. In the hysteric this psychic damage is transformed into a physical illness.

A number of decisive points were implicit in the discovery that began with the case of Anna O. and was furthered in later cases. What was shown primarily was that *mental* illnesses could be traced to experiences that were repressed. As a result of the repression, they were "forgotten." And it was also demonstrated that most of these experiences could be traced back to childhood.

Repression is an apparent forgetting "on purpose," but unconsciously. Through this "forgetting," the experiences that were formerly *conscious* become *unconscious*. And together with consciousness, the pain vanishes, at least temporarily.

What are repressed are experiences having to do with unfulfilled "punishable" wishes, which can be given up only if the individual forces himself to forget them. The wishes are "punishable" because they are directed toward forbidden sexual pleasures. The traumatic disturbance lies in the entire experience of the compelling wishes, the fear of discovery, the sense of guilt, and the final suppression of the wishes. It was Freud's view that all such experiences are ultimately connected with sexuality.

This view became the cornerstone of his theoretical thinking. On it rests his *libido theory*, which, in its original form, declares that ultimately all striving can be traced to the sexual drive. The sexual drive is regarded by Freud as a force, indeed the fundamental force. He sees it as the *energy* that is the determining factor for life processes and that becomes operative in the dynamics of mental life. Even though the concept of "energy" as used here has not been completely explained—obviously it concerns more than purely physical forces—the idea of the dynamics of psychic processes is universally accepted.

Freud gradually modified his early, quite radical concept of the libido. The concept of sexuality was broadened to comprise all *pleasure* in the widest sense. Freud then assumed that there are different stages of development and forms of pleasure. The earliest form is the infant's pleasure in sucking, called *oral pleasure*. The second form is the feeling of pleasure at expelling or at holding back feces, which Freud called *anal pleasure*. He ascribes to this an important role in the mental life of the child from ages one to four. He sets the beginning of the stage of *phallic pleasure*, arising from the functioning of the genitals, at ages three to seven. They all represent stages in the development of sexuality. Freud's thesis at this period of his work was that the basic motive of all striving is *to gain pleasure and to avoid pain*.

Freud finds the drive for pleasure least inhibited in early childhood. He was the first to show the beginnings of sexual impulses at this period of life.

In the course of the development and expansion of his theory, Freud gave it a more scientific formulation. Until recently, it met with extraordinarily wide acceptance, especially among American psychoanalysts. Today, Freud's psychological pleasure-pain principle has been replaced by Gustav Theodor Fechner's more scientific concept of tension discharge. Now the theory reads: *The organism strives for discharge that is pleasur-*

able, but increase of tension is painful to it. Under American influences, this theory was later equated with the *homeostasis* theory of the great physiologist Walter B. Cannon (1871–1945). According to Cannon, homeostasis is the tendency at work in every living organism to bring about inner equilibrium in the body. For example, the body regulates its temperature in such a way that, despite slight ups and downs, it always returns to normal.

Freud's theory of the tension-discharge principle was looked upon as the psychological parallel to physiological homeostasis, that is, to the organic principle of the re-establishment of conditions of equilibrium in the body. It is assumed that the re-establishment of equilibrium depends psychically as well as physically on the *fulfillment of certain basic needs.* If these basic needs remain unfulfilled for any length of time, there arises a condition of tension, which finally results in disturbances. Corresponding to these happenings are emotional experiences of pain, unrest, nervousness, and frustration. If the need satisfaction repeatedly remains unfulfilled for long periods, it can cause illness.

A Psychosomatic Case

This important theory may be clarified by an example, a case of *psychosomatic illness*—physical illness that is strongly influenced or caused by psychic factors (Greek *soma*, "body").

Bob, the agent for a major typewriter firm covering a large territory, is an unusually capable, hard-working, ambitious man of forty-five, a conscientious husband, and the father of two young daughters.

For some years he has suffered from a duodenal ulcer. Here is the history of his illness: In his first years as the representative of this large firm, Bob overworked excessively and never kept to any regular schedule of meals. Even today when his doctor warns him that he must take his meals regularly and slow down, he maintains that travel and visits to his customers often make it impossible for him to arrange his working day in a consistent schedule. So it often happens that Bob goes hungry for an hour or two before he takes the time to snatch a hasty bite. He does not want to admit that the tension to which he subjects his body can be responsible for his illness. He declares, "Others live at the same pace that I do, and they don't have an ulcer. And when for a whole year I took time to eat regularly, my ulcer didn't go away."

Bob's statement is correct insofar as rushing and an irregular schedule in themselves are generally not the cause of illness. Mental overexertion over long periods, however, is almost never undergone without nervousness, headaches, and other somatic symptoms of threatened or beginning illness.

Added to his physical overexertion, as the psychiatrically oriented physician pointed out to Bob, there is the emotional burden he has been carrying. This is generally the case with ulcers.

Bob's mental state becomes evident in his chronic worry, fear, and anxiety at the prospect of failure. He has a great sense of responsibility. Then, too, he gets angry very easily and becomes very impatient with the members of his family. Thus, in addition to the physical, there is a strong mental strain.

To return to our theoretical considerations, what are the unconscious basic needs that, in this case, are unfulfilled and repressed?

Various Views Concerning the Causes of Mental Illness

From the purely physical point of view, we note that Bob's need for food and rest is being satisfied irregularly and insufficiently. Added to this is the fact that he worries excessively. Just what does this signify with respect to needs that are unsatisfied and then repressed into the unconscious?

In the case of a businessman, various things might be involved. He may be *unsure* of himself and feel that he cannot cope with the problems of his job. He may be ambitious, but directed toward a perfection that cannot be attained; he may never be satisfied with himself. He may take his responsibilities too seriously and let himself be weighed down by them. Bob's psychosomatic symptoms might be understood in a variety of ways by various theorists.

Alfred Adler was Freud's first adversary in the dispute over whether sexuality is the principle that explains everything. In his psychology, the motive of *insecurity* and of a perfectionism based on such insecurity would be sufficient to explain Bob's case. Karen Horney, like Adler, looks upon the *striving for security* as man's basic motive. Both psychiatrists consider the social factor to be of greater importance than the sexual one. In other respects their theories differ. But both of them, like Freud, would trace Bob's insecurity and perfectionism back to *childhood experiences,* although in so doing they would ascribe the decisive role to different experiences than would Freud.

Adler and Horney would look for early experiences that had made Bob an insecure child. In his case they would find that he had been corrected and admonished a great deal by his parents, who had made many demands on him. Thus, he was never sure of success unless he performed in a way that was practically perfect.

One of the author's patients, who grew up in a home like this, told her that he remembered exactly how, at the age of four, he made up his mind never to make a mistake. We have already met this patient, Allen. Just think of a four-year-old who is so definite in his mind as to just how he must behave to win the approbation of his parents!

"When we went out to dinner," Allen reported, "I used to think, I'll see what Margie orders. If I order the same thing, then I'm sure I'm not making a mistake." Margie was Allen's older sister, who always knew just how to behave. His parents wanted to bring up their children to be independent and to assume responsibility, so the children were allowed to choose their own dishes in a restaurant. At the same time, however, they were supposed to be aware that being economical was part of their responsibility to the family. Thus, they would get scolded if they ordered an expensive dish.

Allen reported how important it was to him to *belong* to the family circle and to count as an important family member. "At that time," he said, "we were apparently still closely connected. That gave me a great sense of security. When later my father left us, I felt unhappy and insecure."

Here, in his own words, Allen confirms that security was extraordinarily important to him. It is clearly seen how his perfectionism results from his need to be included in the family. Allen's parents, just like Bob's, made great demands on their children far too early. Such parents make it difficult for their children to live up to such demands and to feel secure in the face of them. Demands, as used here, can be quite different from those in Allen's case. They can, for example, be more obvious and insist on strict obedience to too many regulations and prohibitions.

A child can be made insecure by lack of demands as well as by demands that are too high. Complete absence of order, regularity, and guidelines confronts a child with tasks that his limited judgment and ability cannot cope with. Here, too, though in a different way, the demand is too high.

The explanations given so far of the need problems in Bob's case would appear adequate to those psychologists who see a basic motive in the striving for security. The origin of Bob's illness would appear adequately explained if they could point to a childhood influence of strong-willed and ambitious parents.

Franz Alexander, who attempted to apply Freud's theory of unconscious conflicts and their dynamics to certain physical illnesses such as asthma, arthritis, skin diseases, and stomach and duodenal ulcers, was not satisfied with this explanation. Instead, he held that the degree of insecurity and perfectionism that results in an illness as serious as Bob's, indicates causes deeper than just parental demands. It was his opinion that in such cases it could always be shown that as a child the patient was not only subjected to strict discipline but was also deprived of sufficient love and affection.

The intensive studies on the psychology of psychosomatic illnesses made by Franz Alexander and his co-workers are among the most highly regarded in this important field. In patients with stomach and duodenal ulcers, time and again they found a strong desire for emotional dependence on someone who would care for them. This *desire for dependence and being take care of* was combined, however, with a feeling of *shame* at this desire, which was therefore repressed. In other words, the simultaneous desire for and defense against this desire put these patients into an insoluble state of inner conflict.

Does this mean then that all people whose childhood needs for care and love were not fully met and who were, in addition, confronted with great demands, will later fall ill with stomach or intestinal ulcers? Of course not. In addition to the emotionally harmful experiences, there must also be present certain physiological and mental *dispositions*, that is, *tendencies*, for such serious illness to result.

It is a fact that such illnesses always arise at a weak spot in the organism. Most people have one or another weakness, often from birth or early childhood. They may tend to digestive disturbances or to frequent colds, to skin irritations or other mild illnesses. An illness resulting from an organic weakness is often the starting point of a more serious illness that develops together with the neurosis.

Alfred Adler's original theory started from the connection between organic inferiority and neurosis. Later he gave up this theory, holding instead that in the development of the neurosis there is always some weakness that leads to a so-called *inferiority complex*. At the same time the person attempts to *overcompensate* for the weakness with particularly good performances in other fields. One often observes a child who is physically awkward at sports throwing himself zealously into reading of books or pursuing some other interest to excess to compensate for the weakness.

Definition of Neurosis and of Mental Disposition

Most mental illnesses, often combined with physical symptoms if not with an actual ailment, are *neuroses.* The cases of Allen and Bob are examples of neuroses. We have seen how insufficient satisfaction of needs and repression can lead to this condition, But, for a neurosis to develop, there must always be a mental disposition toward it. Both concepts, neurosis and mental disposition, are intricate and controversial.

Only recently, long after the discovery of neuroses, has some unanimity been reached with respect to the definition of this so-called disease of our times. It is now possible to point out some generally recognized symptoms.

In situations that demand unusual mental strength, as when life is endangered, neurotics behave with unexpected strength and adaptability. In everyday life, neurotics are often perfectly able to cope with their tasks and problems. But at some point they encounter insoluble problems or conflicts.

Bob appeared to his wife and associates as a competent businessman. His wife, who had little understanding of her husband's inner life, felt that "he has himself to blame for his nervousness, because he rushes around unnecessarily and worries unnecessarily." Her view is frequently held by laymen, who often believe that these "so-called" illnesses are self-made and therefore unnecessary. They do not take their "nervous" friends seriously, often thinking their behavior an affectation or exaggerated finickiness. Indeed, it must be admitted that in certain neurotics there is a hypersensitivity that seems "exaggerated" or "affected" to the healthy person.

It is now fairly well established that *hypersensitivity* is part of an inborn disposition. But hypersensitivity is not the only disposition toward neurosis. Freud's view was that excessive *strength of instinctual drive,* as he called it, makes an individual incapable of giving up pleasure satisfaction and of adapting self-limitingly to the reality of family life and society.

Excessive instinctual drive makes it difficult or impossible for a weak ego to defend itself against an overstrong id. The conflict that thus arises is heightened if the weak ego is under the pressure of a strong superego. The superego arises from a second conflict, which Freud called the *Oedipus complex,* based on the myth of Oedipus, King of Thebes, who unwittingly fell in love with and married his mother, Jocasta.

Every child, says Freud, has a natural sexual desire for the parent of the opposite sex—the son for his mother, the daughter for her father. The child gradually comes to understand, however, that this wish cannot be fulfilled and has got to be given up. In the normal course of the renunciation, the child, according to Freud, is capable of substituting for the possession of the mother or father by identifying with the parent of the same sex and "introjecting" the parental demands. Out of this so-called symbolic introjection there arises the superego.

If, however, the instinctual drive is so strong that renunciation cannot be brought about, then the Oedipus conflict is not resolved but is only repressed into the unconscious, where it develops into the so-called Oedipus complex.

By the word "complex," Freud means the fixation on a wish that was repressed into the unconscious and that continues to exist there.

Freud assumed that when there is an excessive instinctual drive we are dealing with an *inborn sexual constitution*. Today, however, we use the expressions "inborn" and "tendency" with great restraint, and then only in the sense of *dispositions,* which are regarded as extensively modifiable by experience.

Freud emphasized that precocious and excessive excitation of the sexual drive in young children does not result exclusively from great strength of instinctual drive, but can also be the result of *excessive parental affection*. He speaks of a sexual drive "that has become demanding through spoiling," meaning that in certain circumstances the *environment* is responsible for the development of a neurosis.

Let us return to Allen's case. This child, at the age of four, made up his mind never to make a mistake. We cannot avoid assuming in his case a great hypersensitivity to blame and criticism and an unusual insecurity. Indeed Allen knows that as a child he was loved by his parents. Although they were quite strict and punished their children for being naughty, their punishments were not of such a nature that a child would fear making a mistake. Such an *overreaction* must then have its cause mainly in the particular individuality of this child. He identified very early and to an unusual degree with his perfectionist mother, who used to say to the children, "Whatever is worth doing at all, is worth doing well." But none of the other children was so impressed by this as Allen was.

Allen exhibited what today is generally called *ego weakness*—a lack of capacity for self-assertion. Allen suffered from this lack in his later life until he went into therapy.

Now, just what was the nature of Allen's neurosis? A short description will provide the opportunity to finish our definition of the concept of neurosis.

In his last year of his technical studies, Allen decided to go to a psychotherapist because he suffered from inability to concentrate and from frequent insomnia. He found that his work performance was never good enough. Instead of studying systematically, he wasted his time endlessly with all sorts of unimportant things like little repairs around his mother's house (he was still living at home with her). Or he would make all sorts of little purchases. He did everything with unnecessary conscientiousness and dawdled so that they took a lot of time. Although he criticized himself for the way he was behaving, he was apparently unable to do otherwise. He was acting in a compulsive way.

We mentioned earlier Allen's insecurity and his perfectionism, and also referred to his strong identification with his mother, whose love he perhaps wanted to secure by making himself perfect. Allen seems to have felt, rightly or wrongly, that he could never do enough to satisfy his mother. Even now he has feelings of guilt in connection with things that his mother wants attended to, things that he, in his newly awakened rebellion, has delayed doing or has not sufficiently completed. He also has strong feelings of guilt because he feels that he has not yet thoroughly mastered his studies.

In the uninterrupted argument with the demands of his strict conscience, Allen became increasingly more compulsive, less free, and more anxious in the exercise of the many duties he assigned to himself.

This *lack of freedom* in action is generally recognized as the second main symptom of all neuroses. As has been said, a neurotic can, especially in dangerous situations, forget himself. But in general he is more or less exclusively occupied with himself, his problems and conflicts, and the argument with his compulsions.

The New Ego Psychology

Early students of Freud concerned themselves almost exclusively with the mentally ill and their cure. In their psychoanalytic work with their patients, who were for the most part seriously disturbed, they were faced with the task of understanding the often irrational problems of these people.

When modern psychologists tried to apply Freud's system to an understanding of normal development and to their work with individuals, couples, and families, whose problems and conflicts were much easier to understand and solve, it became apparent that the incidence and role of the Oedipus complex had been overestimated by Freud. In its place *ego development* and *value finding* have been found to be of greater importance in understanding the problems of normal people. A new ego psychology has emerged from these experiences.

CHAPTER 3

DEVELOPMENT

What Development Is

A mother, sitting next to another mother on a bench in the park says:
"Maxie is developing much more rapidly than my older boy did. Probably
it's because he learns so much by watching Earl. Whatever Earl does,
Maxie wants to do too; that's how he learned to talk and walk and climb
so quickly—and he wants to do everything by himself."

To which the other mother replies: "Yes, but you know all children
are different. My Betsy is much less independent than our first two children were. Even though she has the other two as examples she wants to
be helped in whatever she does, in getting dressed, in feeding herself,
and even when she's playing."

"Maybe that's because, as the youngest, she's being spoiled by the
others," Maxie's mother says. "She enjoys being made a fuss of, and
loves to be waited on."

Even though these mothers have never studied psychology, they are
aware of a great many things that are scientifically correct. First of all,
both apparently know that, parallel to growth in childhood there is a
proper *succession* and a regular appearance of certain accomplishments
and ways of behavior, and that this is called *development*. They know
that, in general, the accomplishments and ways of behavior can be expected at a certain *average age*. However, they also know that development can be affected by *environmental influences*. It can be accelerated
by example, and it can be slowed down if too little is demanded of the
child or if the child is hindered in its progress in other ways. And, finally,

one of the mothers points out that children, from the time they are born, display certain *individual differences* as a result of which they develop at different rates of speed and in different directions.

Maturation and Mental or Psychical Development

Anyone who, like these two mothers, has watched the growth, the unfolding, the changes to be seen daily in the looks and behavior of a child will agree that development is one of the most fascinating facts of life. Frequently it seems almost to border on the miraculous, especially when totally unexpected interests or talents come forth in a child.

"Charlie, Charlie," the mother cries out in delight, coming back from her little daughter's room to where her husband is shaving. "Just think! Susy has perfect pitch. Just look at her, the way she's dancing all over the room. And listen to her humming the Blue Danube Waltz."

The father and his music-loving wife tiptoe toward the nursery and watch delightedly through the half-open door at their two-year-old, who is dancing about and humming the waltz in tune. Nobody taught Susy that. It's a miracle!

Fig. 13

Fig. 14

A six-month-old baby can grasp only one block at a time.

At seven months, the child can hold a block in each hand simultaneously.

Fig. 15
At eight to ten months, the child can hit two blocks together.

Fig. 16
From ten to twelve months, the child begins to build with blocks.

Fig. 17

A one-and-a-half-year-old child is an accomplished architect with blocks.

On the other hand, the child may show defects or poor development.

"Paulie just can't understand what I tell him," his mother reports to the pediatrician. "Do you think he doesn't *want* to or just *can't* understand? He still doesn't say a single word."

The doctor looks concernedly at the two-year-old, who has an expressionless face and somewhat mongoloid eyes. How can he tell this poor mother that here perhaps is a case of mental retardation? Very carefully he suggests that the child should be given psychological tests, and the anxious mother continues to hope.

While talents and defects such as these often become apparent in a completely unexpected way, in general, *maturation* proceeds step by step and in a regular fashion. By maturation we mean the processes of unfolding that are conditioned by the organism. These manifest themselves particularly clearly in the infant's early movements. It is extremely interesting to watch the sequence in which they appear.

Anyone who has an opportunity to stand at the crib of a one- to five-month-old baby should watch the play of the tiny hands and fingers. From one day to the next, he will notice the increasing assurance and coordination, movements that reach out more and more, and the increasing goal-directedness of the movements.

The *sequence* or succession of the maturing movements at this stage is so regular that it is possible to predict what each stage is going to be. Experiments like the following are an example. We offer the children a set of five brightly colored hollow blocks that fit one inside the other. We are able to predict with considerable success that the six-month-old will grasp only *one* block and shake it in his hand; the seven-month-old, using *both* hands at once, will grasp one in each hand; the eight- to ten-month-old will put one inside the other, and the one- to one-and-a-half-year-old will set them up, one on top of the other.

In the succession we find important progress in the mastery of movement as well as recognition of the relationship between two objects.

The step from putting two or more blocks one inside the other to placing one on top of the other was pointed out by the writer as one of the most important steps in human development. She considers it comparable to the discovery of the meaning of words. Here is progress from manipulation to the first *creative producing of a new structure.*

At the beginning the structure comes about by chance, but soon the child becomes aware that here he has something newly created before him, and often he points triumphantly at it.

Not many parents are aware of the significance of this moment. The importance of this first creative act is not considered as important as the child's first steps or first words, but it ought to be. The special stimulation that hollow blocks provide for the one-year-old is, regrettably, almost unknown. Only recently has sufficient attention been paid to the educational role of toys *suitable for the age* during the early years.

Children who grow up without the stimulus of the right toys also mature in certain movements according to their inborn abilities, but they lack the skill that comes from thoroughly trained muscles.

In his laboratory at Yale University, Arnold Gesell studied the extraordinarily regular progression in the maturation of bodily movements during the infant's first year. Children were put into a domelike space in which cameras recorded their movements and bodily positions. Gesell's *Atlas of Child Behavior* is probably the most complete pictorial inventory of bodily movements during a child's first year.

It is not by chance that the study of bodily movements represents the acme of developmental research on maturation. For in motility the maturation factor is relatively least disturbed in coming to the fore. In and of itself the scheme of the successive steps in maturation dominates all life functions. For example, the infant is first interested in succession in sounds, then in optic stimuli such as colors and shapes, then in grasping and touching. And he makes sounds in a regular succession until he produces combinations of sounds and, finally, words.

However, from the start, *environmental influences* and *experiences* get mixed in, and *individual preferences* complicate the picture.

For example, if a baby shows a greater interest in musical tones than in all other stimuli, it is quite possible that this child will pay little or no attention to colors, whereas a newborn baby that has been frightened by many loud sounds may later turn away fearfully from any type of music.

I recall a three-month-old boy whose parents had frequently left him with his grandmother when they were away on trips. The grandmother thought she could train her grandson in "harmony" and "appreciation of music" by exposing him very early in life to the "right" stimuli, that is, fine music.

What happened was something entirely different. At the age of three months the child was already dulled to sounds and did not exhibit the lively interest in tones that is general at this age.

The sphere of life that is most conditioned by environmental influences is that of social behavior—and the emotions that develop in social intercourse. In a certain way, emotionality and the capacity to adapt socially, two effects of maturation and environment, represent the counterpart to motility. That is why we can best study in them the role that the environment plays.

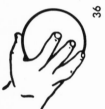

56 44 36

24 16 8

Ball

60 52 44

32 28 24

Marble

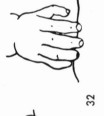
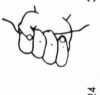

60 52 44

36 32 24

String

The development of a child's grasping ability is illustrated by a ball, a marble, and a piece of string. The numbers show the child's age in weeks (from H. M. Halverson, A Further Study of Grasping, 1932).

Fig. 18

Environment and Mental, or Psychical, Development

One of the most impressive books on the mother's role in the life of the infant is John Bowlby's comprehensive work, *Maternal Care and Mental Health,* written in 1952 for the World Health Organization. In simple words he provides facts and figures that give an overwhelming picture of what a tremendous and fundamental influence the prolonged absence of the mother or of a loving mother-substitute has on the emotional life of the child.

Children who before their fifth year experience long periods without maternal care lose their capacity to feel and love. They become cold, self-centered, sexually disturbed, and almost invariably tend to steal. Bowlby says that one of the earliest cases, described by David Levy in 1937, can still serve as an example.

Levy describes an eight-year-old child, born out of wedlock, who was passed from pillar to post before she got to the foster family from whom, at the age of six, she was adopted. Despite all their efforts, the foster parents could not get close to the child. The little girl is lively, well-mannered and, in a superficial way, affectionate; she is good in school and makes friends with other children—although there are few real friendships—and yet she is at the same time completely reserved and withdrawn. She lies and steals, although there is no apparent reason for either.

The development of infants who have been kept in institutions for some length of time lags behind that of babies who grow up with their mothers —even in the most poverty-stricken circumstances. Severe depressions occur in orphans brought up in institutions even when they have been well, but impersonally, cared for.

It can therefore be stated unequivocally that psychopathic character traits, lack of feeling, and other emotional disturbances can be largely traced to an *absence of mother love* in early life.

There is general agreement among workers in this field that the three most unfavorable conditions for development are: complete absence of a "mother figure" (that is, the mother or a correspondingly loving substitute) during the first three years; the mother's absence for more than three months during the first three or four years; back-and-forth change from one mother figure to another within the same period.

The worst cases of disturbed children are those of *childhood schizophrenia.* The concept of schizophrenia was established by the Swiss psychiatrist Eugen Bleuler to describe a group of mental illnesses having in common the characteristic known as a "split personality." In a schizophrenic person the thought life and the emotional life are greatly disturbed. And he lives in a reality different from the one that actually exists.

Since Bleuler, most psychiatrists are agreed that schizophrenia is mainly the result of faulty reactions to frustration and conflicts. The neurotic produces substitute solutions of his problems; the schizophrenic cannot react in an integrated manner. An individual usually produces schizophrenic reactions only after having been exposed to excessive pressure.

This excessive pressure often consists of *lack of maternal love* or rejection by the mother. Because of maternal indifference, the sensitive, or frequently oversensitive, child withdraws into himself from a world that is unbearably damaging. Such withdrawal is one of the principal symptoms of schizophrenia. According to the severity of the case, it may go hand in hand with disturbances of speech or other functions, fits of rage, aggression, and inability to do anything for oneself.

In view of the relative frequency of schizophrenia—it accounts for half the mental illnesses treated in institutions—it is of great importance to point out what a powerful role the lack of love and indifference of a mother plays.

On the other hand, if a mother shows any interest at all in her child, her other weaknesses never have a catastrophic effect on him. It must be admitted, however, that babies with nervous mothers tend to become nervous themselves and to develop unevenly.

The relative importance of *hereditary factors, psychological influences,* and *socioeconomic conditions* in the development of childhood psychoses is shown in a study by Yerbury and Newell, who compared fifty-six mentally-ill children with fifty-six average children with reference to these factors.

In Figure 19 the first five rows point to influences that are due to heredity and are a result of illness; the next six to psychological influences; and the last five to unfavorable socioeconomic factors.

Among the factors conditioned by heredity, the most conspicuous is the extraordinarily high percentage of siblings among the disturbed children. In second place are the defects inherited from parents by the mentally-ill children.

In the group of psychological factors, the first two places are taken by disturbed family life and the conflicts of the parents about the upbringing of the children.

In the third group, most conspicuous are the low economic circumstances of the family and the unfavorable neighborhood in which the child grew up.

Next to the unfavorable environment, *bringing up* represents the most

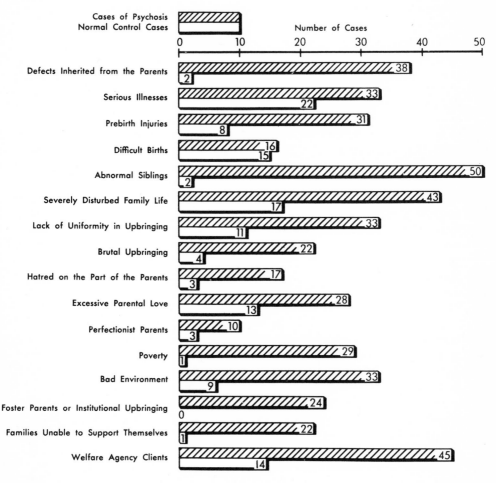

Fig. 19

Comparison of the effect of hereditary, psychological and socioeconomic factors in normal and psychotic children (after Yerbury and Newell).

important psychological factor. The psychiatric experience of the last decades forces us to conclude that too much or too little affection and too much or too little discipline are the most frequent basic causes of neurotic development. However, as has already been said elsewhere, there are always cases in which children develop much better or much worse than would be expected in their circumstances.

Natural Tendency and Mental or Psychical Development

Let us return to the beginning of this chapter, where Betsy's mother said with such assurance: "Of course children are different; Betsy is much less independent than my other children."

The problem is not that simple. Even without having studied psychology, Maxie's mother explains that Betsy, as the youngest child, may be coddled and spoiled.

It is very difficult to make absolute statements about natural tendencies. The heredity factor in mental illness is high, but it is by no means 100 percent. The same can be said in reverse about unusual talent.

The problem becomes even more difficult when we are dealing with so-called traits. The word "trait" is used by scientists with great caution. Most traits, which were formerly looked upon as constant and decisive, are today thought to be subject to change. This realization is important because from it emerges a completely different attitude toward the problem of the *re-education* of human beings. Today, even criminals are not regarded as incorrigible—granted, of course, that proper therapeutic methods, such as depth analysis and pharmaceutical treatment, are employed.

Faulty and undesirable so-called *character traits* are, to a great extent, capable of being corrected, although the methods of educational influencing most frequently used, or conscious self-guidance, are generally unsuccessful when deep personality changes are involved. The results achieved by these means are either superficial or temporary. Or they may merely get rid of certain symptoms, in whose place other symptoms develop.

Among the most scientifically reliable investigations of the role of natural tendencies are studies of *identical twins,* those one-egg twins that resemble each other "to a hair." Because the heredity of such one-egg twins is the same—they come from a single fertilized egg cell and not, like fraternal twins, from two egg cells that were fertilized separately—they possess the same natural tendencies. Everything that remains the same in the course of their development is thus undoubtedly conditioned by natural tendencies, and everything that makes them different from each other is caused by the environment. Identical twins brought up separate from each other but displaying similar developmental traits indicate the effects of the heredity factor.

Yet the life evaluation of a person on the basis of his inborn capacity is not predictable, because *motivation,* the decisive second factor, contributes to the determination of development. In general, those who are highly talented are superior in professional life, and those whose endowment is inferior contribute in a high degree to juvenile delinquency. But predictions of development based only on talent or other inborn characteristics are not reliable.

In recent approaches to the problem of *individuality,* the emphasis is no longer so much on the question of what is innate as on what is uniquely characteristic in a particular individual. The reason for this change in perspective is that we know that, from the beginning of his existence, the individual is being molded by his environment. We know, too, that at no point is there a clear separation between what is inborn and what is acquired. But, from certain consistencies in reaction to stimuli and in motivational trends we also know that from the beginning there are uniquely individual traits.

Functions and Accomplishments in Development

In this "century of the child," as it has been termed by Ellen Key, interest in childhood development surpasses that in all other branches of psychology. The reason may be the steadily increasing need in Western cultures for a scientifically based self-understanding. In this endeavor, the more philosophy makes room for psychology, the more the problems of development in the child, and of human development in general, step into the foreground.

Development, seen as an *unfolding of functions and performances,* begins with an extraordinarily rich inventory. From birth onward the infant has the use of all his sense organs as well as the potential for great motility, although this is not coordinated at first. Motility begins as mass activity in the "self-starting" organism, that is, one that is spontaneously active. With this—the activation of his limbs and his entire body—the newborn infant, one might say, thrusts himself into life. With this mass activity, which is at first undirected, the infant also reacts to many of the stimuli that impinge upon him. At the same time he is capable of a large number of specific reactions to stimuli. At first these appear principally in the form of *reflexes,* which are direct, unconscious, and involuntary answers to stimuli. For example, the salivary reflex at the sight of an appetizing dish is to "make our mouth water."

The time from which the newborn infant can be said to have a *consciousness* is a question still under debate. But it is clear that, even during its embryonic existence, the child experiences changes, in the sense of adaptations. The *learning* that has begun in this way, and that is interwoven with *maturation,* makes it possible for the infant to take in his surroundings *perceptively* within a few months and to recognize objects and persons. The child between six and nine months old can normally distinguish tastes and smells, sounds and noises, colors and shapes, tactile impressions of various kinds, as well as objects and faces. Such an infant has *mastery over his body* when he is sitting, creeping, moving to and fro, and in his defensive movements. He has a rich inventory of *emotions,* and he gets into contact with his environment by screaming, smiling, laughing, crying, and making *speech sounds.*

At about one year the baby is often able to stand, take steps, and speak his first words. At the same time, he begins to solve problems by thinking —by using objects as tools.

All this means that at the end of the first year the child normally can perform many functions. These are the functions and performances that serve the development of cognition; the development of *play* and *creativity*; and the development of *social* and *sexual relationships.*

The Development of Cognition

Cognition encompasses *perception, memory, thinking,* and many supplementary functions.

During the first year, the *perception* of objects in the mind of the child is made up of many qualities. At the end of the first year he begins to recognize pictures, but it takes him longer to distinguish between what is alive and what is not.

Even at preschool age the child recognizes resemblances and other qualities of form as well as units and quantities. He also achieves awareness of space and time relationships, although the grasp of distance and perspective develops more slowly.

By puberty the capacity for perception is fully developed and thereafter remains constant until middle age, when a diminution in sensory keenness may bring with it a lessening of perception.

Memory, the development of which has always been of great practical interest, is at work from the beginning of life, first in unconscious learning processes and then in short conscious memories. These are to be found from the very first months of life, indirectly documented in actions that show expectancy. From the second year, events are remembered for more than a day, and soon for weeks and months. In the third year, memories can be retained from over a year earlier.

Although events in the first and second years cannot be remembered after a short interval, some early experiences seem to make such an extraordinary impression that they live on in the unconscious. Later, in certain circumstances, these can rise to the surface again. Only in this way can one explain "age regression" experiences, in which unconscious memories return in the course of deep psychotherapeutic treatment or under hypnosis.

Training and Intelligence

Most parents take pains to train their child's memory early in life. Karl Bühler theorized about this early *training,* which is provided by the environment as well as by the child himself. Bühler placed this mechanical learning in juxtaposition to learning through insight. In an experiment, Bühler proved that learning based on insight is possible from about ten months and that mechanical training can take place successfully from at least the middle of the first year.

The experiment was similar to one that had been carried out with chimpanzees. A banana was laid outside the chimpanzee's cage. The animal could not reach it by stretching his arm outside the cage, but could reach it with a stick. The stick was placed in the cage before the chimpanzee entered it. The question was whether it would occur to the animal to make use of the stick to reach the banana.

Almost all the chimpanzees proved themselves capable of this performance. It was considered an *intelligence performance* because it was done not by chance and in play, but was *goal directed* and performed with insight into the *relationship* between the arm, lengthened by the stick, and the banana. This process is termed *tool thinking.*

This same tool thinking represents the beginning of a child's problem solving by insight. Karl Bühler put a piece of zwieback just out of reach of the child's outstretched arm. Tied around the zwieback was a string, the other end of which was close to the child's hand.

Although a nine-month-old was not yet able to grasp the idea of getting the zwieback by means of the string, a ten-month-old conceived of it. Later, eleven months was set as the average age for this type of performance.

In contrast to mechanical learning, which is based on numerous *repe-*

Fig. 20

The same tool-thinking of Koehler's chimpanzee . . .

Fig. 21

Fig. 22

. . . was found by Karl Bühler in ten- and eleven-month-old children to be the beginning of intelligent problem solving. Here the child pulls toward him with a ribbon the cracker he could not reach with his hand.

Fig. 23

Fig. 24

Fig. 25

titions, no repetition is necessary in learning by insight. Once the connection is understood, it remains in the memory. This sort of learning process is to be preferred because it can be successfully undertaken in higher age levels, whereas mechanical memory begins to decline in the twenties. That is why a professionally trained person, even at an advanced age, can acquire new data related to his particular field of knowledge but is prone to forget his doctor's telephone number or a friend's address.

Development of Learning

Even though learning acquired by insight remains in the memory in later years, mechanical memory, which is essential for the learning of such data as words in a foreign language, historical dates, or chemical formulas, reaches its high point early in puberty and begins to decline in the early twenties.

After the middle of life there is generally a decline in memory and learning ability. However, here as everywhere, there are exceptions. Cases are recorded of men and women in their fifties who were successful in studying for their doctorates; one octogenarian, after a long professional career as a chemist, took up the study of medicine and passed his state board examinations.

It is becoming more and more common for aging persons to continue to work and learn in all fields of endeavor. This is the result of better health, due to vastly improved hygienic conditions and progress in medicine. In addition to good health and motivation, aging persons have intellectual powers that are obviously still developing, although they are usually limited to specialized fields. Here, however, insight and thinking play decisive roles to an even greater extent than memory.

Thinking has already been mentioned in connection with the ability to use tools. The development of creative intelligence, the preliminary steps of which manifest themselves from the beginning in many of the child's assertions of life, reach a new plane with the grasping of *relationships* between objects. The realization that one can make use of one object to reach another object comes to a child at about the same time as the realization that certain groups of sounds comprise an object's name.

The Beginning of Language

With this realization we have the birth of *language,* the development of which raises thinking to a higher and specifically human level. Karl

Bühler, in extensive investigations, took up the subject of *language think-ing* as compared to *tool thinking,* and also the difference between *human* and *animal speech.* In a model study that has become widely accepted he distinguished three basic functions of language: *expression, appeal,* and *description.* He showed that animals use their "language" only to give expression to their needs or emotions or to appeal to their kind. Man alone is capable of expressing himself objectively about circumstances, without bringing into play subjective factors such as feelings and needs.

Beginning with the first cry of the newborn, all an infant's utterances are important preliminary steps for the first word—that is, for the first syllables to which a meaning is consciously assigned by the child. In the sounds and syllables of the pre-language stage, the child acquires the material with which he later builds up language.

One's mental life and ability to communicate manifest themselves to a high degree in vocabulary. That is why, more than any other, this phase of mental life requires cultivation of interest in the environment. If the little three- or four-year-old who is strongly disposed to talk and to ask questions meets with a lack of friendliness and understanding, he will soon get out of the habit of talking and asking questions—and perhaps of thinking and reflecting.

It is understandable, of course, but it is surely not in the interest of her child's development for an overworked mother to react impatiently to his endless string of questions. Not only can the questions be endless, they are not always logical. Here is an example of a four-and-a-half-year-old reported by Rust:

Child: I'm four, aren't I?

Mother: Yes, four years old.

Child: What's a year?

Mother: (Explains.)

Child: Is that a long time?

Mother: Quite a long time.

Child: How long?

Mother: That's hard to explain. It has a great many days. Three hundred and sixty-five of them, in fact.

Child: Yes, but how long?

Mother: Well, you know when it was Christmas.

Child: Yes, I remember. I had a tree, and once I had the tree in the corner and once I had it on the table.

Mother: Well, that was twice—and it takes a year till Christmas comes around again. From one Christmas to another Christmas, that's a year.

Child: Yes, that's very, very long. When I was little, we had Christmas. Is a year a birthday?

Mother: Well, you have a birthday, and then there's a year—that's the time till your next birthday.

Child: Yes, three, then four—then five. Tell me, how old are you?

Mother: Thirty.

Child: How did you ever stretch up that far?

Incidentally, the female often talks earlier and more than the male, a tendency that could be taken as a sign of women's greater need for contact.

Many primitive cultures expressed their inner wealth in works of art, but Western culture is primarily scientifically oriented. It is pre-eminently a language culture, built on language thinking, even though nonlanguage tool thinking finds extensive application in technology.

Early Thinking and Reflecting

Thinking, in the narrow meaning of the concept, consists of grasping relationships between objects. Such relationships can be of diverse kinds: space-time relationships; cause-and-effect relationships; logical reasons; intentions; goals; and a great many more.

In two children whose vocabulary was recorded up to their third year, we found that the "where?" question first appeared between one and a half and two years, and the "why?" question between one and three-quarters and two and a quarter years. The "when?" and "what is it?" questions do not make their appearance until later. With these, as well as with the first namings, observations, reporting, interpretations, and judgments, the child at the age of two to three enters the mental world of his environment.

No one has been more occupied with building up the mental world of the child than Jean Piaget, who studied the thinking of the child and his way of looking at the world in many careful observations and brilliant experiments. Piaget recorded children's questions and remarks, beginning from the very earliest expressions, and at the same time asked questions to stimulate the child's thinking. His studies investigating the child's thinking about causes are particularly valuable. He sought answers to such questions as: what is a child's conception of the world and what goes on in the world? Here are a few examples to illustrate thinking in early childhood.

J. is a little girl who since the age of three has thought a great deal about where human beings and animals come from: how they come to be, whether they make themselves, and what they are made of.

At five and a half she declares: "Babies are at first air, I think. Isn't that right? They are so little, they have to be air at first. But there must be something or other in the air the babies are made out of. I know. A tiny little thing, like this." And she points to a grain of dust.

L., not yet four, thinks a great deal about dreams. One morning she reports: "I didn't have any dreams last night because it was light. It's got to be dark for dreams to come. Dreams are in the dark."

Still another example is J.'s explanation of natural phenomena. Piaget shows the development of her thinking from month to month and from year to year. At three and a half she notices the clouds as they float in the sky. "Is the cloud an animal?" she asks. Piaget asked her why she thought it was an animal, and she replied, "Well, because it moves."

At four and a half she expresses herself somewhat guardedly: "The clouds move because it's cold. They come when it's cold. When it's sunny, they're not here. When it's cold, they come back." When asked *how* they come back, she answered, "They know how."

At five and a half her question is already put more scientifically: "What are clouds made of?" "Well, what do *you* think?" she is asked. "Out of some fluid. Out of water, water that has turned to steam."

The questions as to where things come from, what they are made of, and what are their causes occupy the child at a very early stage. It is important to know that the earliest thinking about causality—the connection between cause and effect—does not yet operate in a scientific way. Before the child can grasp that what is happening is self-contained, he looks for personal forces that may have brought it about. Physical-scientific thinking is preceded by *symbolic* and *magical thinking*.

Magical and Symbolic Thinking

In Western culture and education, the scientific form of thinking is considered the only one of importance, yet magical and symbolic thinking, often repressed into the unconscious, play a significant role. This happens even more in most other cultures. To understand human mentality, we must consider briefly the prescientific modes of thinking.

A *symbol* is something that stands for something else by virtue of being assigned to it by someone. This something can be a word, a name, an action, a thing, or an attribute of a thing.

One-year-old Jacqueline starts to say "bow-wow" as soon as she sees a dog; but she also says it when a bicycle or horse goes past. She has understood that "bow-wow" is a word that has been assigned to certain rather long, moving objects. At one year and four months, however, as Piaget found, she uses the word only for dogs. "Bow-wow," as Jacqueline now understands, means a dog; earlier it meant long objects that moved.

When a two-and-a-half-year-old boy struts about the room and puts a small stick of wood into his mouth like a cigarette, then holds it between his fingers and blows out "smoke," this action means "smoking."

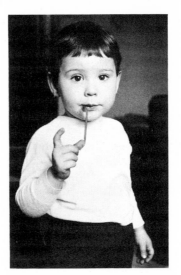

This little boy pretends that he is smoking a pipe—an action of symbolic thinking.

Fig. 26

This lending of significance is symbolization. In the choice of symbols, similarity may play a role, as when a small stick of wood is used as a cigarette. But a symbol can also be arbitrarily chosen. This is familiar to us from the secret or private languages one used as a child with other children or from learning stenography. It is not known whether human language owes its origin in part to such arbitrary assignments. Children, however, seem to be deeply imbued with the feeling of the arbitrariness of words used as names and invent symbols of their own.

We must distinguish between the conventionally established symbols of language systems or cryptic languages and *symbol thinking,* in which signs or symbols are invented and used in games or for the purpose of giving expression to emotional needs. In the play of three- to five-year-olds, in all artistic creation, and in various rites, the symbol thus comes to serve creative thinking. It plays another, no less important role, as Freud has shown, in sexuality and in dreams. The picture language of which symbolic thinking often avails itself conceals that which arouses anxiety and which is forbidden, just as it also helps in the revelation of what is only partially understood. In certain mental illnesses, symbolic thinking has a similar function.

The mentally ill also make use of *magical thinking,* something that is banned from the mental horizon of rational people in our Western culture but that plays an important role in the magic formulas and cults of primitive peoples, and also in our children's thinking. Magical thinking is based on the assumption of secret powers and secret relationships.

A first step to magical thinking can be seen in a nine-month-old infant who throws a second toy after one that has fallen down, with the obvious intention of having the second one retrieve the first.

Still another preliminary step is termed *evocation,* which is a conjuring up of objects. The children Piaget observed provided a classic example of magical thinking.

L., aged three, says: "See, that wagon went over there because I didn't want it to come here." When L. is four and a half, she says: "When I stamp my foot, the soup is good, when I don't stamp my foot, it's bad." And even at five and a half, meditating on how the sun moves across the sky, L. explained: "I think a giant behind the mountain makes it move."

Creative Thinking

All thinking is creative to the extent that it involves making connections and seeing relationships. *Creative thinking* has a more specific sense— *new* connections are discovered or invented. *Discovery* and *invention* are the two processes through which new things are created by thinking. Things may be "new" only to an individual; but they can also be new to larger groups, to a whole culture, or even to all mankind.

In this sense, solutions to problems in theory and practice can be new, but so can playful and artistic creations. Besides, understandings and relationships that evolve from human beings getting together can be new, as well as insights into mental happenings gained by self-observation or in the analytic process. The human mind constantly brings forth what is relatively or absolutely new in this sense from the very beginning of life.

Our knowledge about the beginnings of creative thinking is still limited, since it is only recently that intensive research has specialized in this area.

Observers have always been impressed with the creativity of young children at the beginning of their speech development, in make-believe and other play, and in early art work. Delight in fairy tales is an indication of a child's predilection for fantasy.

A comparison of two groups of adolescents resulted in a number of interesting findings regarding the most creative students and those with the highest I.Q.'s. Although all were superior in scholastic achievements, their values, attitudes, fantasies, imaginative productions, and career aspirations differed significantly.

Those with high I.Q.'s tend to converge on stereotyped meanings, to perceive personal success by conventional standards, to move toward the model provided by teachers, and to seek out careers that conform to what is expected of them. The highly creative students tend to diverge from stereotyped meanings, to move away from the model provided by teachers, and to seek out careers that do not conform to what is expected of them.

The developmental curves of both groups, as we know from other studies, are also different. Intelligence as measured by I.Q. tests culminates around twenty years of age. Creative productivity, however, may culminate at varying ages, but on the average reaches a peak in the early thirties.

Play, Creativity, Performances, and Interests in Human Development

It is probably correct to say that the child's creative powers are nowhere expressed as in his *play* and in his *graphic productions*. With increasing age, these creative powers lead to accomplishments of varied sorts.

To many an adult, play and games are not to be taken seriously. They are something a child does when he "can't find anything better to do." And many mothers judge play and games by how well they keep the children busy and out of the way. The fact that play and games are important functions in life is not yet sufficiently known and valued.

Play and games are of enormous importance for the development of the child, and also later in life. Mental health and well-being depend on a proper balance, appropriate for each particular age, between play activity and work. The focus gradually shifts from playful activity to work, and their importance changes place.

The Pleasures in Functioning

Play has primarily a *practice value* similar to what takes place in animals. In play the infant, like the animal, learns many movements and ways of behaving that it will need in later life. Its "excess energy" permits it to use time and effort in being active and thus to gain experience and knowledge. From the subjective point of view, the motility of play seems to be of the same nature as its goal: it is, first of all, the pleasure that activity provides for the player—"function pleasure," as Karl Bühler designated it. Strictly speaking, only the play and games of the first year are based solely on the function pleasure. Later, winning becomes important, and the competition for prizes or for victory changes the character of the game. But even then, the function pleasure is of importance.

Besides this function pleasure that governs a child's early play, we are often able to observe, even in the first year, the effectiveness of the *social factor*. The eight-month-old delights in playing "peek-a-boo," a game of hiding in which the mother or child disappears behind a blanket, only to reappear again. The seven- or eight-month-old, when he has for the first time successfully handled two things at once or knocked them together, may happily show off his tricks to his mother, and this should be interpreted as an early experience of success.

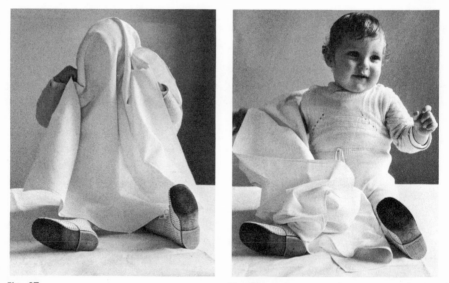

Fig. 27   **Fig. 28**

This infant is happily and enthusiastically playing peek-a-boo with his mother.

The sense of *mastery*, of which the child is already aware, undoubtedly heightens the pleasure in functioning, and the pleasure grows with increasing mastery. After complete mastery is achieved, however, the child's pleasure can change to boredom. This outcome can be seen not only in play and games, but in sports and other activities that are perfected through practice.

The Beginnings of Mastery

Mastery, performance, and success, in small things as in big ones, in play and in work, in human relations and in tasks one undertakes, in separate phases of life as in life as a whole, are the principal goals of our existence. The orientation here is obviously very complicated. To apply the concept of "instinct" to this desire for mastery seems incongruous. For instincts are more rigid and more specific than the great variety of techniques needed for obtaining mastery.

Wanting to be able to do things, which spurs us on throughout life, can be correctly understood only in the context of life as a whole. Later, we shall take up further the nature of wanting to overcome and to master. Here let us just point out how it is indicated in early play.

Besides the acquiring of mastery through practice with the help of play, another kind of mastery occurs, which Freud pointed out. This is the surmounting of traumatic experiences by release in play action.

A child who was hurt by the doctor when he was examining his sore throat plays "Doctor" with a younger sibling. He has his little brother open his mouth wide and makes the helpless little one feel pain the way he himself did.

In this connection Freud spoke of a *repetition compulsion,* that is, the need to assimilate painful experiences through a repetition in words and deeds. In this way the anxiety connected with them is mastered. Freud thought he saw here the meaning of play in general. The repetition compulsion in connection with the assimilation of traumatic experiences is only *one* form of the tendency to repeat. Besides, repetition not only serves to conquer fear, but can in itself be pleasurable. This is especially true when it culminates in the mastery of a situation that one wishes to master.

Make-Believe Play

In the child's second to his fifth year, there is extraordinarily rich activity in *fantasy.* It appears first in speech and play and later in constructive activity. The *motor play and games* of early childhood serve primarily the pleasure in functioning, the mastery of movement, and, later, social success. *Social play and games,* however, aim first of all at sociability and at competition, while the make-believe games and dramatic play of the preschool child, in which he plays a "role," are of great importance in the unfolding of the child's fantasy life.

One usually views make-believe games as *imitation*. It should be pointed out, however, that through imitation of what the father, mother, doctor, storekeeper, conductor, airplane pilot, or any other grown-up does, the child is trying to appropriate to himself the rights and the capabilities of the adults. Often children say that they want to be like Mommy and be able to do what she does.

The child in his play, however, does not only imitate grown-ups, he also brings the adult world nearer himself when he reproduces what they do.

In make-believe play, there are many emotional releases in the Freudian sense. In other words, make-believe play, like all other forms of play, serves a number of purposes. Fantasy, which finds expression in the elaboration of activities assigned to grown-ups by the child, later assumes an increasing role in art.

Constructive Play

Fantasy finds its strongest expression in the child's artistic productions, which are important constructive activities. The great psychic significance of play and games is not always correctly estimated by adults. The same holds true of *constructive play*. In a child's play activities, beginning with the tower that he sets up at a year or a year and a half and continuing on up to technical constructions, artistic portraits, and poetic or musical compositions at school age, we have proof of a responsibility taken on voluntarily, in the face of a self-imposed task, that has no parallel in other strivings. What the child acquires in these activities is the ability to dedicate himself to a piece of work with patience and persistence, with the will to overcome difficulties and to complete the structure, and with a wealth of ideas and a pleasure in creating that cannot be replaced by any other activity.

The child who concentrates on drawing, painting, building, or other construction develops by these activities an attitude toward *performance* that will stand him in good stead in later life.

Physical and Social Skills in Play and Games

The healthy child enjoys continual and diversified *activity*. By practicing the various movements that give function pleasure, the child gradually acquires *skills*. As he develops his aptitudes in running, climbing, swimming, skating, wrestling, athletic training, or other sport, the growing child wants to acquire prowess in addition to pleasure. And he wants to excel.

The desire to excel may develop into a desire for *competition,* depending on the individual and the situation. This means that the aspiration to achieve physical skills seems to bring out social competitiveness. The same applies later to games in which mental skills are practiced. But the main area of the child's *social interaction* is his outdoor play in groups of both sexes and, often, of mixed ages.

Perception and Projection

It is interesting how the *perceptive grasp* of the world is mirrored in a child's drawings, paintings, and graphic presentations, which are at first schematic and later realistic. Here the development of perception and intelligence so obviously finds expression that several psychologists have standardized as an intelligence test the child's drawing of a man's figure.

At the age of four many children are still in the "scribble" stage, that is, they do not yet know how to reproduce an object graphically. Even so, they pour out their feelings in their scribbles, as the great diversity of scribblework shows us. In the scribble stage, man's inborn tendency to "mix up, mess up, and mash up," as Goethe put it, provides great satisfaction for the child. According to Freud, the scribbles express emotional needs.

As soon as the child is able to produce forms and represent objects, he begins with the unconscious objectification of personal feelings that we call *projection.* This manifests itself in all art creation, beginning with the first drawing of a house, in whose solid or swaying form the child personifies himself, to the later reproductions of moods in landscapes or scenes.

Most children have a natural need to give expression in artistic creations to their feelings about life. In other words, children's paintings and adolescents' poetry are produced not so much to gratify artistic needs but to satisfy more general needs for creativity and for expressing feelings. That is why they often represent a diagnostic goldmine to the child psychologist. And because of their great significance as the carriers of emotions, creative productions should be taken seriously by the adults in the child's environment and should find warm appreciation.

The technical productions that begin in childhood are the result of more specifically directed needs to create.

What a child creates, in common with what the adult creates, structures material and expresses psychic experiences. The difference is only that, in the case of the child, the accent is on self-expression, while with the adult it is on the structuring. Thus playful activity becomes professional work.

Performance and Work

Play and constructive activity can be understood from the psychology of the individual. *Performance and work,* on the other hand, are a result of the individual's belonging to society. As soon as a product is created to be viewed as a performance, and, beyond that, as work, it has claims to a place in society.

We mean to stress here that the same activity and the same production that were formerly brought forth in only a playfully creative fashion can by their social implications become a performance and work.

Thus the four-year-old who in play and "for fun" is dusting furniture with her mother becomes aware only in consequence of the praise she gets that she is doing work for her mother. The five-year-old who goes to the store for his mother and carefully carries back the box of cereal and the correct change is already proud of the work he is performing. It generally also gives him pleasure.

Soon, however, the child and, in increasing measure, the young adult see themselves confronted with tasks the fulfillment of which is not pleasure but *duty.* The idea of duties that have to be performed, even when they are unpleasant, is carried from the world of adults into the life of the child. However, some children seem to develop a sense of duty without being expressly directed to it. They apparently pick up the idea of duty from the way people around them act and treat them.

A child performs duties primarily through obeying and from a desire to do what will gain him recognition. Other motives, such as fear of punishment or the conviction that through performing duties he will make himself liked and will "belong," also play a part in varying degrees. In normal development, the fulfilling of duty gradually becomes a need.

A feeling for perfection in performance originates in the environment. Later it becomes independent, functioning by itself without requiring an impetus. Hence the need to create something good.

In contrast to playful activity, which serves primarily as personal emotional satisfaction, the emphasis in performance is on objective factors of quality and quantity that are appreciated by others.

The development of a *striving for good performance* depends for the most part on influences from the environment. Extensive investigations show that a definite combination of environmental influences in childhood and youth bring out the most successful performances. Most favorable in this respect are demands made early on the individual appealing to his independence and responsibility, as well as discipline. The latter may be strict, but must not be authoritarian.

A striving for good performance that has been developed in this way inevitably leads to high performance. This has been proven in two investigations undertaken independently of each other and for different purposes. One was made on young people in school; the other on 200 engineers and bookkeepers in factories.

The investigation on school children was concerned with social performance in the group; the one on adults with work performance in the plant. The results of the second study on the motivation for work show that high morale and good performance are closely related to a striving for recognition, to a sense of responsibility, and to an interest in the work itself. When there is low morale and poor performance, other motivations play a larger role. These may include salary raises, working conditions, personal treatment, and personal relationships.

Similar findings were obtained among the school children. Thus, under two very different conditions it was shown that maximal performances are primarily connected with the *striving for performance* and the *striving for recognition.*

The second fact indicates that for good performance the social factor is of fundamental significance. In other words, the self-realization of the human being in society does not depend solely on his performance as such, but also on the recognition he receives for his performance.

These examples clearly show how levels of performance depend partly on motivation for performance as such, and partly on a social factor. In addition to these, the kind and degree of *capabilities,* the particular *life situations,* and whether the *occasion* is favorable or unfavorable play a decisive role. Through the working together of these and other factors there comes about the life performance.

Vitality and Mentality as Factors in Performance

When we were considering the building up and decline of various functions, we became aware how much most of them depend on age— hence they depend on vitality. Some performances, particularly speed and strength of movement, reach their high point in early youth. Experience, on the other hand, increases with age. Performances that depend on experience improve continually (unless failing memory or ability to concentrate lessen the usefulness of the experience).

Some performances depend more on *vitality* and others depend more on *mentality.* In general, however, the working together of both factors is the most favorable, and therefore the *middle period of life* is the most fruitful. However, certain performances are typically achieved early, and others late. Biographical material demonstrates that there are four different *periods of performance:* some people reach their summit early; others reach their high point in middle age; others culminate late in life; some people are productive at varying ages, without a definite peak becoming apparent.

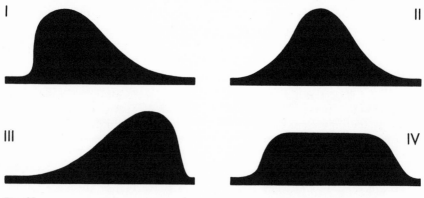

Fig. 29

Quantitative division of four types of performances in the life cycle (from C. Bühler, *The Human Life Cycle*, 1959).

Interest

In all types of performance, in play as well as in work, *interest* also plays an important role. Just what is interest?

Everyone knows, of course, what interest is—the Latin word means "being in between or amidst something." It signifies the most diverse grades of participation—from passing attention to an object to enthusiastic and complete dedication.

As Anne Roe has shown in her studies of interest, most psychologists consider intensity to be a complex process, in which the focusing of *attention* as well as *predilection* play a role.

Intensity

There are babies who, from the very beginning, respond with intense interest to the stimuli offered them in their environment, while others of the same age take no interest. Whether such interest goes hand in hand with greater physical activity is not known. The state of being interested appears to be a *pleasure in mental or psychic activity,* whereas physical activity seems to be a *pleasure in physical movement.*

Many people recount their dreams with intense interest. Even though the dream may be unpleasant, shameful, or unhappy, they are unable to shake themselves free of it. These people also find life interesting and are inclined to greet each new morning enthusiastically so long as they are not confronted with things that are definitely unpleasant. The author once heard a Viennese woman who later perished in a concentration camp discussing the subject of suicide in case it were impossible for her to flee from her native land. She declared with great conviction (and she later translated this conviction into action): "I could never take my own life. I find life much too interesting. It doesn't matter what happens. I'm just too curious about the future." It is not known just how this poor creature's interest in what actually came to pass was finally extinguished.

Those who take such an interest in life are the antithesis of those who, as the folk song has it, look forward to each morning with sorrow and dread—"Soon a new day will dawn, would it were gone"—or who look upon its coming with indifference and who long for death, the deliverer. The way in which these people cling to losses or disappointments, and are unable to develop new interests, points to the fact that interest is a *mentally creative activity.* The new life that a brilliant orator, a fine writer, or a gifted musician can impart to an old idea or to a piece of music is the result of the interest with which he approaches the theme.

We can, therefore, define interest as a *mental endowing of material with life* accomplished by an interested person's strong involvement with the material. The awakening and maintaining of interest are essential for any education that is to turn out well. The state of being interested is one of the most important concerns in life. Only by this mental participation, this endowing with life, can we make our lives worth living.

The things that we call our *interests* are characterized by the fact that we are more than just generally interested in them. A great deal has been written about interests, their origins, development, and the changes that take place in them. From the point of view of developmental psychology, interests first correspond to physical factors, such as skills. Later the interests correspond to the individual's heightened mental or psychic factors, with which we are already familiar from the curves of vocational summit performances.

It will be no surprise to hear that, among the young, all investigations show greatest interest in active sports, dancing, and social entertainment. Adult interests tend toward spectator sports, music, art, books, flowers, and gardening. With respect to attendance at lectures and concerts or going to church, investigations show no age difference.

Because the role that interests play can be mentioned meaningfully only in connection with the life cycle as a whole, a more detailed discussion of this topic will be taken up later.

Social Functions in Development

At three to six weeks a baby smiles back at another person or when he hears a voice. Just exactly what smiling signifies is still a matter of controversy, but one thing is certain: the infant's smiling is a social reaction—a reaction to another person.

The first question is whether the social reaction to another person is *primary* (inborn) or *acquired.*

Those who consider it primary point to the fact that the human being has an inborn need for companionship with those like him. He also has needs of belonging with other people. Hence he reacts positively to other people as soon as he becomes aware of them.

Another opinion is that the social reaction to another person is acquired —the infant associates the appearance of his mother with the warmth and nourishment she brings him. According to this theory, the satisfaction of need is experienced as pleasurable. This feeling is transferred to the person who does the nurturing.

This view can be called behavioristic. By *behaviorism* we mean a school of psychology founded by John Watson which introduced the technique of observing the most minute behavior. This school regards as unwarranted speculation all conclusions that cannot be proved by observed behavior. Although the behavioristic method enjoys wide acceptance today, many of its theoretical assertions are rejected by present-day researchers.

Many observations and experiments on newborn animals, especially birds, have shown that they lose certain instincts when they are not provided with the stimuli that call these instincts into play. A baby's smile might be comparable: it may be that it is inborn, but that it cannot develop if the stimulus that sets it in motion is not given, in other words, if the opportunity for social contact is not provided.

The Psychoanalytic Theory of the Mother-Child Relationship

A second theory, which also regards the social reaction to another person as conditioned by the other person, is held by psychoanalysis but is explained differently from the way the behavioristic theory explains it. In the psychoanalytic theory two phases in the development of the first social relationship of the newborn can be distinguished.

In the first phase the baby is a purely instinctive being and therefore not yet capable of any perception of objects. He experiences only the satisfaction of his needs and the *affective climate* that the mother creates for her infant. In this affective climate there is an exchange of affects in which the foundation is apparently laid for the emotional relationship between mother and child. According to René Spitz:

> The psychoanalytic theory has since its very beginning insisted on the fact that all mental or psychic functions, whether they be sensations, perceptions, thinking and acting, must have a libidinous charge as a prerequisite, that is, an affective process. The system of communication between mother and child, from the birth of the child, consists of a reciprocal exchange of affects and affective processes.

The concept of the libido introduced by Freud is very difficult to define because he several times changed his definition of it. In any case, in Freud's theory the libido is the *basic drive*. In Freud's later thinking it includes the drive for pleasure, for love, and for life. To have pleasure, to want to have, to feel, to be an individual, and to want to exist—all these flow together in the magic word *libido*. In the psychoanalytic view it represents the early desire for, and the early basic relationship to, everything in life. It is the original single process in the individual, but also the affect that sustains this process, from which it arises and to which it returns.

Spitz is of the opinion that these affective processes represent structuring forces from which there gradually emerges a specific emotional relationship of the child to the mother.

The second phase in this development, then, is the one in which, from about the third month of life, the child begins to *recognize* the mother or any other person who approaches him by the attributes of the human face, especially by the eye and nose configuration.

We are dealing here with the deepest and most important question that exists for human beings: *What is the origin of our relations to our fellow men?*

Does everything that we put into this relationship stem from what we *learn* from the environment, as the representatives of an all-embracing learning theory see it? Or does the origin lie in *affect experiences,* as psychoanalysis sees it? Or is there a third possibility?

Evidence is available for the opinion that, although at the beginning the child does not yet recognize objects, it does receive *perceptive impressions* to which it reacts in an individual way.

Jean Piaget points out that by one month, and more definitely by two months, there are reactions to sounds as well as attempts to imitate sounds. Furthermore, he noted that infants of this age stared at his face in motion and tried to imitate the motions.

Of two-month-old T., Piaget says: "I made the sound *aa*. T. made a number of unsuccessful attempts, with his mouth open and an almost inaudible sound following. Then a broad grin ensued and a real imitation."

At the same age, T. followed with his eyes a movement of the head that Piaget made. Then he smiled and moved his own head a little.

What we witness here are attempts at perceptions as well as at controlled movements. Furthermore, we find an expression of pleasure and the first signs of a relation to another person. This pleasure, however, is not the same as the pleasure of the sucking infant. Little T., who grins so happily, is experiencing the *pleasure of successful functioning*, which is different from the pleasure of sucking.

T. is furthermore experiencing a contact with the experimenter—h' feels a sense of community. They are playing this game together; it is an *interaction*. An interaction is a reciprocal effect that takes place between people and to which both partners contribute in their individuality. Interaction forms the basis of a sense of community.

Interaction and Successful Community

This working out of interaction, however, has definite prerequisites. Just as in the interchange of affects the experiencing of love comes about only when there is an actual giving of love, so in interaction a sense of community results only when doing things together is successful. From the very beginning of life, *success* in the social relationship appears to be as important as love.

We find excellent examples in Sybille Ezvalona's and Sylvia Brody's studies of mothers with four-week-old babies.

The first mother was rigid, slow, and awkward in her movements. She showed little affection for her child and little pride at having a baby, which she always held somewhat stiffly and straight. She also remarked that one shouldn't hold babies in one's arms too much. She always held the little fellow somewhat away from her body. The infant was well nourished, well cared for, and well developed, but was somewhat restless in his movements. It was noted that the baby smiled when the observer lifted him up, held him close to her, or spoke to him gently and not once did he smile when his mother lifted him.

Everything Mother No. 2 did with her baby was done with a light touch and with easy and skillful movements. She talked a great deal to him and about him, often full of admiration. In her behavior, a great sense of security and of responsibility was expressed. Her child was strong and well developed; he looked older than he was, and made many energetic and free movements. Every time the mother picked him up, the child smiled and crowed with delight.

Mother No. 3 handled her baby with care but without expressing any feelings whatever. She never talked to him and did not believe that he could understand anything. She said that he was "nothing but a tiny creature. What is there to see in him yet?" The infant was in good health; he was well developed and seemed quite relaxed. Yet he took no notice of people or things, did not smile, and made no movements as though looking for something.

Mother No. 4 was somewhat restless in her movements and referred to all sorts of worries and anxieties. She handled her baby gently and skillfully, but she was overly concerned with protecting her and keeping her quiet. She was uneasy about the baby's feelings, but did nothing to stimulate the child. The little girl lay there, usually with a serious look on her face. She showed an interest in being stimulated and in faces, but she did not smile. She reacted oversensitively to being touched and to being stimulated.

Mother No. 5 was loving and protecting. Although she was not always skillful, she was very eager to make the baby as comfortable and as satisfied as possible. Her attitude was that infants can sense whether their parents love them, and she was very proud of her little daughter. The child was particularly well developed and excellently cared for, very relaxed and at the same time very much interested in being stimulated. She stared repeatedly at the faces of her mother and the observer, followed their movements, and smiled every time they spoke to her.

When we stop to think that all these observations were made of babies only four weeks old, we marvel at the great variety of ways they behave.

Reciprocal Steering

The *interchange* between mother and child was aptly described by Karl Bühler as *reciprocal steering*. Mother and child continually direct each other in a subtle way. Hence, a sense of community emerges, which will develop in different directions—better in one way, worse in another—and certain tendencies are formed as a result. In these contacts the baby behaves as an individual, and, although he is also unquestionably influenced by the mother, he expresses his own *individuality* from the start.

In the interchange of affects the baby satisfies his life needs, while in the common functioning with another person he utilizes his adaptive tendencies as well as his expansive ones. With selective receptivity of the influences that stream in on him, and with *trust,* as Erikson called this attitude, the newborn infant opens himself up to the external world in order to function in it and master it. With trust in the possibilities offered, with experiences of succeeding and failing, the child shows from the beginning a striving for *mastery* that is just as fundamental as the libidinous drive.

In summary, we can say that, at the start, a person's social relationship to another person is based on two things. The first is an *interchange of affects* of unstructured feelings that flow into each other and produce an affective climate between the partners. The second is a sense of community arising from the *functioning together* of two partners, who steer each other reciprocally in selective receptivity. Obviously, primary dispositions as well as learning processes play a part.

The forms that a sense of community assumes in the first year of life go through a considerable development. In the writer's studies of contacts between babies from the age of five months on, one can find very diverse kinds of relationships. There was smiling at each other, friendly touching, the giving and taking of toys, and attacks on each other; gestures and expressions of subservience, aggression, superiority, rivalry, and triumph. Between six months and a year, there are attempts at a friendly exchange of toys, showing off, watching the other child, and community in playing.

Isabel, aged five months, touches the foot of Frances, aged seven months, whereupon Frances touches Isabel's foot, smiles, and says "Da-da."

Arthur, aged eight months, laughs at Frances, who is watching him, while he shakes his rattle before her eyes and utters sounds of satisfaction. Frances then tries to take the rattle away from him. He holds on to it tightly and smiles triumphantly while Frances begins to scream.

Brent, nine months old, and Mary, eight months old, have a rattle and a bell to play with. Mary plays happily with the bell, babbles, utters sounds of satisfaction; Brent smiles at her, she laughs back. She plays and he watches. Now he begins to get active and pushes the rattle over to her; she takes it although he reaches for it, too. He has the bell and rings it. She gives him the rattle and reaches for the bell; she takes and shakes the bell. Both children are beaming. She gives him back the bell.

Angelus, aged one and a half, and Marguerite, eleven months, really play *together.* He gives her a drumstick and holds out a drum to her so that she can beat on it. Both children drum together and laugh.

Having observed these beginnings, we can put some order into the enormously complex study of social and sexual development by distinguishing phenomena *dependent on maturity,* phenomena *dependent on the environment,* and phenomena *dependent on personality.*

Dependent on maturity are certain stages of sexual needs and certain capacities for *belonging to a group.*

The baby that grows up in friendly surroundings shows pleasure at contact with people. Between the ages of six months and a year many children do not want to let their mothers out of their sight. In the last months of the first year they begin to understand such social play as "Peek-a-boo!" and the rolling of a ball back and forth.

Belonging to a Group

In his first year, the baby is able to get into contact with only one person at a time. By his second year, the capacity for belonging to a group has developed in such a way that the child can play with two partners. After the age of two he likes to be "along" when older children are in a group. Actual participation in their games, however, occurs only after the age of three.

In spontaneous group formation, such as can be observed in kindergarten, only the four- and five-year-olds are found in larger groups. In increasing measure, children of school age seek to belong to a group. Eight- to twelve- or thirteen-year-olds love to go about in groups or gangs. In these groups there occurs, consciously or unconsciously, a ranking order, in which each child is assigned to a place that corresponds to his social qualities. In the gradual structuring of such a ranking order, *leaders* come to the fore.

The tendency to be a "loner" in the middle school years is a divergence from the norm, while in puberty the desire to be alone appears to be conditioned by maturational changes. Thirteen- to seventeen-year-olds seek to be alone because of the need to develop their individuality. At the same time, *friendships* and sexually colored *pairing off* play an increasing role.

The group formations now gradually take on the character of structural, goal-directed social formations. In these later associations, clubs and other adult organizations are anticipated.

The desire to belong, which leads the young child toward a group of children, draws him even more strongly to the *family.* Beginning at a very early age, the healthy child wants to do things together with the family and wants to take part in everything. He is proud to be allowed to eat at the table with the family, and when evening comes he does not want to go off to bed alone. He is happy when Mommy or Daddy sits by his crib and tells him bedtime stories.

Beginnings of Sexuality

Before Sigmund Freud, no one thought that sexuality plays a role in the early development of the normal child. And no one would have imagined that early sexual development represents an essential factor in the making of personality, particularly in its social aspects. In this respect, we all have been enlightened by Freud, although not quite in the radical way in which psychoanalytic theory was originally taught.

For example, the view that was seriously held by several of Freud's co-workers, if not by Freud himself, that every child wants to have sexual intercourse with the parent of the opposite sex has been generally abandoned. Also, Freud's *Oedipus complex* theory—that the child wishes to get rid of the parent of his own sex, whom he regards as his rival, and to possess sexually the parent of the opposite sex—is now probably ac cepted only by exponents of so-called classical Freudianism. The same probably also holds true for the theory of the *castration complex* as a stage of the maturation process. In a boy this is the fear of being castrated; in a girl it is the conviction that she has been castrated as a punishment for her early childhood masturbation.

Although we reject the assumption that these complexes are universal, we do not deny that they occur. There are certain neurotic developments in which these complexes do play a role. In some children there are often certain beginnings in the direction of these complexes in, for example, jealousy and psychic impulses toward possession. Castration fantasies occasionally occur in children, though not always with the tragic flavor that Freud gave to this experience.

Quite well known is the charming story in which a little boy, seeing a little girl in her bath, asks: "Was it cut off?" "No," she replies. "It's always been this way."

Partial Sexual Drives

While modern psychology, built up along analytic lines, accepts Freud's theory of complexes only with considerable limitations, it has widely accepted the theory of partial sexual drives.

According to this theory, also developed by Freud, the sexuality of adults is built up of partial drives that manifest themselves in early childhood. Their coming into being is possible because, besides the sexual organs of the body, there are various *erogenous zones*. These are parts of the body that can be sexually aroused and that, in the beginning, play a greater role than do the sexual organs. To Freud it appeared that, in the child, the mouth and the anus were particularly important in this respect. The partial drives are termed by Freud *oral, anal,* and *genital sexuality*. His theory holds that these appear successively from birth to about the fifth year of life, at which time the development of the partial sexual drives normally comes to an end.

The idea of oral satisfaction—that is, the satisfaction of the infant in sucking—as sexuality demanded a change in the earlier concept of sexuality. In fact, Freud broadened the concept of sexual desire, of the *libido,* to include all types of satisfaction and love. Accordingly, he conceives of neither love nor friendship nor the desire for social contact as separate from sexuality. He assigns their origin to one and the same instinct, and assigns to them all the same goal—gaining pleasure-satisfaction and love.

Neo-Freudians are inclined to distinguish between love, friendship, and the desire for social contact, on one hand, and sexuality in the narrow sense on the other. They turn to other, secondary processes as decisive in the development of these relationships.

Yet the concept of sexuality as including the functions of the erogenous zones has remained. It has met with wide recognition and confirmation from scientific investigations. Although Freud based his theories on pathological material and applied them to normal development, many studies of normal individuals support his theory of the way sexuality is built up out of partial drives.

The *oral phase* represents the first phase in the life of the infant and normally lasts until about the middle of the second year. In this phase the baby derives his principal pleasure from sucking and eating. He requires this satisfaction to such a degree that he provides substitutes if he has been deprived too early, either in part or altogether, of the pleasure of sucking. Substitute satisfactions consist of sucking the fingers or other objects, or masturbation. Researchers have proved that, in the case of too early weaning from the bottle, the sucking of objects is the substitute activity.

Freud goes even further. He assumed that adults find substitute needs for unsatisfied oral needs. For example, many analysts trace alcoholism to an unsatisfied oral drive, and the same holds true for "sucking" cigars or pipes. In this connection, Freud speaks of an "oral character" as an immature personality that is fixated in oral needs.

The *anal phase* follows the oral one; normally it lasts to the age of about three and a half or four. The child's interest in his excrement is aroused by the parents' emphasis on its importance. Pleasure-feelings result from the physical stimuli that occur in evacuation and also from holding back the excrement. Freud pointed out that there are also mechanical excitations of this area, for example, in swinging or other games of movement. He also called attention to the fact that repeated physical chastisement on the buttocks can cause sexual excitement.

As a result of active or passive participation in the processes of evacuation, *sadistic* as well as *masochistic* impulses are imagined. As Freud says in his famous *Three Contributions to the Sexual Theory:* "This form of sexual organization can . . . preserve itself throughout life, and can draw to itself a great portion of sexual activity." The instinctive drive toward withholding feces, which is normally developed in the same way, is at the basis of so-called *ambivalence,* that is, the tendency to be pulled in two opposite instinctive directions.

According to Freud, in the development of anal sexuality there lies one of the roots of *aggression.* Another lies in frustrations to which the individual responds with hostility and aggression. Freud saw a third origin in a destructive or death instinct that works against the life instinct. The origin of aggression, however, as well as its developmental phases, must for the present be regarded as controversial.

The way in which the child is toilet trained is, according to Freud, of extraordinary consequence in the development of certain character traits. In reaction to the pressure to which the child is subjected during this period, especially if he is being trained very early and strictly, he enjoys the power that he gains over the persons training him by holding back his bowel movements, thereby being able to make them worried and anxious.

To anyone who is not accustomed to analytic thinking, statements of this sort are often impossible to believe. However, it does not require searching analysis to receive from patients, or even in answers on questionnaires, responses that confirm these statements.

Thus twenty-eight-year-old Leonie, a few months after the start of her psychotherapy, reports that her mother was always more occupied with Leonie's three sisters than with her, the youngest, because she was less lively and affectionate. "The only way to attract her attention was for me to hold back my bowel movements for days at a time so that the whole family got all excited and anxious. All three sisters had to help to hold me when I was given an enema. I defended myself with hands and feet, but I did enjoy being the center of interest."

In this way, stubbornness and constipation are brought about. Other characteristics that belong to what Freud designated the "anal character" arise under such conditions; for example, the simultaneous appearance of stubbornness, an exaggerated sense of orderliness, and stinginess. Freud calls these three characteristics "the anal triad," which develops out of injudicious toilet training. He makes a connection between children's love of smearing and anal eroticism.

A further partial drive of sexuality in early infancy is the choice of the *sexual object*. As Freud says, "Various sexual strivings are directed toward a single person in whom they desire to reach their goal." According to this theory, the object-choice proceeds in two thrusts. The first thrust begins in the years between three and five and comes to a standstill or a regressive movement during the latency period; it is characterized by the infantile nature of its sexual goals. The second thrust begins at puberty and determines the definitive structure of the sexual life.

The Latency Period and Puberty in Freud's Sexual Theory

The period between the ages of about six and ten is termed the *latency period*. In this period sexual interest subsides. Freud probed intensively into the question of whether the restraints—among them disgust, feelings of shame, and aesthetic and moral demands—that work against sexuality during this period are the result of upbringing. He holds that upbringing has a good deal to do with it, but that this development is essentially an "organically conditioned, hereditarily [that is, inherited] fixated one [that] occasionally results without any help from the bringing up. . . . Bringing up remains throughout in the realm which has been assigned to it, when it limits itself to dragging in its wake that which is organically indicated and stamps it somewhat more clearly and deeply."

Freud interprets the latency period as serving purposefully to redirect instinctive sexual forces toward cultural performance.

Since such external influences as education and upbringing exist everywhere in the world, even in primitive conditions, it is difficult to determine to what degree the latency period must be regarded as a maturation process. There are obviously great cultural and individual differences that correspond to the extent to which sexual activities occur in this period of childhood.

Freud is of the opinion that it is not until *puberty* that the primacy of the *genital zone*, as he calls it, is realized. Genital excitation and the "end pleasure" that is achieved by the functioning of the mature genital apparatus is introduced by "forepleasure," which results from the excitation of the erogenous zones. Genital stimulation can, however, also come about from the inside of the organism or by mental processes. The sexual excitation that is thereby engendered is then converted into "a peculiar feeling of tension of the greatest pressure" and into a readiness of the genitalia—the erection of the penis and the moistness of the vagina.

Corresponding to physical genital development there is, psychically, a progress in the development of *object finding.* This ought actually to be designated "refinding," because preparations had been made for it from earliest childhood.

Freud wrote:

> When the very earliest sexual satisfaction was still connected with taking in nourishment, the sexual drive had a sexual object outside one's own body, in the mother's breast. This is lost only later, perhaps at the very time when it became possible for the child to form the total image of the person whose organ provided him with satisfaction. The sex drive as a rule then becomes autoerotic, and only after passing through the latency period is the original relationship re-established. Not without good reason has the suckling of the infant at its mother's breast become the model for every love relationship.

Freud's Theory of the Origin of Anxiety

In the course of this development Freud also saw the origin of *anxiety,* which, he declared, comes about through missing or losing the beloved nurturing person.

The explanation as to the origin of children's anxiety Freud felt he owed to a three-year-old boy whom he once heard begging from a dark room: "Auntie, talk to me; I'm afraid because it's so dark." To which the aunt replied, "What good will that do? You can't see me." The child called back: "That doesn't matter. If somebody talks, it gets light."

Thus we see that he was afraid, not of the dark, but because he had lost a beloved person. He could promise to be quiet as soon as he had received a proof that his aunt was present.

In later studies Freud saw the origin of *primary anxiety* in the experience of birth. His pupil Wilhelm Reich expanded this assumption into the theory of *birth trauma,* that is, that anxiety begins with the shock of the birth process. Other analysts put more emphasis on the helplessness and the "flooding" of the newborn organism with emotion as the causes of primary anxiety.

Freud sees development as completed, in principle, when all the partial drives have flowed together into the fully developed sexuality of puberty. He considers the later up and down fluctuation of sexual needs conditioned in the main by personality and cultural factors. These, as is generally known, play such a decisive role that it becomes almost impossible to single out the maturation factors as such.

There are, of course, a great number of physical occurrences that are essential to the development of sexuality, but no one knows precisely how the reciprocal effect of physical and psychic factors on this most complicated of all human spheres comes about.

Hormonal Influences in Development

One example of the physical factors in development is *hormonal influences*. Hormones are complicated chemical substances secreted in certain glands and carried in the blood to other organs, where they produce specific physiological effects.

There are male and female sex hormones. At this point we shall turn our attention only to testosterone and estrone. Both hormones are produced by both sexes, but in different quantities. In addition, these quantities undergo changes in the course of life.

In children under the age of ten, secretion of sex hormones is relatively low. Then it rises sharply; in both sexes the secretion of testosterone reaches its highest point in the twenties and then declines. The production of testosterone in men is significantly greater than in women until old age, when approximately equal amounts are produced by both sexes.

The production of estrone is greater in women than in men. The high point, interestingly enough, lies between the ages of thirty and thirty-nine; in the fifties and sixties there is a strong falling off.

Estrone affects the development of the sex organs, the beginning of *puberty,* and the *climacteric.* There are age variations in sexual development whose causes are not yet fully explained. Generally speaking, the beginning of *menstruation* occurs between the ages of eleven and fourteen; sexual maturity in boys comes somewhat later, between fourteen and sixteen. *Menopause*—the ending of menstruation—comes between the ages of forty-five and fifty-five; today forty-seven is considered the average age.

This presentation of sexual development has, up to this point, remained incomplete. Not mentioned, aside from its basis in early childhood, has been the development of *love,* the central phenomenon in human life. Nor have we touched upon *sexual life* at various ages and under different cultural and other conditions.

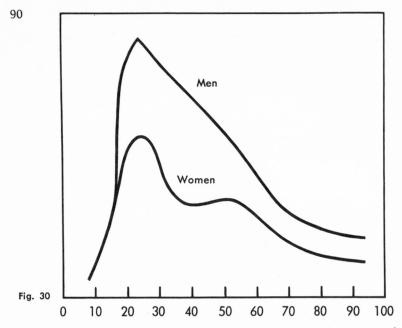

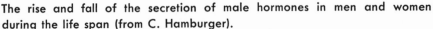

Fig. 30

The rise and fall of the secretion of male hormones in men and women during the life span (from C. Hamburger).

Developmental Research in Longitudinal Studies

The facts discussed in the preceding section were gathered mainly through systematic observations and experimental studies. In these studies the procedure is for groups of individuals belonging to different age categories to be examined comparatively with regard to certain problems of development.

There is, however, another method for finding out facts in development —the technique of *longitudinal studies*, which are investigations carried out over a number of years on certain people. With the individual, the work can be done by observations, interviews, tests, or by a combination of these. It is of great importance that the project, by means of which a *single individual* is to be dealt with continually and as completely as possible, be systematically planned and carried out.

Investigations of this type have been conducted since the 1920's, especially in the United States. Today we are in a position to survey their results and assess their value.

The main problem is: *Just exactly how does the development of an individual proceed?* Just what does development consist of? It seems so simple, and it sounds so matter of course, when Maxie's mother speaks of how quickly her little boy is developing. But when we look into the matter more carefully the question arises: Just what does she mean when she says "development"? And what do we mean when we use this expression?

Gradual and Sudden Development

On the one hand, Maxie's mother is obviously speaking of the changes that take place *gradually* and continuously. Every day, for example, Maxie learns how to walk better or to climb, or to do this or that, and he learns at a fast pace. On the other hand, she also has in mind sudden or spasmodic changes, although she is not necessarily aware of just what that means. When a child learns to talk, for example, something entirely new enters his life.

When my little daughter understood a word for the first time, it was a dramatic event. She was just nine months old; I had her on my lap and held my wrist watch up to her ear. Playfully I said "Tick-tock, tick-tock." She listened attentively, then she wanted to look at the watch herself and to touch it. Again I said "Tick-tock." She looked at my mouth, at the watch, and then with unbelieving wonder straight into my eyes. I nodded and said "Tick-tock," at which she asked in a whisper, "Ta-ta?" And as I nodded again, she repeated in a louder tone of voice, "Ta-ta," and kept repeating it; finally in a jubilant voice she said "Ta-ta," and swung the watch back and forth.

For the first time, she had grasped that the sounds, the syllables, belonged to this object, and that by using this word she was referring to this object.

Once the principle was recognized, the child learned to speak very quickly by pointing questioningly to objects and wanting to hear the names for them. With her understanding of the first name-word, there thus opened up by leaps and bounds a whole new world of understanding.

In my daughter's case, as with Maxie, progress was rapid. But does this mean that progress will be equally quick in all fields and at all times? Obviously not. There are fields as well as periods in which progress is less rapid and is possibly held back by unfavorable circumstances.

For example, Maxie was later a great disappointment to his parents; he became very rebellious and had to be punished frequently.

It all began when Maxie, who was a very intelligent child, became bored with school. As a consequence he engaged in all sorts of mischief and talked continually to the other children while lessons were going on.

His teacher had no understanding of this sort of naughtiness and gave him low marks.

Maxie considered this unfair. When a conference between his teacher and his mother could do nothing to change the teacher's attitude, the boy got even by neglecting his school work.

The development of a person is a very complicated procedure depending on a great many influences, and no one knows exactly how the various aspects of a personality hang together and which ones change more than others.

The Process and Concept of Development

The *process* of development, although it may seem natural to the observer, is actually extremely complicated.

At the beginning, development accompanies *growth*. In this period, it appears as the unfolding of the growing organism. But growth of the organism ends at a certain point, while development continues.

In development, organisms grow or change at characteristic rates toward their maximum size, form, and function, with the final state or limit representing a relatively steady state of forces. Form, size, and function appear to have a durable or persistent quality in adult vertebrates. Thus, individuals change in appearance after maturity, but they change within boundaries determined by the end of the early adult years.

The process that takes place after maturity has been reached is called *aging,* which may be defined as beginning at the point in time when the forces of growth of the organism in size, form, and function have arrived at a relatively steady state.

The development that goes on throughout life is characterized by a *sequential order* of normal *irreversible* stages. It is a process in which both certain *gradual* changes and *abrupt* transformations take place. These changes are brought about primarily through the two interlinked processes of *maturation* and *learning,* both of which are *continuous.*

The organism's passage from birth to death through growth and decline is shared by the individual's psychophysical system and personality—in fact, by the person as a whole. The interrelationships between the different physical and psychological forces that come into play is to a great extent still problematical; nor is it known exactly how genetic and environmental influences are integrated into a particular individual.

The extraordinary number of determinants results in every individual being *unique* from the very start. This uniqueness increases even as time goes on. Today it is thought that from the beginning and increasingly so as time goes on, everyone develops a *life style* of his own.

In spite of this uniqueness of the individual, there are likenesses among all human beings. There are certain characteristics that people of the same *biological age* have in common. There are likenesses in what is called *psychological age,* which is determined mostly by emotional development. The term *social age* is used to characterize an individual's aptitude to fit into certain social institutions and to perform according to social norms.

While the process of development is a continuous one, it shows certain marked *turning points,* which usually coincide with a change of the roles that society assigns to the individual, such as the beginning of school, marriage, retirement, and the like.

Some turning points offer useful criteria for the description of the developmental process through life in terms of a succession of stages, or *phases.*

The Phase Theories of Development

The various phase theories of human development refer either to childhood and youth or to particular functions. Examples are, on the one hand, Arnold Gesell's divisions of childhood and youth; on the other, Freud's phases of libido development, Piaget's phases of intellectual development, and, more recently, Erikson's phases of ego development. The author has suggested five phases of childhood and youth as well as five partly corresponding ones for the entire life cycle. Her phases are conceived of in terms of the goals pursued at consecutive age levels.

In establishing a theory concerning life phases, it is obvious that different points of view may be emphasized. This means that any theory will be somewhat arbitrary as to the progression of changes during an individual's lifetime.

A simple principle by which such difficulties can be avoided is a division into phases determined by practical life. Robert Havighurst suggested the concept of "developmental tasks" corresponding to the performance to be expected at each age.

Havighurst distinguishes six life phases according to developmental tasks. These are: early childhood (0-6 years), middle childhood (6-12), puberty and adolescence (12-18), young adulthood (18-35), middle age (35-60), and later life (over 60).

The performances to be expected at every phase are not conceived of as sharply differentiated; each set of new performances comes about in a gradual metamorphosis of what the individual is capable of performing and of learning.

In the first phase the child is expected to learn to control his body and to take on his first relationship with the environment. In the second phase he learns concepts and skills that are necessary for life. In the third phase he begins to free himself from his parents and assume his sexual and social role in society. In the fourth, he is expected to find a mate, marry and start a family, and assume his first duties toward society. In the fifth phase, the older adult is supposed to have assumed his social and community duties and to have set up a definite standard for his life. Finally, in the sixth phase, he should be capable of facing the fact that his powers are waning and that often material success also diminishes, and he should become resigned to the idea of death.

Rise and Decline of Functions and Performances

A different sort of *description* of development gives us *norms* for what to expect in various respects from persons at different age levels—in other words, they are instructive as to the particular *average age.*

All parents are familiar with the concept of average age. A conscientious mother notes carefully her baby's increase in physical and mental ability and might use a diary containing printed advice about what to look for. And most mothers know that around the end of the first year their baby ought to begin to walk and talk. Expressing this psychologically, one can say that, on the average, all *basic functions* are acquired during the first year.

However, few parents have a clear idea of when and why a child should be toilet trained. Neither do they know when the child should be able to eat by himself, wash himself, keep his toys in order, acquire certain conventional behavior, and help his mother.

Traditions, customs, and changing ideas of the optimal conditions for development are determined by the times and the circumstances in which the children acquire their earliest *habits.* The development of cleanliness, independence, manners, and the capacity to perform duties only rarely comes about without any direction. There are children who almost toilet-train themselves, want to be independent, and like to help. In general, however, development depends on habits, which determine the mastery of one's body and the first fitting into society. It also depends on upbringing and education, and even more on *example.*

Looked at purely from the standpoint of developmental psychology, the first step toward independence is to be expected at preschool age. The first consciousness of duty appears at that point when, in both modern and primitive cultures, the child begins to obtain education that is directed toward practical life.

When school age is reached, the school sets the norms for the progress that is to be expected in learning, in mastery of one's body and oneself, and in behavior in the group. Many parents, however, want their children to be not only above average but precocious.

Precociousness, however, is almost as undesirable as late maturation. It appears that there is a correlation between staying within the average age in development and physical and mental health. With all the happenings that are subject to the effects of culture—and psychic maturity is among these effects—there are great variations in the average age.

Developmental Tasks According to Havighurst

Despite the variations, there is some usefulness in applying the concept of average ages, as Havighurst shows in his setting up of what he calls *developmental tasks.*

Entering upon a vocation, marrying, starting a family, and assuming one's place in society are to be expected, on the average, before one is thirty-five. The stabilization of one's income and mode of life comes about, on the average, before the fiftieth year. The release of the next generation and the objective and subjective proofs of success in life occur, on the average, in the years of the climacteric. After the middle sixties there are forms of withdrawal from active participation in life.

There are, of course, exceptions to all this, and everywhere we find variations brought about by many factors. On the one hand, psychophysical development and social roles are correlated to a great degree. On the other hand, in a society like ours, in which one's capacity to perform, one's social position, and one's success all depend to a great extent on education, many events are delayed. Thus, marriage and starting a family occur much later than sexual maturity would permit. Yet, in the decision as to how long an individual may be profitably employed, the position he holds in economic life and in society carries more weight than his age or his ability to work. According to the comparative strength or duration of all these factors, a person develops his physical and mental powers in inner harmony or disharmony.

The pragmatic description of development, whether a course that is average or one that deviates from the average, provides us with useful knowledge of what is *factual* in life. It cannot satisfy us, however, when, beyond this, we want to understand life as something that has *meaningful connections.*

Human beings in all ages and in all cultures have tried to understand the "meaning" of life, to give it an interpretation that places everything that happens in life into relation with a principle that transcends all this, that is, to a principle that lies beyond the mere happenings. Various things can be looked upon as this principle—a purpose, goal, task, or symbolic meaning. The desire to provide such meaningfulness is human and universal; all religions and philosophies are based on it.

A psychology of human development is incomplete if it does not include the *development of providing meaningfulness*. This means that the facts of development must be seen in the connected meanings that man gives them.

If we are to understand the facts of development as a series of meanings instead of merely random functions and performances, then we have got to introduce a new concept—that of *personality*.

Only when we consider development as the history of a personality does it become more than a multiplicity of psychosomatic processes held together by an individual.

CHAPTER 4

PERSONALITY

The Concept of Personality

Defining the word personality is a very complex and complicated task. It is extremely difficult to describe a personality, and it is even more difficult to give a satisfactory definition of the concept.

First, let us make an effort to describe a personality. Let us assume that someone is thinking of a person he knows very well, for example, his mother. Where will he start with his description?

Anyone who is systematically inclined will look for some sort of principle of organization; perhaps he will begin by pointing out external indications: "My mother is a woman who is still good-looking, of medium height, not at all fat. She is approaching seventy, but she is still full of energy and almost always in good health." Here we find a description of physical attributes combined with an indication of age.

"She is interested in everything." Here, perhaps without being aware of it, a son is describing his mother's inner characteristics, signs of her nature, and relates ways of behavior in which these characteristics are expressed.

"When we children visit her, she always wants to know everything that has happened. She asks us about everything, and she has a very good memory for anything we've ever told her. Her mind is active; she reads everything she possibly can. Full of life and warm-hearted, she is one of those people who also show their love. She is very affectionate, and she always has some good food on hand that she has prepared for us. There's always something for other guests, too; as a matter of fact, she is extremely hospitable. She used to love to give parties, and of her former large circle of friends, a great many still visit her."

For this systematic fellow, everything about a person is a part of personality: his physical and mental qualities, the way he behaves, the circle he moves in and his personal relations, the goals and the values that he pursues, and the life and actions that are appropriate to his age.

Less systematic observers often point directly to any quality that seems to be particularly conspicuous or characteristic.

"My mother," says Linda, an exceptionally happy and accomplished woman in her fifties, "is, first of all, an exceptionally loving person. This great love, which she always showed for us children, was my great good fortune from my earliest childhood on. I shall always be grateful for this love, because it gave me joy in life and a feeling of my own worth."

In Linda's description the whole personality is focused on a main point, her mother's love, and the lasting effect it has had.

The same thing may be said of the opposite characteristic, which a woman patient in psychotherapeutic treatment reports about her mother:

"My mother was a terribly selfish person," Wanda states in great excitement. "She always made enormous demands on us children, and if we did anything that did not please her, she would often not speak to us at all. For example, she hasn't spoken to me since my marriage, because we didn't celebrate our wedding the way she wanted us to. Throughout my life she burdened me with a sense of guilt; even my present illness has something to do with the fact that I feel guilty."

In this description, everything else fades into insignificance in the face of the effect of this personality on Wanda.

While the men included more or less everything when describing their mothers, Linda and Wanda started out from a *central* characteristic, by which the whole person is made understandable to them and by which she seems to be exclusively determined.

Gordon Allport, who was one of the first modern psychologists to attempt to get to the bottom of the difficult problem of personality and who is one of the leading research workers in this field, would call the men's descriptions *omnibus* definitions, because their characterizations of their mothers are like an omnibus, that is, they load onto the vehicle everything and anything that can possibly be taken along.

This type of description of personality may be very graphic, but according to Allport, its fault lies is that it does not allow for the point of view of the inner organization of the personality. In this, we come upon perhaps the most significant factor in the understanding of human personality, namely, the factor of its *inner organization. The healthy human personality is an organized whole.* Mental illness generally starts when this inner unity is lost or threatened.

Gilbert, for example, described his mother this way: "My mother has a frightful temper. When she gives free rein to it, we all run away from her. My sister Martha says, 'Mother is in a bad mood. You'd better get out of her way—she has one of her headaches again.' Yet, at other times she can be loving and friendly. Then she would read aloud to us children or take us to the museum. We never could understand it, and one could never tell in advance whether she'd be in a good mood or a bad one."

Here is a man describing his mother from the standpoint of her moods, the unpredictability of which, to this day, when he is a man of thirty-seven, is still a complete riddle to him. He was never able to understand the inner connections of these mood changes, nor could he recognize the basis for her inner distraction. Nobody really knew why she was tossed hither and yon by her emotions.

It was discovered that this woman was mentally as well as physically ill. A brain tumor (which was later operated on successfully) was the objective cause of her pains. But in addition to this, she had been spoiled by her parents and her husband. In her attitude toward life, she was both immature and without any goals.

This description gives rise to a number of further points that are important for determining the concept of personality. People expect a personality to be *understandable.*

"There's no sense in this woman," Gilbert once said, speaking of his mother.

What did he mean by that?

The *understandability* and *sense* of a personality arise from the fact that the behavior of a person as a whole exhibits certain tendencies, or *principle of organization.* The main tendency in Linda's mother was her loving attitude, while in Wanda's mother it was selfishness—or at least seemed so to her daughter.

Traits and *quality* are words that many would prefer to use instead of "tendency." But many modern psychologists wish to avoid the word "trait" because they regard the human being as a *dynamic system* rather than a being with definite traits or qualities. Qualities belong to an object more or less unchangeably, like size or color or purpose. Thus, a landlady might say to a tenant; "This big brown wardrobe is meant for your clothes." In saying this, she mentions the qualities that directly and unequivocally characterize the object.

Personality, then, is not a composite of qualities. Rather, it represents a system that is continuously in a state of development, that is subject to change, that is surrounded and limited by a physical body, that is in a continual reciprocal relationship with the environment, that possesses a core of strength, and that, in its progress from the beginning to the end of its existence, pursues certain goals. The way in which the individual behaves in these circumstances gives the impression that he possesses certain qualities.

This impression is correct only insofar as the structure of the goal-setting of a person makes possible the predictability of certain individual qualities. Such qualities—the way, perhaps, in which loving and selfish mothers make themselves known and behave—we speak of as the *essence* of a person. In so doing, we are expressing the conviction that in the flux of ever-changing happenings and in all the vicissitudes through which a human being may pass, there is a core that lies at the base of everything, an innermost indefinable something that keeps a person intact and determines him as an individual. We call this core the *self*.

The self, the definition of which is still very controversial, is now recognized by many theoreticians as the *core* of personality. It is from the self that the various goal directions arise.

The self is the core of a *hierarchical organization of processes* that constitute the personality system. This hierarchical system makes possible the personality's inner unity.

The various strivings that proceed simultaneously at various *depth levels* and in various *layers* of the personality are kept in *order* by the hierarchical structure. This hierarchy is not firm and unchangeable but is, to a certain extent, constantly renewed. An example will make this clear.

Gilbert, the son of the unaccountably moody mother, is employed by an advertising agency. He is in charge of the advertising that appears in two weeklies of wide circulation. He enjoys his work very much and is happy that at last he has found a position that interests him; for a good many years he was unable to find the right position. Today, at the age of thirty-seven and married for two years, he feels he has a solid foundation under his feet although, as he well knows, it has all come about pretty late for him. He had not concentrated on a goal, he had not had any inner organization—just like his mother, he sometimes thinks. He has often felt that her influence on his development was most unfavorable.

Today, however, he believes that he is on the right track. The hierarchical organization of his personality follows.

Most important to him is success in his career. He knows that his endowment is just average, but he believes that his interest in his work, his conscientiousness, his energy, and his popularity with his associates give him a prospect for a secure future and a good income. His goal of an appropriate and secure way of life is important to Gilbert.

But at the same time he has an intense desire for happiness in his marriage. He often asks himself whether this doesn't really take first place, whether he would be at all interested in a secure future without happiness in his marriage.

Could it possibly be that both goals are equally important? Gilbert's hierarchy of goals in life is perhaps two-pronged. He is unable to decide. Career? Or marital happiness?

The question often troubles him because his marriage is not so satisfactory as he had hoped it would be. Diane does not love him so much as he loves her. Often she seems depressed and irritable. At such moments, Gilbert immediately suffers stomach upsets. He is nauseated; he experiences feelings of panic; he breaks out in a sweat. His body does not seem able to cope with such trials. Although he is of athletic build and in excellent health, Gilbert feels that he is adversely affected by these weaknesses, which he considers his psychosomatic reactions to be. At such moments he thinks of himself as a "weakling."

Conquering both his weaknesses and his tendency to lack concentration appears to him to be a third important goal. He regards *inner organization* as the hallmark of a personality able to cope with life. In this respect, Gilbert's father was a much better model than his mother, but as the parents were divorced when Gilbert was a child and his father moved to another city, the boy did not see as much of him as he would have wished.

We might now proceed to show how secondary strivings, interests, duties, and problems of daily life fit into this picture of the principal goal-strivings. Countless large and small, superficial and deep desires play diverse roles in the personality structure of a person: feelings of anger, professional triumphs, questions of appetite, digestion, and fatigue, having a cold, even bathing and retiring at night.

One important factor that Gilbert seriously considered was his *capacity to adapt* to his tasks in life as well as to the conditions in which he finds himself. This capacity to adapt is taken into consideration by many theoreticians in their definitions of personality.

When, at the close of this section, we try to find a useful definition of personality, it would appear that the one coinciding best with what we have just said is Gordon Allport's: "Personality is the dynamic organization within the individual of those psychophysical systems that determine his characteristic behavior and thought."

In this definition the question naturally arises as to what kind of organization and what kind of structure are under consideration.

The Structure and Development of Personality

A human being's personality has an extraordinarily complicated structure. According to the impressions people make on us, we consider some "simple" and others "complicated." Our judgments are based on the motivational structure of the particular personality. But even the simplest people have complicated personality structures, just because they are human beings.

First of all, there is the extensive *action system,* from which all human action proceeds; in this action system there come into play the *inborn tendencies,* which are continually being modified by *learning.* This has already been discussed in detail in previous chapters. At the basis of the action system are the complicated *psychosomatic events* in which, whether by mutual interaction or in some other way, the happenings that are *physically conditioned* and those that are *mentally conditioned* are integrated.

Second, the personality processes are, to a certain extent, subject to change. This change consists in part of *development,* in part of other *alterations,* among which illnesses or other disturbances of the regular course play a part. Accordingly, within the over-all continuity of personality there are discontinuities.

Third, the personality processes are time-bound. The personality is always partly determined by both its *past* and its *future,* while it lives in the *present.* This means that *looking backward* and *looking ahead,* in individually different measure, have an influence on the experiencing and the handling of practical life problems.

So we arrive at a fourth point, perhaps the most complicated part of personality: the structure of motivations and goal-settings. *Motivations,* as we saw in an earlier chapter, can be *unconscious* as well as *conscious.* A mixture of conscious and unconscious motivations becomes the determining factor in mental or psychic happenings.

From *motivations* on the one hand, and from given *situations* on the other, there arises a fifth point: the enormously rich and complicated structure of goals, with which the human being is almost uninterruptedly concerned. Although we can determine individual variations with respect to continuance, variability, complications, and limits of goal settings, there is no human existence in which *goal directedness* does not play a fundamental role.

Even a person absorbed in play or in recreational relaxation simply cannot do otherwise than concern himself with goals that touch his daily life. He must know, when he comes from the sunny bathing at the seashore, in what direction to turn his steps, when, where, and what he is going to eat, and how he intends to spend the rest of the day. So long as he is a human being, he cannot avoid the necessity of having intentions, even if he were to attempt to live a purposeless existence.

These goal settings occur, just as do the motivations which are the basis for them, in the most diverse realms of life, the most varied strata, and the deepest levels of the personality.

While on vacation, the man returning from the beach may occupy himself with how and where he will get some satisfaction for the rumblings in his stomach or what he is going to do in the afternoon and evening. Then, on his way to the restaurant, it may occur to him that he should write his mother a letter and send his wife a check. And while he is doing this, a worry about money may pass through his mind. Perhaps he is then overcome by a feeling of dissatisfaction that his vacation isn't interesting or stimulating enough, not the way he had imagined it would be. And at a still deeper level he may unconsciously be troubled by a longing for a sense of happiness that is missing and by the foreboding, still unconscious because it is repressed, that he is missing what is essential in life.

All these partial processes operate relatively independently of one another. This relatively independent and yet inwardly connected method of functioning of the *partial systems* of the personality is the sixth important characteristic of its structure.

In the various theories of personality, the partial systems, as we will show, are separated from one another and their operations are described in very different ways. A number of research workers, especially those of the German schools, are more impressed by the functional connections of the lower and higher levels in the personality structure. American theories of personality derived from Freud pay more attention to the conflicts among the impulses that arise from the diverse partial systems.

Despite the relative independence of the partial systems, the personality is held together in a *unity* in an individually characteristic way. This unity of the person is, first of all, the purely external one determined by the physical limitations of the individual. Internally, however, there is not always a complete unity of structure to correspond with it.

Where it exists, *integration* toward *unity* is the result of a performance that begins with the integrative activity of the embryonic organism.

Arnold Gesell describes the first bases of unity formation in certain happenings in the embryo. He shows that in the fetus in the mother's uterus, five factors have to be integrated with one another in the proper way: homeostasis—the regulation of the inner equilibrium of all processes (see page 41); breathing processes; states of consciousness that start as impulses in the nerve tissue; muscle tone; motor activity. The health of the psychophysical foundations of personality depends on the proper working together of these basic factors during embryonic growth.

All observers agree that schizophrenic children exhibit extreme *anxiety*. They can be so overwhelmed by these anxiety states, which are often continuous, that they are incapable of any organized behavior. The complete failure to build up any equilibrium integration or unity formation seems to result in that depth of anxiety, we might even say torment, that can be observed in certain schizophrenics.

"I have a hole, a great big hole in my leg," screams three-year-old Nina, while in her madness she tears her hair and throws herself around in her bed where she has been laid for her afternoon nap.

There is nothing the matter with her leg, but Nina stares, screams, and points to her leg where she "sees" the hole. This disturbance of body image is an example of how perception of one's wholeness may be lost or absent in a schizophrenic.

The sense of well-being that the healthy person experiences when he is conscious of an *inner equilibrium,* inner *order and unity,* stands in sharp contrast to the anxiety of a person whose unity-formation is disrupted by a lack of inner equilibrium.

For inner unity and order, a further factor is required. We will use the example of our vacationer to make this point clear.

Here he comes, a man of medium height, from the sandy beach at some seaside resort. He is on his way to lunch. We know that he is concerned with where he is going to eat, with plans for the afternoon and evening, with remembering the letter and the check, both of which he has got to attend to, with money problems, and finally with a certain dissatisfaction about how the vacation is coming off and about the course of his life as a whole.

The picture is clear: the feelings we have mentioned give the impression that he possesses an inner organization and an inner equilibrium even though there may be certain disturbances in that inner unity. But something essential is lacking for real understanding of this man's personality.

"What's his name?" Mrs. Sommer asks as she sits chatting with some other ladies on the porch of the summer hotel as our man walks past. For many people, of course, the name is very important in determining the identity of a person.

Mrs. Sommer's daughter Hilda says, "I think it's Robinson."

"He looks a little Negroid, don't you think?" Mrs. Aldrich asks.

"So what?" Hilda shoots back. "Does it make any difference?"

"Oh, no. No, perhaps not," Mrs. Aldrich replies.

"Well," says Hilda, whose liberal views have been strengthened by the courses she has taken in sociology and anthropology, "racial and cultural signs may be important, perhaps, but as far as I'm concerned, it's much more important what kind of person a man is."

"So that's what they teach you in college!" Mrs. Aldrich exclaims, unable to conceal her irritation.

"What do you mean by 'what kind of person he is'?" Mrs. Sommer asks her daughter.

"For me it means that I'd like to know what a man really is and what he wants; whether he is a selfish person or whether he's ready to help others, whether he knows what is truly worthwhile in life, or whether he is content with superficialities—things like that."

After a moment's thought, Mrs. Sommer says, "I think I understand what Hilda wants to say. She's interested in what a person ultimately wants and is."

"That's exactly right, Mother," Hilda says. "That's it exactly. In psychology class we talk of a person's self, of the innermost core of his being."

The *self*, which in the last analysis constitutes a person's *identity*, what he is, and what he wants, is what determines inner unity. The question whether there is such an innermost core and how it functions is still controversial and is answered differently by different theoreticians. Without such an inner core a unity formation would, to our way of thinking, be incomprehensible.

Only when we assume that there is a *centralization* does the generally accepted fact of the *hierarchical structure* of goals become comprehensible. We still know little more about the hierarchy of goal formations than the fact that it exists. This hierarchy is normally subject to change and development. Moreover we know that there are day-by-day, and beyond these, more permanent goal formations in one and the same individual.

Thus, at the moment, Mr. Robinson's lunch may stand at the very top of the hierarchy. But, in a broader text, his family life, the letter to his mother, and the check to his wife take primacy, along with the money matters in connection with his job. As to proper utilization of his vacation, the problem of greater satisfaction pushes itself into the foreground, even though it may be insoluble. In his view of his entire life, however, his longing and the foreboding that something is lacking are perhaps the deepest and final goals, although for the present our vacationer will not let these come into his consciousness.

But so long as his feelings and problems do not overwhelm him, he is master of them by the very fact that he keeps them in order and that he sets now one and now another at the head of the list.

The mentally healthy person who functions in a well-organized way has a more or less clear idea of his principal and secondary intentions and of his near and future goals. The person who is mentally unorganized often has no clear picture of what his principal and secondary goals really are. And the person who is mentally ill is torn by conflicts and strives simultaneously for many goals, no one of which can be combined with the others.

In healthy persons, the hierarchy of goals is definitely structured but is at the same time flexible. The healthy person can—in accordance with his satisfactions and his disappointments—reorganize himself, for, in the course of becoming mature, he learned to give up certain goals and exchange them for new ones.

Where does he get the *principles* for the order that he creates? Everyone is influenced by various points of view about what is important or unimportant. A child generally learns from his parents what they consider important and unimportant. The rest of the environment, too—the school, the community, the nation, and the cultural community—are influential in this respect.

The most important role, however, as has been described in Chapter 2, is played by the individual's own *basic tendencies*. These basic tendencies, experiences, and the continuing effects of the environment provide the individual with the points of view he selectively makes use of in order to determine what is important and valuable for him. This means that the *importance in life* that a person accords to certain goal attainments and the *ranking of values* he has set up for himself determine his inner organization.

Linda, whose childhood was such a happy one because of her loving mother, throughout her whole life exhibited a personality that is definitely established and, at the same time, very flexible. Even as a child she had a few clear guidelines, even though they had not yet been integrated into the unity of her personality. However, we were already able to see in the three- to four-year-old a definite partial goal direction beginning to work itself out at various levels.

As a little girl Linda wanted, first of all, to be close to her mother in mutual *affection* and mutual *help*. By the time her younger brother was born, during her third year, Linda, the second of five children and the oldest girl, had experienced enough love to be able to help her mother with the care of this child and with the other children without jealousy. *To help others* and understand them became an important goal for Linda early in life. Later it became her main goal, to which all the others were subordinated.

Another goal of Linda's was to know and to learn a great deal. At four she let herself be initiated into the mysteries of the alphabet by her patient brother Ted, who was two years older than she. Linda's *eagerness to learn* was just as great as her curiosity. Her mother supported and furthered this eagerness while her father, then and increasingly later on, expressed his disapproval at having Linda brought up to become an "intellectual." In his view, women's place was in the home—they should learn to cook; a scientific education would only ruin them.

In his hostility to higher education, so rare in this country, her father's disappointment at his own development was expressed. He had lost his father at an early age, and his mother had been poor. He had had to work hard from morning to night to earn a living. Under these conditions—the family lived in rural California—it was considered a great success that he worked his way up to become a ranch manager. His education had been a purely practical one, and he was of the opinion that his children should work just as hard as he had. In this attitude he expressed a certain envy and a rejection of the higher education he had been denied. He was a very irascible man, and it required great tact and humor on the part of his wife to keep him in good spirits.

A conflict soon developed in Linda's relations with her father. She loved the huge ranch where she grew up with her brothers and sisters, but very early she determined to make her way to the city and attend the university.

Here another personality trait that Linda had acquired from her mother played a part. When she was three or four years old, her mother had explained to her that, while everybody has *duties,* they also have *rights.* This pointing out of rights, omitted by most parents when they speak of duties, made a great impression on Linda. As she told me when she was fifty, from that moment she was deeply touched by the dignity of human existence—a singularly precocious observation for such a little girl. It became one of the most basic components of her personality and of her way of life.

Linda recalls a humorous little scene, an episode in which she applied what she had learned from her mother about people's rights. The mother explained to her older brother Ted that he must rise when a lady enters the room and offer her his seat. Linda, aged four, who had heard this conversation from an adjoining room, thought that there was a fine opportunity to test her rights. She promptly marched into the next room and, without beating about the bush, reminded the astonished Ted that he must offer his seat because she was a lady. Grinning, he did so. Linda's practical as well as her tactical skill, which later stood her in good stead in her sociological work, here showed itself in its early beginnings.

She also applied this skill to her duties. Frequently she was in an inner conflict, full of anger at her father's narrowmindedness and tyranny. But gradually she adopted her mother's gentle advice that it was not only wiser but also her duty to bow to her father's wishes. Even as a little girl at school, when her teachers encouraged the gifted child to study and to work for a college scholarship, she knew that despite her present *conforming* to her father's wishes, she would later go her own way. In this decision she was supported by her mother, who saw to it that the child had time for reading and study.

We see that Linda, earlier than most children, was strongly influenced by the future, although she thoroughly enjoyed her school life and her carefree life at the ranch.

Moreover, she exhibited unusually early a clear rank of values and a hierarchical goal structure that was as temporary as it was oriented to the future.

What is most unusual is how early Linda found her *self*. Her idea of a life of helping others, a life built up on the basis of a good education, and consideration for her own happiness was envisioned by her in early years with greater clarity than we generally find in young people. She did not go through periods of uncertainty and fighting in order to find herself. The direction and the timing of her creative expansion were obvious to her in her youth. She was certain that proper ways and means would be found.

Such was the case. When Linda graduated from high school at eighteen, an uncle living in Honolulu offered her a small job there. Linda told her father that she was going to take it, was going to become self-supporting, would study at the University of Hawaii as soon as possible. She had some misgivings about telling him of her decision, but she was encouraged by her mother's support and was relieved to find that her father no longer had any power over her.

Linda's development shows us a picture of the gradual strengthening of a personality, the partial goal strivings which became harmonious unusually early and culminated in a principal goal. As a result of her mother's love and help the child's burgeoning was spared serious inner conflicts. The conflict of her father's wishes did not touch Linda so deeply as would have been the case if she, as is the case of many other children, had suffered under his lack of recognition. At an unusually early age she was capable of distinguishing between his love for her as his daughter and his rejection of her goals. She did not feel hurt by this rejection. Thanks to her mother's intelligent guidance, she saw her father as a person with certain weaknesses that were not her problem but his. This inner freedom is rarely met with. So much the more, then, can this case be regarded as an example of a healthy and strong personality.

When Linda left her parents' home, her goal structure included, first of all, the plan to study and to take up a profession in social work, besides earning money. Soon, however, it became clear to her that, like every other healthy young girl, she also wanted to find happiness and personal fulfillment in love, marriage, and a family. Linda, a gay, blonde, and pretty girl, was very popular with young men. But she postponed sexual experiences until later. In Hawaii she had her first love. Soon after that she met Hal, a young newspaperman, in whom she recognized the right man for her. He loved her, and in a few months they were married.

Now for the second time she was faced with the task of maintaining a complicated goal structure. On the one hand, she was determined to study and complete her training. On the other, she had to consider interrupting her studies in order to earn money to help her husband at the beginning of his career. Also, as it soon become evident, her husband was a difficult personality; he was stubborn and moody and at times had difficulties with his associates.

Linda, who at the time was studying psychology, asked herself just why she married a man whose personality was in many respects similar to her father's. And when, some years later, she met a very attractive, charming man, she thought seriously of divorce. But, not unlike her mother, she decided to stick to her marriage because she considered Hal a valuable person. She loved him. His work interested her; she considered it important, and she wanted to help him. She sealed this decision by becoming pregnant for the first time when she was thirty years old. She gave birth to a daughter.

In the hierarchical structure of Linda's personality, we find at the top the creatively expansive tendency of the healthy person to develop fully and to find realization in love, marriage, family, and career. With an extraordinarily constructive and comprehensive basic attitude, Linda attempts to do justice to the many tasks that arise out of the multiplicity of her principal goals. She succeeds in this only gradually, but it leads, in her fifties, to a life whose outcome completely satisfies her because she was always flexible and adaptable enough to relinquish or postpone certain satisfactions and to put into the foreground the goals that were right at the time.

Thus, it was not until she was about fifty that she completed her training as a social worker. Up to that time she had been compelled by financial and health problems, and by the demands her husband and daughter made on her, to interrupt her career. Then she succeeded in taking up an extremely satisfying position with the good feeling that her husband was more contented than he had ever been before and that her daughter, who had just entered college, was well provided for and happy. To fulfill herself by helping others had been her goal; her deeply felt need and her scientific training had finally led her to success.

In this life, in one sense so modest and simple, in another so complicated, the goal of comprehensive self-fulfillment through the helping of others and through personal family happiness constructively worked for and achieved stands clearly in the forefront. In all this, Linda's great flexibility and adaptability stood her in good stead. Pleasure in the ordinary meaning of the word, that is, entertainment, wealth, luxury, are unimportant to this woman. She is uncommonly simple with regard to the satisfaction of needs of this kind.

She lives in a simple little house with her family, wears simple clothes, and leads a simple life corresponding to the middle-class income, to which she contributes of late, since she is once again working.

In creative expansion with self-limiting adaptability, under continual maintenance of her inner organization, with few demands waiting to be satisfied, this personality represents an individually molded, healthy structure.

Healthy and Pathological Personality Structure

In Linda's firm yet elastic personality structure there was displayed throughout her entire development a great strength in the way the child, the young girl, and the adult woman understood how to cope with the conditions of her fate. This *strength of personality* obviously helps Linda to a mastery of her life, which she undertakes in a *constructive* manner. Perhaps the expression "talent for life" best characterizes these capacities of mastery, constructiveness, strength of direction, and adaptability.

Talent for living is among the factors conducive to inner unity and organization and therefore to a healthy personality. If, however, it is lacking or inadequately developed, then life is not coped with and the personality structure shows signs of illness.

Before we turn to pathological structure, we must mention that a healthy structure does not necessarily have to be as comprehensive and as many-sided as Linda's. A healthy structure can be considerably narrower and more limited. What is important is that a person should plan his life with a view to mastery, and not undertake more than he believes himself capable of.

The example of another woman, Elizabeth, will show us a narrower *healthy* personality structure.

Elizabeth was well aware of her limitations when at the time of her marriage she broke off her plans for a professional career. She did complete her university studies, but after that she devoted herself entirely to her husband and her home. As she said, she could do but one thing in her life, not a number of different things; for her it would be impossible to divide herself between marriage and a career.

The sick personality is generally evinced very early in childhood when the given circumstances of an individual are too difficult for him to cope with. In the following examples we shall describe some of the forms of sick personality structures of persons who were not up to coping with various circumstances.

One expression of neurotic personality structure is a *rigid,* inflexible personality.

Ellery, in his late thirties, was the owner of a successful manufacturing plant producing machinery, which he had built up from nothing. He went into psychotherapeutic treatment because, despite his unusual success, he did not feel the slightest pleasure in life and suffered from nervousness and insomnia.

He reported that from his earliest childhood, when he and his widowed mother often had to go hungry, he had had but one thought: to earn a great deal of money. As he was very talented, he decided that with the aid of a scholarship he would become an engineer and use his knowledge and inventive talents to design machinery. He wanted to become independent as soon as possible.

Since Ellery worked day and night without permitting himself the least recreation or pleasure, he soon achieved his goal. After completing his studies at the university, he married a distant relative. This young woman, Laura, admired him very much, but because she was not particularly good-looking she had inferiority feelings. Laura brought some money into the marriage, which Ellery used to open his first small workshop. Ellery thought he loved Laura; in any event he felt he was her protector and helper, and for a short while he thought they would be happy.

But soon he found that Laura bored him. Neither knew what to do when they were together, and this so much the more because neither had any hobbies or any experience in social intercourse with other people. Laura had been brought up in lower-middle-class milieu; she had learned to cook and sew but, with the exception of the movies, radio, and television, had no cultural, social, or sports interests.

After a short interruption, Ellery returned to his treadmill of uninterrupted work. Although his position gradually removed all financial worries, he could still not conceive of any goal other than making money. Love, marriage, later a family of two children, meant nothing or very little to him; entertainment of various sorts didn't appeal to him. All his thoughts compulsively and continually returned to his work in the factory.

Ellery's personality provides an example of the inflexible structure of a *compulsive personality* whose main goal, wealth, *compulsively* permits no other goals to arise beside it or any change in organization to take place. This type of personality is not capable of any change without long and deep psychotherapy.

Another type of neurotic personality structure is that of the person who is *torn* or disrupted. Disruption of goal-setting is met with in diverse forms. A person can be torn because he wants to pursue two incompatible goals at the same time. Or he is disrupted because, although he follows a principal goal, he believes that he can never attain it and therefore always wants to give it up.

Many of these disruptions can be traced back to early childhood, where they have their origins in, for example, unresolved conflicts between pleasure and renunciation or between obedience and self-will. This has already been mentioned in the chapter on motivation; we shall consider this further in examples.

Besides disrupted personalities, we also encounter other problems of personality structure that begin in childhood and that result in an absence of goals, indefiniteness of goals, or failure of goals.

An example of lack of goals is seen in Joe, who, at twenty-six, does not know what he should be or what he wants to live for. His childhood and youth were spent in strong opposition to the domination and regulations of his mother. When Joe left home at eighteen he found himself completely without any plan or goal; he had no idea what he should undertake. At first he let himself be caught up with a group of toughs with whom he sat around in cafeterias, drank, and rowdied and felt a vague sort of hostility toward society. As Joe had not learned any trade, he earned his living as an unskilled laborer. His only goal was to get along by doing as little as possible.

When, at last, dissatisfied with himself and the world, he sought psychotherapeutic treatment, he confessed that he had never given the slightest thought to any goal in life or to his future.

Joe's compulsive resistance and the lack of goals resulting from it had a relatively rational basis, and he could be treated as a neurotic. The following case of lack of directivity presents a psychosis.

Eric, a student, also twenty-six-years old when he came into psychotherapy, was diagnosed as a borderline schizophrenic. He was a borderline case insofar as, at times and in certain circumstances, he was able to function rationally, while in others he completely lost any sense of reality.

This was the case in all his relationships as soon as his extreme sensitivity was hurt in the slightest degree. A question awkwardly put, the slightest indication of criticism or doubt, an apparently unfriendly word —all this would put Eric into a terrible excitement and panic; he would be unable to get over it for hours or even days. On the other hand, he was able to attend lectures with other students; so long as no classmate or unpleasant noises disturbed him, he would take notes along with the rest and was able to learn quite rationally. He was a keen thinker and, when he was in a good frame of mind, spoke of wanting to become a lawyer.

Then, however, there came a disturbance and every goal was lost from sight. His whole personality seemed constricted into nothing but anxiety.

As a child Eric had exhibited the extremely susceptible personality, easily injured and incapable of adaptability, that is found in certain childhood schizophrenics. In this group, inborn extreme hypersensitivity plays a decisive role. As a result of their incapacity to adapt to reality, these personalities are disrupted and confused at an early age.

Personality Research and Personality Theories

In describing the *structure* of personality, we presented, as far as possible, everything that concerns the personality system and the way it functions. The questions of how *personality as a whole* comes about, how it is maintained, and how it functions are answered differently by research workers for two reasons. First, personality research is still a very recent branch of psychology and our knowledge of it is correspondingly fragmentary. Second, because of the very complex structure of human personality, the task of understanding it can be approached from different standpoints. According to the point of departure that appears most important to the particular researcher, and according to the method he chooses, the answers will differ. Here we shall present six approaches to the problem.

Personalistic Psychology

The "personalistic" approach to psychology was developed by William Stern in the 1930's. This view offers an interpretation of all psychology from the point of view of the individual. Stern's basic assumptions are that everything mental is at the same time personal and that everything personal is either a totality or part of a totality. The abstraction of personality dimensions, and the description of an individual in terms of these dimensions, is seen as violating this functional wholeness. The person himself is the locus of every mental event, and it is the relevance of the self that determines even such things as perception of time and space. For instance, a friend toward whom one is traveling may seem nearer than the stranger in the next seat on the train. The relative degree of consciousness or awareness is also described in terms of whether at the moment something has or has not special significance to the individual.

Memory, according to Stern, conserves the past, thereby providing salient features of experience for the present in the service of future goals. This aspect of goal directedness leads to Stern's treatment of volition and will as valid concepts. For, in his view, the person is not only the locus, but the generator of every psychophysical event. He is not only reactive, but is a spontaneous organism having a creative role in determining his own behavior.

Gordon Allport criticizes Stern's departure from the personalistic stand in his recourse to the concept of universal drives, such as hunger or sex. Allport suggests that personalistic psychology abandon its dependence upon all doctrines of generalized, categorical motivation. He would employ a more flexible framework that includes interests, desires, attitudes, traits, inclinations, and tastes. For he sees the individuality, uniqueness, and personal experience of the human organism as the most meaningful subject matter for the exploration of personality and considers self-report as the most reliable source of data.

Like Stern, Allport cannot see trying to understand the individual in terms of preconceived dimensions that might not even be relevant for that individual. He objects to what he calls the "response set" of psychologists whose only interest in the individual is as a source of hypotheses and generalizations, which they then apply to the human personality in general.

This actuarial approach to the prediction of human behavior has its limitations. It can tell us that x percent of boys with such-and-such a background become delinquent, but it cannot tell us whether John will become delinquent. Actuarial prediction may be highly valid for a large population, but not for an individual. Whether or not John becomes delinquent depends on certain unique and idiosyncratic factors. This view is not unlike the modern existential one that emphasizes that the individual is a unique being whose system of meanings and value orientation is unlike anyone else's.

Allport is not abandoning scientific technique in his approach, and he does not suggest the use of intuition for the understanding of the individual. For the morphogenic interpretation made with respect to a given individual must be testable, communicable, and have a high measure of predictive power.

Gestalt Psychological Personality Theories

At first, Kurt Lewin used the Gestalt theory mainly for an interpretation of the processes of perception, memory, and thinking applied to the field of human *action*. Action is understood as a process in a *field* in which the person and the environment enter into reciprocal relationships. This psychological field is the *living space* in which the person and the environment affect each other.

An example will help us to understand Lewin's theory.

Let us suppose that a child walks past a candy store, looks in the window, and wants to have a bag of candy. The sight of the candy arouses a *desire* in him. Now three things happen. First, the desire releases *energy* and results in *tension* within the personality, that is, in the personality system that wants to have the candy. Second, the field in which the candy is becomes imbued with desirability, a positive value that Lewin calls *valence*. Third, it produces a forces that pulls the child in the direction of the candy. This directed force is called *vector* by Lewin. Suppose that the child wants to go into the candy store but he hasn't any money. Then the boundary between him and the store becomes a barrier. The child presses his nose against the window but does not dare enter the store.

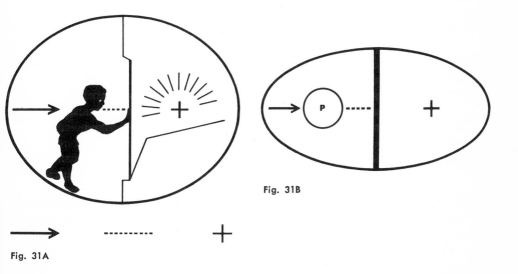

Fig. 31B

Fig. 31A

A child in front of a candy store. **P** is the personality. The arrow is the drive that the will exerts. The heavy black vertical line is the window of the store—a barrier. The plus sign represents the positive attractive force of the candy behind the window (after Lewin).

But the matter may become even more complicated. The child might say: "I'll go to my mother and ask her for some money." This desire to get some money is called a *quasi desire* by Lewin. If the mother refuses, she provides a new barrier. The child must strike out in a new direction, perhaps to a friend.

In Lewin's theory, the personality is a system of forces in a field of forces and the relation of the personality to the environment is essentially an interplay of forces. In this interplay, the organization and differentiation within the personality assume significant roles. Lewin sees development mainly in the light of increasing differentiation. The regression that results from time to time in the course of development, that is, the falling back upon earlier or more primitive levels of behavior—originally a Freudian concept—is experimentally shown by Lewin to be the result of *frustrations,* or denials of desires.

In our example, not having any money is a frustration that represents a force holding the child back. There now results a conflict in which the child asks himself whether he should get the money from his mother or from his friend. The path that he finally chooses, to his mother, becomes "the designated path."

In Lewin's theory, the degree of conviction with which the child presents his wish to his mother, or, in other cases, the degree of ambition with which a goal is pursued, is called the *aspiration level.* This is a straightforward and enlightening concept that fits into our daily manner of speaking in a natural way.

Another important concept is that of the "resultant force," which proves to be the strongest force from every standpoint. With this concept, recent theoretical ideas about the integration processes in systems were anticipated.

Although Lewin's thought system has had an extraordinary influence, especially in the United States and, because of the results of his extensive experiments, has had a very stimulating effect on the examination of group processes, it has been criticized as a theory of personality.

The principal criticisms are the following: first, although a new type of presentation of actions is provided in Lewin's method, no new knowledge about the connections of behavior is transmitted; second, the purely formal description of the way action proceeds, with no consideration of the actual facts of the environment or of the individual's history, is not sufficiently revealing; and third, Lewin's use of physical and mathematical concepts is misleading because they are only used metaphorically.

The Factor Theories of Personality

The factor theories of personality are the result of quantitative research, that is, research that counts and measures. The data on which these processes are based are obtained by observation, questionnaires, and experiments.

In his investigation of intelligence, Charles Spearman was the first to point out the existence of "factors." Factors are *basic dimensions* that cannot be divided into further constituent parts. Suppose any two intellectual performances are being tested, for example, visual memory and vocabulary. Two factors can always be established in these performances, a general one and a specific one. The *general factor* is the general intelligence of an individual or his educational level. The *specific factor* might be a particular language talent or a good visual memory. Thurstone further developed the two-factors theory when he showed that besides general and specific factors there are *group factors* as well, which in their distribution hold a place between the specific and the general.

The personality theory based on the analysis of factors that is most discussed today is H. J. Eysenck's. Primarily because of him the analysis of factors has been carried over into the clinical field.

In his theory of personality, Eysenck distinguishes four sectors, which he names the *cognitive sector* (intelligence), the *conative sector* (character), the *affective sector* (temperament), and the *somatic sector* (constitution). He calls the details that he attempts to determine statistically *personality traits* and *personality types.* Examples of the traits that Eysenck has examined are "dependency feeling," "lack of energy," "depression," "apathy," "anxiety," etc. The types that Eysenck examined are principally those set up by Ernest Kretschmer and Carl Jung. Thus, Eysenck examined *extroversion* and *introversion,* by which Jung understood personalities that are directed outward and those directed inward.

Eysenck finds the following traits united in the neurotic introvert: tendency to depression, anxiety, fixed ideas, irritability, apathy, and lability of the vegetative nervous system. Introverts admit that their feelings are easily hurt, that they are shy and nervous, that they tend toward feelings of inferiority and to moodiness, that they fall easily into daydreaming, and that they remain in the background socially. In their body build they are tall rather than broad. They do not secrete much saliva. Their intelligence is relatively high, their vocabulary excellent, and they are tenacious and precise but slow. They are splendidly fitted for meticulous work. Although they make abnormally high demands on their own performance, they tend to underestimate their productions. They are rather inflexible as regards the aesthetic sphere; they prefer quiet, old-fashioned pictures. When they produce any art work they tend to depict real things. They have little sense of humor, and sexual jokes are particularly offensive to them. Their handwriting is legible.

One must admit that the wealth of characteristics that were objectively found by the statistical method is surprising and extraordinarily informative. The *psychometric* personality traits that were found are defined by reciprocal relationships.

As the final goal of research into personality, Eysenck names "the setting up of a mathematical model of the personality organization, and deriving from this model, hypotheses that can be proven with the aid of the hypothetical-deductive method." The factor theories undoubtedly have the advantage of contributing definite facts to a field that is otherwise difficult for empirical research to approach.

Of the objections raised against these theories, we shall mention two. First, Allport points out that the personality made up of factors is an artifact, the inner organic connections of which remain hidden. A collection of traits is by no means a living human being. A second objection is that the naming of the traits selected for examination is arbitrary and that even the various research workers in this field are unable to agree on them.

Typological Theories of Personality

The theories previously discussed result from factors research and rest on a statistical basis. The theories generally designated as "typologies" are of older origin and are based on the assumption of constitutional types, that is, inborn types.

The theory of constitutional types goes back to the classical Greek period. Hippocrates taught that there were four human temperaments corresponding to the four basic elements (air, water, fire, and earth), which come about as a result of different mixtures of body fluids. The Roman physician Galen, continuing with this idea, set up four types, the names of which are still in use today: the *sanguine,* the *phlegmatic,* the *choleric,* and the *melancholic.*

Among the many modern theories of types, Ernest Kretschmer's theory holds first place. In the United States his theory has been further developed by William Sheldon.

Kretschmer conceived his constitutional typology while working with the mentally ill. He distinguished two basic types of mental illness, the *schizophrenic* and the *manic-depressive psychosis.* We are already familiar with schizophrenia as a mental illness in which *the relationship to reality* is severely disturbed because of abnormalities in feeling and thinking. The manic-depressive psychosis consists of extreme fluctuations of feelings between excitement and depression. In the manic phase, hyperactivity and flight of ideas are in evidence; in the depressive phase, anxiety and tendency to suicide appear. Kretschmer discovered that these two mental illnesses often appear in connection with definite forms of body build.

In his progress from the pathological to the normal, Kretschmer established that tendencies toward certain well-defined forms of body build together with certain basic mental attitudes are also to be noted in the mentally healthy. He distinguished three types of body build: the pyknic, the leptosomic or asthenic, and the athletic.

The pyknic form of body build, described as medium height, a figure that leans forward, fat deposits in the abdominal region, an apparatus for graceful movements, and a soft, broad face, goes hand in hand with the *zyklothymic* temperament. This temperament displays a tendency to mood changes in a personality that is predominantly directed by feelings. The type is described as good-natured and sociable.

The leptosomic or asthenic type is depicted by Kretschmer as narrow-shouldered with weak musculature of the arms, narrow hands, a tendency to shoot up in height but not to get fat, a narrow chest, a long narrow face, and a long nose. Kretschmer sees the *schizothymic* temperament connected with this type of body build. It consists of hypersensitivity, lack of warmth, an unsocial, critical attitude, and is inwardly directed. Further signs are a capacity for keen and abstract thinking, endurance, and often a strong will without consideration for others.

The athletic type tends to have a well-developed skeleton and musculature, exhibits broad shoulders, medium to large height, has compact hands and a compact, long head. Kretschmer calls the mental type that goes with this body build *viscous,* which he describes as wavering between phlegmatic and explosive, slow and steady in thinking, clumsy, lacking in buoyancy, but faithful, solid, and reliable.

William Sheldon altered Kretschmer's theory of types in certain directions by describing the types physically and mentally and examining their statistical relationships in greater detail. Among other things, he introduced indications of the differences in *male* and *female* body builds.

Research on constitution and temperament has found many supporters and just as many critics. One of the principal objections is that average people seldom correspond completely to one type. Eysenck and other statisticians of personality traits have often reached completely different results. The assumption in Kretschmer's theory—that certain bodily traits are connected with certain mental ones in such a way that the one necessarily has the other as a consequence—is much disputed. We do not yet know enough to be able to affirm these connections unequivocally, but it must be said that, despite all objections, there is a nucleus of truth in the assumption of these body-mind connections.

As a result of disagreements on constitutional and temperamental types, a group of theories have been formulated that deviate in principle from the first three. In these theories the method of functioning of the personality is described through abstract concepts and is broken down into its constituent parts, out of which the whole person has to be put together again.

In the group of theories that begin with the constitutional theory, on the other hand, the person is considered more as a whole and is looked upon in actual relationship to life. This is the case particularly in the social-psychological theories.

Social-psychological Theories of Personality

Supporters of social-psychological theories of personality ascribe the decisive role in the development of personality to the *reciprocal relation between people* and the effects of the *cultural environment,* in other words, to the *social factor.* In so doing, they start at an opposite pole from the constitutional investigators, who make *heredity* responsible for personality structure.

Theorists in this category place people's *social needs* ahead of all others; they are of the opinion that an individual feels *isolated and alone, unsure of himself,* and *helplessly exposed* to a potentially hostile world.

Erich Fromm calls this inner loneliness "the human situation," because no animal experiences it. He says that the more freedom man has acquired over the centuries, the more lonely he feels. As a result of this unbearable loneliness and of his responsibility as an individual, the free man feels himself driven to a "flight from freedom."

Since the human being has a need to establish roots, identify with others, and form close relationships with others, he depends on the society in which he lives for the development of his potentialities. If modern society were such that the individual could see himself loved as a brother, society would help him out of his despair and alienation. It would also favor the development of his *creative powers,* a point that Alfred Adler has emphasized. Instead, however, society hinders and disappoints the individual, who is forced to conform to it. From these established facts, Fromm sees the necessity for a new structure for society.

Karen Horney expresses herself more emphatically on the harmful effect of society by declaring, in contrast to Freud's view, that conflicts are not inherent in the individual but that society is responsible for these conflicts, for it sets people in a state of conflict.

While the older social-psychological theorists of personality mentioned and in part indicted "society," the newer researchers, many of them in the train of Margaret Mead and other anthropologists, concern themselves with an examination of *specific cultural environments* and their specific effects on human personality. We shall have more to say on this subject in Chapter 9.

Emphasis on the social and cultural influences of the environment on the development of personality is proving an extraordinarily fruitful method of observation. Recent social psychiatry, particularly in the United States, has shown in extensive studies that many deficiencies in development that were formerly laid at the door of the individual can be traced to social and cultural conditions.

But many social-psychological theories pass too lightly over the question of why different individuals from the same environment are not affected in the same way. The question of to what degree the individual himself and to what degree the environment determine the developing personality is still controversial.

A further objection to Adler, Fromm, and Horney is that they draw too simple a picture of human nature and of the possibilities of reforming society. Human existence is not free of anxiety, as the existentialists have shown, nor does it seem realistic to imagine that mankind will ever be united and rational enough to create a perfect society.

The Depth Psychological Theories

Although important contributions have been made by the personality theories mentioned so far, the depth psychological method appears to be the most advanced and most promising in spite of much sharp criticism leveled at several important theses of the depth psychological theories.

Depth psychological theories stress the belief that human personality can be understood only on the basis of individual motivation.

Because of the extraordinary multiplicity and many-sidedness of depth psychological theories, it is almost impossible to provide a short, adequate description. In the limited framework of this chapter, we must limit ourselves to just a few essential points.

First, a study of Freud's view of the motivational structure of personality is essential. According to Freud, the human personality has at its disposal *three motivational systems,* which are independent of one another but which nevertheless affect one another. At an early age these systems come into *conflict* with one another. As Peter Hofstätter says in his description of the depth psychological theories of personality, they all have "in the final analysis . . . something to do with the fact of the inner split and disruption of human beings."

The so-called Freudian *triad* of drives comprises the *id, ego,* and the *superego.* Freud considered the principal section of personality to be the wholly unconscious id. The id, the reservoir of both the life and the death instinct, is the source of almost all psychobiological energy. According to Freud's original concept, the id desires pleasure gratification. It also has *aggressive* tendencies. It has no awareness of time or reality, and wants only the satisfaction of love and hate. Freud believed that at the beginning of life the infant is nothing but an id.

This condition, however, does not last long. *Reality* soon becomes noticeable, primarily through *frustration*. Thus the infant becomes a conscious being. The ego develops both as a defense against anxiety and as a means of resignation to the inevitable. It seeks to cope with the world, and concerns itself with adaptation and defense.

The superego is the last system to develop. It has its origin in the relations of the child to his parents, making itself known the first time the child realizes that he *should* do something his mother wants him to do.

Most frequently the infant's awareness of the demands made on him begins with toilet training, when his mother demands that he "produce" something. When she greets his "productions" in his diaper with clearly expressed distaste, possibly with a scolding or even a spanking, the one-to two-year-old can no longer disregard the character of her "should do" demands.

The moral principle of *should,* according to Freud, is born of man's relation to his environment and his relation to society. It is based on the individual's need for love and recognition from his environment, which he would lose if he were to satisfy his needs without restraint. Adaptation to reality and obedience are, accordingly, indirect satisfaction of needs, that is, they substitute for direct pleasure.

This compromise would lead to a harmonious development of personality if insurmountably strong instincts, unconditionally demanding satisfaction, did not emerge in the individual. These instinctive needs are understood to be *sexual partial drives.* The first partial drive is to gain pleasure through suckling or sucking. This is followed by a period in which pleasure is experienced in the anal processes. The anal stage begins the period of the first narcissistic experiences (experiences directed toward one's own body) of pleasure. It is followed by heterosexual phallic experiences of pleasure.

As a result of the strength of these drives, the individual finds himself involved in *conflicts*. His id demands satisfaction of these drives, while his ego and his superego rebel and demand control of the drives.

The conflicts now lead either to *repression* of the drives or to self-indulgence. These processes are accompanied by *anxiety* and *guilt feelings*. There are still other "mechanisms," as Freud called the various methods by which a person obtains his substitute and quasi satisfactions, besides repression and instinctual satisfaction.

Despite its one-sidedness and its vulnerability to criticism, the Freudian theory of human personality proved to be of revolutionary significance both for psychiatry and for mankind's general awareness about itself.

Through Freud, personality disturbances were made comprehensible in a new way, and this new understanding permitted many such disturbances to be seen as curable.

By the very fact that attention was directed to the inner disruption of man's nature, to his early conflicts, to the role of unconscious drives, particularly the sexual drives, to the interplay of defense and repression mechanisms, to the self-deception that is connected with these mechanisms, and to the experiences of anxiety and guilt that are bound up with them, people gradually came to recognize Freud's theory as a system that threw light on the abysses of human personality that up to that time had been unfathomable.

Freud's theory has undoubtedly destroyed many illusions that mankind harbored about itself; today we can speak of naïve pre-Freudians and realistic, self-critical post-Freudians.

Now that the revolutionary significance of Freud's theory of personality has been acknowledged, we must mention the criticism against it. This criticism has directed attention to many weaknesses of the system; however, no one has succeeded in replacing it with a depth psychological personality theory that is satisfactory in every respect.

The following are the six principal objections to Freud's theory.

1. Some of Freud's most important students, particularly Alfred Adler, Carl Jung, and Otto Rank, objected that Freud related everything to sexuality and instinctive life. They felt that this was underestimating both the role of *the creative* in man and his genuine urge to realize *values* and be socially related to other human beings. Freud's declaration that all value strivings are only secondary considerations derived from social rules may well be the most objectionable bias of his system. He has unquestionably freed us from many illusions, but at the same time he robbed us of the consciousness of our inner freedom.

2. Freud held that human value striving is only secondary, that it is derived from renunciations that are forced upon us. The discomfort felt by many with regard to this devaluation of value striving has led to many new theoretical approaches.

Gordon Allport's principle of *functional autonomy* is based on the fact that, in the course of personality development, motives change in a natural way, without the exertion of any compulsion. Allport describes two different ways in which such changes in motives can come about.

The first corresponds to the principle of *canalization* introduced by Gardner Murphy; this means that in the routine of daily life many things get to be "second nature." The boy to whom the daily repetition of brushing teeth or washing hands was a horror will as a man have become so used to these ablutions that he will feel uncomfortable if he must omit them.

The second rests on the fact that the interests of an individual undergo changes. For example, a student who takes a course only because it is required may later continue enthusiastically in this originally disagreeable field.

The principle of functional autonomy is of great importance in the evolution of personality. But even beyond this, from the very beginning of the development of the self there is a selective and value-creating self-determination toward goals other than need-satisfaction that comes about with relative freedom.

3. This relative *freedom of choice* and *value setting* is emphasized by those who proffer a third criticism: that Freud divided the psychic wholeness of the personality into a triad of drives, which toss us back and forth between the slavery of our drives and the slavery of society.

In opposition to this, Karen Horney, Erich Fromm, Kurt Goldstein, Abraham Maslow, and the author have emphasized the *global unity* of human personality, the strivings of which have the self as a basis. Even though the structure and method of functioning of the self is still a matter of controversy, it is to many an established fact that value realization is essential to the self. In other words, morality and other values are sought by man out of his own need, not only in obedience to society.

In this objection, Freud's theory of the superego and of obedience to the values represented by society are not necessarily eliminated. Rather, two kinds of values are to be distinguished: the individual's own and those that are taken over by him. Freudians, who set up the ideals of the superego as belonging to a different category from the *ego ideals,* have in part supported a similar idea.

4. The acknowledgment that value realization is partly primary leads to the fourth objection: that the theory of pleasure as the ultimate goal fails to recognize the essential needs of mankind. Horney, Fromm, Goldstein, Maslow, Rogers, the author, and others consider self-realization the final goal of the unfolding personality.

This, then, in contrast to Freud, includes the assumption of a primary positive reality, into which one moves because one expects to find in it the possibilities for self-realization.

5. The fifth principal objection relates to Freud's theory of *personality development.* Since pleasure is only a partial goal and the personality as a whole is directed toward more substantial satisfactions—for example, self-fulfillment through self-realization—development cannot be looked upon merely from the point of view of its sexual genesis. Apart from the phases of maturation and learning that developmental psychology has

differentiated, the most important need for the personality as a whole is for the *development of the self* or the *identity* of the individual.

The problem of the development of the self has been explored particularly by Erikson and by the author; in many respects it is not yet resolved. However, the statement may be made with some certainty that the self represents the *central system* of the personality.

6. The sixth objection comes from modern anthropologists and social psychologists who criticize Freud's disregard for the entirely different effects of particular *cultures* and *cultural groups* on the individual. They regard Freud's view of the way in which the ego and the superego developed as distorted and one-sided. They point out that in some cultures prohibitions, and consequently guilt feelings, are nonexistent; difficulties are pushed out of the child's way.

Character and Personality

"He is quite a character," one often hears someone say of a friend. By this he usually means that the person has very specific, sometimes *peculiar,* and somewhat set *personality characteristics.*

This usage comes close to some of the original connotations of the Greek word "character," which refers to something that has been engraved or cut in.

There is a different connotation when one speaks of a person's *moral* character or of *character education.*

The two meanings of the word, however, are not unrelated. As psychoanalysts have shown, character traits are acquired in the individual's attempts to cope with life. Wilhelm Reich, whose book on *character analysis* is considered basic, says in this connection: "Analysis of the different characters shows that they are merely forms of armoring of the ego against the dangers threatening from the outer world and from the repressed inner impulses. . . . The character consists in a chronic alteration of the ego which one might describe as a rigidity. It is the basis of the becoming chronic of a person's characteristic mode of reaction. Its meaning is the protection of the ego against external and internal dangers. As a protection mechanism which has become chronic it can rightly be called an armor."

The main difference between the *healthy* and *neurotic* character lies in the degree of *flexibility* or *rigidity.* Reich says: "The degree of character mobility, the ability to open up to a situation or to close up against it, constitutes the difference between the healthy and the neurotic character structure."

While Reich emphasizes the aspect of *self-protection* in coping with life, another group uses the term to refer to the *ethical,* or *moral aspect* of the personality. According to Allport, for example, character enters the picture only when personal effort is evaluated from the standpoint of some code. "Character," he says, "is personality *evaluated;* and personality, if you will, is character *devaluated.*"

As Allport points out, American psychology has not as yet concerned itself very much with the problem of character. Only recently have empirical studies been attempted.

Robert J. Havighurst was particularly interested in the question of *character development* during adolescence. He selected five traits as representative of moral character: honesty, responsibility, loyalty, moral courage, and friendliness. He investigated the factors related to and responsible for character formation, and also delineated personality types within which the different character structures develop in different ways.

Havighurst and his collaborators raised serious questions about the effects of educational and religious practices on character development. They investigated the sources of moral values in the life of the growing individual and tried to establish a scientific basis for future ethics. This is a truly basic trend in modern thinking.

CHAPTER 5

THE HUMAN LIFE CYCLE

Previous chapters have shown how biology, motivation, development, and personality contribute to success or failure in life. We experience success or failure time and again in all our physical and mental performances, in our human relationships, and in our material and occupational under- takings. For a thoughtful person, success and failure represent a con- tinuity. They also represent a gradually all-inclusive experience of the *total result* of one's life.

How Do We Experience Success and Failure in Life?

When we hear people talking in clinical interviews or study what is set down in diaries, correspondence, and other biographical documents, we begin to see that in the buildup of success and failure over the years there is an *accumulation*. Even those who do not, in the actual sense of the word, set up life goals, nevertheless have such summarizing feelings as "I'm successful in everything" or "I'm a failure in everything"; or perhaps a qualifying "In the main, I'm successful and life has treated me well," or "Much too much goes wrong in my life. I'm just an unlucky fellow."

By saying this, people hold *fate* or conditions responsible for their happiness or unhappiness. In the modern attitude toward life, however, it is considered a sign of mental strength, health, and inner honesty for a person to admit some responsibility for his successes, and, more espe- cially, for his failures.

Whether the person who always holds fate responsible for his failure is sick, weak, dishonest, or all of them put together, he is no longer taken seriously today. The determination of this is all the more important since we live in a time in which great political catastrophes thrust humanity hither and yon, uproot the individual, deprive him of what is essential for life, and expose him to situations of horror, suffering, and death the likes of which the world has not seen for centuries. Many people can face these frightful blows of fate with a surprising serenity and strength. With admirable resourcefulness and imagination, they carve new existences for themselves out of nothing. However, just as many succumb, often in appalling numbers, as the result of brutal extermination or overwhelming hardships.

Psychology is not yet in a position to give us scientifically based information on all the reactions of individuals, groups, and masses. For the present, we must content ourselves with very limited studies of individual fates.

We understand by the word "fate" circumstances over which the person, for external or internal reasons, has no influence, that is, events that are beyond his control. If someone has only limited intelligence or too much sensitivity, or if he sets up the wrong goals for himself, these factors, too, contribute to his fate. Fate is, then, the sum total of the circumstances that determine the course of his life.

But what is there besides fate? Isn't the will power by which one person rises while another sinks ultimately also part of his fate? Yes and no. Insofar as final internal and external given conditions are concerned, the answer is yes. Yet all given conditions, including the internal ones, are to be considered as *potentialities*. In other words, there appears to be, in the face of the given conditions, an inner *degree of freedom* that, up to a certain point, makes possible a choice, a self-determination.

The attitude toward success or failure can also be either hopeful or pessimistic.

"In spite of everything I really always remain hopeful; I am convinced that in the long run everything will come out all right," a patient told the author right after he had told her of several harsh blows of fate.

Another, named Walter, told me: "In the past I was always pessimistic. My wife always used to complain that I never seemed to have any faith in the future. Now, when I have perhaps greater difficulties to surmount than I ever had before, I am strangely optimistic. True I'm often completely discouraged for the moment, but, in spite of everything, I know I'll be able to succeed."

Walter attributes this *change of attitude* to the success of his psychotherapeutic treatment and also to his divorce from a woman who robbed him of his courage and self-confidence.

But it is also possible for a person to feel like another patient, Sally, who said: "I'll never amount to anything. A person like me *can't* have any success in life."

And why is this? "People like me don't deserve to succeed. First of all, I'm bad . . . they always dinned that into me from the time I was a little girl. And besides, if someone has as bad a heredity as I have, such a lousy family—what can ever come out of anything like that?"

Neurotic factors of the kind that play a part in Sally can influence one's attitude toward success and failure in still another way. As a result of his neurotic personality, Willy Loman, the salesman in Arthur Miller's *Death of a Salesman,* has an attitude toward life that fluctuates continually between false optimism and pessimism. His optimism is false insofar as he misunderstands and misjudges the realities of life. He also misjudges his own capacities and what is really important.

Just as one's attitude toward success or failure in life can be constructive, so one's *judgment of former success or failure* can correspond to reality or be distorted, either by false hopes and expectations or by inferiority feelings and depression. Everyone knows from his own experiences how often he has been mistaken as to the extent of certain successes or failures. He knows, too, how hard it is, even with adequate objectivity, to form a correct judgment about these things.

The awareness of success and failure, which is the same as experiencing success or failure, of course, depends very much on the goals and expectations a person has. We shall now examine the factor of expectations.

Life Expectations and Attitudes Toward Life

The expectations with which a person enters into and goes through life are conditioned by a number of factors, which, to the author's knowledge, have never been systematically examined.

We just referred to optimism and pessimism. Both are based on experiences, yet they probably reflect elements of native disposition. The relative importance of these factors is still unknown.

Furthermore, the *aspiration level,* by which term Kurt Lewin described the great or small expectations and demands that different individuals make on life, has its origin partly in experience and partly in the consciousness of one's own potentialities.

"All that I want is to earn my living in an honest way, and not to get into debt," said Ed, a middle-aged man when asked what he expected out of life. Ed was a highly regarded worker, well liked by his colleagues and his superiors, but he was very conscious of the insecurity of his life. At an early age, as the illegitimate son of a poor, hard-working girl, he had to work to support himself.

Another man, who had worked his way up from great poverty to become the owner of a factory, naturally had an entirely different reaction to the harsh circumstances in which he had grown up.

This man, named Roger, also came from unfortunate circumstances. His father deserted his mother during his childhood and disappeared, never to be seen again. But in contrast to Ed, Roger was aware at an early age of his own capabilities. Besides, in his childhood he had known secure living conditions. To these he looked back longingly and, in a way, as though they were his due. In addition, his mother had kept his ambition alive, as she, too, was expecting a better future through him.

Roger said: "When I was still in school one thing was clear to me: that in all circumstances I would help my mother and myself to a better, pleasanter life. Never again are we going to be poor—that's what I decided."

Helen, a woman in the sixties, the wife of a physician, reviewed her life in these words:

"I never had any interest in having much money and a fine social position. What I needed, above all, was inner order and spiritual peace. Besides that, I wanted to be well thought of in the community and to be economically secure. And it was important to me to have responsibility and to prove myself capable."

As one inquired further into the origins of this woman's ideas, it became apparent that she had been brought up with certain family traditions and wanted to maintain them. Helen came from a strict Catholic family that lived a simple life in a small city among friends and relatives. Her father was a medium-grade factory supervisor. There were few entertainments and little luxury. Great value was placed on the education of the children.

The effect of the cultural environment may be clearly seen in what Helen expected from life. The life experiences of Ed and Roger were likewise determined by this, but in their cases their personal experiences played a primary role, as did the influences of their mothers and the amount of confidence each had in his own capabilities.

All such factors determine the *content of the expectations,* which express the wishes of the individual as well as his concept of life. In the wishes, the basic tendencies of a person, which have already been mentioned a number of times, play a primary role. These tendencies make one person strive for happiness, which he may expect in the form of love, enjoyment, or material possessions. Another may desire above all security in life: he wants to know that he belongs, that he is appreciated, that he cannot be dispensed with. Perhaps he also wants to be liked, and in return he is ready to adapt to given circumstances. A third person may want to conquer the world and leave behind evidence of what he has accomplished. For him it is important to have the opportunity for accomplishments and success. A fourth is desirous of leading a well-ordered and dedicated life.

Life circumstances often have an influence on one's concept of life and the way in which a life is built up. This influence can be more decisive than a person's wishes. There are social psychologists who hold that the attitude of a person toward life is determined much more by his cultural environment than by himself. One's position regarding this important question depends essentially on what degree of *inner freedom* one ascribes to the individual.

Expectations and experience undergo modification at various stages. In general we imagine the expectations and hopes of younger, healthy people to be high, even though they are perhaps still indefinite. However, the insecurity of life in our times, war, uprisings, or other catastrophes result in today's young people often being worried rather than hopeful about their future. It is an unhappy sign of our times that, as the author found in a group of socially and economically well-placed young people, they talk more of *security* as a future goal than of any other.

In general, we assume that a person in his middle years has *realistic* life expectations; in other words, that his expectations correspond to actual conditions. This is the case among those who are mentally healthy inasmuch as their own potentialities play any part.

We often note among older people a tendency to throw a softening light on life's shadows. We speak of the detachment and wisdom of old age. These derive partly from seeing things from a greater distance and from lessening participation. There are certain blessings that come with old age. The aging person forgets many of the disappointments and much of the injustice of life, and he is ready to make his peace with himself and his God, as the saying goes. The Catholic Church particularly, with its sacrament of extreme unction at life's end, responds to this need for ultimate peace.

But not everyone who has grown old tends to detachment and peace. There are also those who go on striving. Here, too, there are individual differences.

Life Goals and Life Problems

When do life goals start to take form? The answer depends on how one conceives and defines the words *life goals*. Conscious goals that span all of life do not usually appear before adolescence. In this period, for the first time, the *life span* is envisaged in its total extent. In the diaries of young people we find *past* and *future* time expressed, and understanding of the relations between past, present, and future. Yet the distant future is at first only vaguely contemplated, just as the goal settings projected into the future represent only designs for possible life forms. They must be distinguished from the *definitive self-determination* that follows in the thirties.

In a certain way, however, one can already speak of life goals in childhood, provided one does not limit the expression to conscious, time-oriented strivings.

Life goals in the sense of tendencies toward fulfillment exist from the time life begins. Life goals in the sense of conscious or semiconscious projections of the self into some future time occur from about the age of four. At about this time, the child also becomes aware of experiences of success and failure. These are experienced from the beginning of life but before this time are not consciously grasped.

Anyone who has observed infants with disturbances in coordination in grasping or other manipulations knows that they react to such failures with signs of distress.

This first awareness of one's own *success and failure* means a first *self-evaluation*. The standards for this may be partly acquired, partly inherent. Even then the child seems to experience *problems* and *conflicts* with respect to his goals and achievements.

Freud saw the origin of these problems and conflicts mainly in the relations of the individual to the environment. He saw them based on the frustrations and obligations imposed on the child. On the other hand, Karen Horney agrees with all those poets and thinkers who have found the causes of man's conflicts to lie "in his own breast." Horney feels there is an inwardly conditioned split or schism in one's own needs.

Both types of conflict, those arising out of the environment's demands on the child and those arising out of his own standards of accomplishment, can be demonstrated very early in life.

Childhood Beginnings of Successful and Unsuccessful Lives

We had an example of early goal setting that worked out unfavorably in later development in the case of Allen (pp. 36–37, 43, 46–47). As a four-year-old he had made up his mind never again to make a mistake, and with increasing stubbornness he fastened on to an *ideal of perfection*.

The origin of this self-determination lay in Allen's relation to his mother, who provided him with a model of a life based on strict principles and spurred him to follow its example. One of her frequently repeated expressions was, for example, "Whatever is worth doing at all is worth doing well." This principle, which is at odds with an easy solution to problems, was accepted with the utmost seriousness by Allen. He was deeply impressed by the significance of this motto and by all the similar principles that his mother espoused. Her influence was all the stronger because, at certain times, she gave her children a great deal of kindness and affection. Through this she bound them to her strongly.

Allen's brothers and sisters, however, did not take their mother's commandments nearly so much to heart as he did. Herein lies a decisive second factor. It was in part Allen's own contribution to his development that he identified himself to such an extreme degree with his mother's standards—not so much because he loved her but because of his oversensitive fear of criticism. Even at the age of thirty, after he had been in psychotherapy for two years, Allen admitted that he still had great difficulty in overcoming being hurt at any critical remark.

Allen's need for *self-justification* caused him to choose *self-determination* toward unassailable perfection. Besides this, his fear of his mother and a certain admiration for her play a part, so his choice really cannot be designated a truly free choice.

The question that interests us here is how Allen's early and stubbornly held self-determination influenced the success or failure of his life. It is easily predictable that his perfectionism would get him into great difficulties. Fortunately, his technical talents were great enough to ensure him professional success, but his personal life was a failure. No girl he met corresponded to his ideal, and until he was in his thirties he could not decide on any permanent relationship, since it might possibly be "wrong." His social life was limited to a few friends. Thus, he suffered a great deal from loneliness and from the absence of a satisfying love and sex life.

Another example of a life spoiled by early unfavorable self-determination is provided by a woman. Not until she was in her fifties did she come to see that she would have to change herself and her life altogether if she were not to consider it a complete failure.

Celia is a childless, still-pretty divorcee. She is economically independent. Her life is filled with social duties, and she is an active member of a charity committee. Yet, despite all this, she is deeply dissatisfied. In her restlessness she tries, now and then, to begin some sort of a business— an art gallery or the like—but always gives up the attempt shortly after. She takes a trip around the world, and comes back full of plans that never become reality.

Even as a little girl of four or five, Celia was impressed by how very different the people in her environment were and what different lives they led. She pitied her mother because she was always serious and sad, with all sorts of troubles. She didn't like this at all. And, much as she loved her mother, she herself wanted to be quite different. Of all her relatives, there was one aunt to whom Celia was especially attached. This was her Aunt Eleanor, who was rich, beautifully dressed, and always happy. Her husband seemed to be much in love with her and was always concerned with her well-being; Celia's father did not bother much about his wife and children.

Celia decided that she would get to be like her Aunt Eleanor—beautiful, rich, and gay. She made the decision early, but for a great many years was not aware of it. She did not become conscious of it until, at the age of fifty-two, she was in psychotherapeutic treatment. But by then the decision had determined her whole life. She grew up into a beautiful and elegant young woman and chose from among her admirers a wealthy young businessman who adored her. Married to him, she permitted herself to be loved and spoiled, just like her Aunt Eleanor. In the course of years, however, she discovered that she was not happy. It required psychotherapy to make clear to her that, from her own lack of devotion to husband, children, or any meaningful activity, she had let her life become empty, impoverished, and unfulfilled, despite all her wealth in worldly goods.

Even before Celia began school, she wanted to be like her aunt. Many children in the preschool years are, to be sure, far removed from setting goals for themselves in such a definite way. They have diffuse feelings rather than clear ideas about themselves and their environment. Unfortunately, parents still know so little about the role of early influences in their children's lives that they often leave them to chance. An upbringing directed toward the development of the personality, such as Linda's, which we have already mentioned (pp. 98, 106–10), is an exception.

As a rule, parents who direct their children toward certain values are satisfied with general basic principles. Good behavior, honesty, orderliness, and a sense of responsibility usually head the list. Only a few parents think so deeply about life that they can transmit to the child in comprehensible terms insights into how life's problems can be constructively solved.

Linda, for example, had a mother who understood this in a unique way. On the occasion of a scolding when the little girl was only four, she aroused the child's interest in the fact that she, like everyone else, had certain duties, but that she also had rights, which she illustrated. This explanation made a deep impression on the child, and gave her a sense of human dignity.

Furthermore, this intelligent mother also taught her child the value of compromise, for example, Linda's father opposed her wishes to continue her studies. The mother knew how to get her daughter to combine a helpful interest in the household with her zeal for learning. She saw that Linda had suitable preparation in both areas so she could, at the proper time, make her decision in favor of what appealed to her most.

At an early age, Linda learned to *think things through,* to *understand* things, and to develop concepts that would enable her to cope with her first conflicts. This strikes the author as an uncommonly happy beginning for success in life.

Here lies the difference between Linda's mother and Allen's mother. Both mothers tried to give their children guidelines for their lives. However, while one mother laid down *rules* as to how things should be done, the other guided her child toward *independent thinking.* She showed how things should be regarded and what can be done, not what the child must do. Linda's mother led her daughter into an *open system* of thinking while Allen's mother taught a *closed system* with no degree of freedom. Linda's mother paved the way for a constructive attitude toward future problems, while Allen's merely laid down inflexible principles.

The author studied fifty cases to find out how the parents of people in treatment had guided them in their childhood. She found not a single case in which there had been any help in thinking through life's problems. Rather, the general attitude was either that the children did not have any serious problems yet or that they ought to cope with them themselves. When children that no one helps to understand life have bad examples before them, or are met with injustice and cruelty, they are even less able to cope with problems. In times like the present, torn by conflict and violence of all sorts, it is difficult to imagine a normal development for the next generation.

Thus, even children who are given love and a suitable upbringing require well-thought-out guidance for thinking things through and for solving life's problems. This is truer today than ever before.

In this connection, something that Fritz Redl and David Wineman wrote in their book *Children Who Hate* appears worthy of note: these children are particularly unable to cope with their feelings of fear and insecurity in serious situations. These eight- to ten-year-olds, who have grown up in the most terrible conditions, have only two possibilities with which to cope with their problems: either they run away, or they attack and destroy.

Eight to ten years is the age at which more or less healthy children already have some idea as to how they can find their way in life, either through adaptation or mastery. But many have neither direction nor examples to guide them and remain helpless into their adolescent years, and sometimes beyond.

Adolescent Problems Concerning Success and Failure

Puberty and adolescence—the span of life from about twelve to twenty —is generally considered one of the two most difficult periods in life. The other is the climacteric. Adolescence leads into life; the climacteric leads out of it. Their particular difficulty lies in the fact that in both periods the individual has to orient himself in a completely new way.

The adolescent's task consists primarily of preparing properly for success in his *vocation* and his *marriage*. By preparing "properly" we mean choosing the field of performance and the human relationships that make the best use of his potential. Having chosen, he must test himself in them and continue to develop himself. One often hears that the adolescent must "find himself." After what has been said in the preceding section about the lack of a suitable upbringing of children with respect to adequate self-determination, one need scarcely be surprised that adolescents have great difficulty attempting to solve this problem.

A severe judgment on the failure of the older generation in this respect is rendered by Percival Symonds in an interesting study of twenty-eight young people. They were examined first when they were between twelve and eighteen years old and again thirteen years later, when they were between twenty-five and thirty-one. Symonds' careful study, based on the results of tests and interviews, reaches the conclusion that these adolescents—from good American middle-class families—had been obliged to use trial-and-error methods in their transition from childhood to adulthood. If the first, unthought-through attempt to solve a problem proved a mistake, then a second, equally blind, attempt was made. Frequently this too turned out to be a mistake.

As Symonds says: "Nothing or very little had been done to help them in the preparation or the planning of their next steps. Each of them had to solve every problem with the means which, by chance, he had at his disposal. What he learned at school turned out to be as good as useless for preparing the young person to cope with the problems that inevitably arise in preparing for a vocation, in pursuing a vocation, and in marriage."

Symonds' conclusion, based as it is on facts, is a severe judgment on our educational methods at home and at school, provided we can draw general conclusions from his observations. The question is: Can we draw such conclusions? Opinions are mixed. Those who grew up in the closed *tradition* of a certain cultural group declare that, now as then, there are traditional values and that these traditional values are still being transmitted between generations.

The case of Helen, which we shall soon discuss, provides a unique example of such a transmittal. However, such a case is, in the estimation of the author, an exception and not the rule. It would seem that deep *insecurity* and *perplexity* with respect to life's most important questions are much more prevalent. Everywhere one comes upon such unsolved problems as, for instance, sex. The parents, like the adolescents, rarely have the courage to express themselves openly on this subject. Most parents and adolescents are not sure in their own minds about the basis for their attitudes toward sexual experiences. Frequently, too, there are problems with inadequate goal-setting in the choice of a vocation or a place in society. And the question of life values—in the sense of a broad and comprehensive attitude toward life—is almost always left unexplained.

True, there are certain rules—one should work hard, earn money, and save for the future; one should aspire to a secure position in society; one should be honest, should win respect, and should make friendships. These are the generally accepted life rules that are passed on by parents to their children. Beyond this, however, there is little serious thought about life and scarcely any discussion as to its meaning and purpose. Nor do parents and children discuss the ultimate questions that concern the world and the universe. In many families the children are sent to Sunday school and to church, but the parents do not accompany them. The church is considered a kind of school that the parents have left behind.

The adolescent is, by his very nature, insecure. He is unsure of his own potential. He is groping in the dark for guidelines he can make his own. A full and positive identification with the older generation is an exception; youth is always striving for something new. If, however—as is frequently the case in our times—the older generation itself is emotionally insecure, it becomes even harder for the adolescent to find himself. He receives neither positive nor negative guidelines.

This may be one of the reasons why today's youth has placed such great reliance on itself. It does not get its orientation from the older generation; instead, it chooses models from within its own ranks.

To today's adolescent, *adaptation to the society* of his own generation is more important than arguing with that of his father. The new generation demands—as David Riesman has shown in *The Lonely Crowd*—that the individual be able to adapt to the wishes and behavior of his own age group. That which he contemplates for himself must appear valuable and appropriate to his peers.

A second point becomes clear from James S. Coleman's *Social Climates in High School.* The discouraging conclusion of this book, which is widely debated today, is that educational goals and the adolescent simply do not jibe. The adolescent moves away from the image of the "brilliant student" toward a "social image," which is personified by the most popular student. Coleman's evaluation of this situation is that the educational approach to adolescents must undergo a change.

With this rejection of traditional examples and ideals, youth, which tends toward *rebellion* against the older generation anyway, moves further away from the older generation, but does not obtain help anywhere else.

It would appear that there are only three groups that are relatively untroubled by conflicts today: those who are firmly anchored in tradition; those whose parents were able to transmit still viable rules for life; and those with such definite talents that they are able to use their talents to point the way.

An example of a tradition-bound child is Helen, who grew up firmly rooted in a Catholic family that enjoyed unusual love and harmony, apparently never experienced problems of self-determination. She was happy at home, with her parents, in her neighborhood, and at school. She especially loved her friendly and jolly father and was on good terms with her many younger brothers and sisters. She went to a Catholic school and a Catholic college, and she valued and respected her teachers. For a short time she had several secretarial jobs but was not enthusiastic about them. However, she did her best in her work and made a good many friends. When she was twenty-four, she married the son of friends of her parents and whom she had known since she was fourteen. In this connection she remarked "I never considered anyone else as a husband. Vincent and I understood each other from the beginning, as long as we've known each other, and that has never changed throughout our marriage, which has now lasted forty years."

Such stability and absence of conflicts as Helen's are unusual today. In the author's voluminous material this case is unique.

Linda, whose life had many problems and was not easy by any means (see pp. 98, 106–10), had learned the principle of compromise from her mother, the weighing of rights against duties, and other things that made it easier for her to find herself. She thus succeeded in making her life a success.

It is interesting to see how Linda, thanks to an inner sense of security that strove toward a goal, never even considered interpreting her life as a failure, despite the fact that she repeatedly had to postpone the realization of her goals. There are not many who, like Linda, could muster enough patience and steadfastness to postpone the start of a career until they were fifty and still not feel that fate had treated them unkindly.

Problems of Self-Determination

An exceptionally large number of people encounter serious *problems of self-determination* in their adolescence. The following is a good example:

Denny is the seventeen-year-old son of a construction engineer who, as a result of personal instability, had an irregular career. When Denny finished high school, the family was in poor financial circumstances. Despite this, his father insisted that Denny go to college, funds for this purpose having been set aside earlier.

Yet, although he was very talented, Denny refused to go, declaring instead his desire to become a factory mechanic. His parents were understandably distressed that he did not want to develop his capabilities and take advantage of the opportunity to continue his studies.

Denny gave as a reason for wanting to work in the factory that he did not want to run around without any money in his pocket and take his girlfriend out in a shabby, second-hand car. Besides, most of his friends had taken jobs. He considered the high value placed on the so-called higher professions to be exaggerated. He would rather have a smaller, but more assured, income than his father. He saw nothing but snobbery in the higher social rating given to an academic career. Denny's father, who had made great sacrifices in order to study at a technical school, was extremely angry at Denny's arguments and made no effort to hide his outrage.

Denny declared that he and his friends simply had values different from his parents'. Through the discussions of a therapy group that his parents persuaded him to enter, Denny came to the realization that he used the example of his friends to punish his father for his authoritarian behavior. But not until his girlfriend, Brenda, whom he was planning to marry, told him that she wanted to go to college did he agree to go.

Thus, it was neither outside authority nor his own potentialities but his friends' points of view that were the decisive factors for this young man.

Nadine is an example of those who do not find any guidelines for their goal setting and who allow chance to arrange matters for them. Soon after being married, in her early twenties, Nadine came into therapy. She had gone along as though in a "fog," throughout her whole childhood and adolescence, and had hoped for happiness in marriage and an awakening into life. But this hope had not been realized.

Nadine's childhood was characteristic for this type. This is how she described it: "As a little girl, I would often sit on the steps in front of the house, hoping that the children would invite me to play with them. Sometimes they did. Often, when it rained on Sunday, I would just look out the window. I didn't think of anything at all. My parents never had time for me. They were more interested in my older sister, who was lively and active and who used to bring friends home with her."

At school, Nadine had a silent crush on some of the boys, but they never talked to her. Since the time a boy cousin lured her into the cellar and had sexual relations with her—an activity she permitted him to repeat—she felt that she was worthy of contempt, otherwise her cousin wouldn't have had the courage to do what he did. Like almost all children, she never told anyone about this experience.

After an unrequited love for one of her classmates—this was in her last year of school—and a short, distressing job as a not very competent secretary, Nadine gratefully accepted the marriage proposal of a young businessman whom she had met at the home of relatives. Naturally, her sexual life was distressing, since it continually recalled her experiences in the cellar.

This not unintelligent young woman, who later blossomed out in therapy, went from puberty into marriage as a completely undeveloped person with a neglected intellect and a diffuse and entirely unintegrated personality.

"I never thought about life, about the future and all that," she said. "I was totally mixed up when I found myself up against any sort of problem."

In this case, lack of thinking and a *diffuseness* of personality existing since childhood made success in life impossible; in other cases, it is a *fear* of life and making decisions, as well as the difficulties of self-preservation, that prevent an adolescent from finding himself and his correct path.

Extraordinarily frequent are cases in which a young person, out of fear or indecisiveness, lets himself be pushed by emotional or economic pressure into an apprenticeship or activity that chance happens to place in his way. Then, from the very beginning, lack of interest and of *inner satisfaction in the work* makes his leisure time appear more important than his vocation, and there develops what is called "leisure addiction." Since his leisure is not used for self-realization but for a flight from reality, there develops, instead of a mastery of life, an extensive loss of reality.

These problems exist for a great many workers who are dissatisfied and especially for the ignorant and unskilled, since they generally do not look upon their work as a vocation. The lives of the great mass of people who just live along far from any ideal of self-realization are all the more depressing when one sees, through happy lives, how fulfilling human existence can be.

When, under favorable conditions, great talent is combined with unusual parental understanding and economically and culturally favorable conditions, the most desirable pattern of adolescent development is possible.

A good example in our own times is Van Cliburn, the young musician. From many points of view, it is hard to imagine a more favorable beginning for a life and a career.

Van Cliburn, whose full name is Harvey Lavan Cliburn, Jr., was born in July 1934 in a small town in Louisiana. He grew up in Kilgore, Texas, where his father was employed by an oil company and his mother was a piano teacher.

When he was only three years old, he surprised his parents by picking out a waltz melody on the piano. Soon afterward he begged his mother to teach him to play. As he had absolute pitch he learned extraordinarily fast. When he was five, he declared to his mother: "Mommy, I want to be a concert pianist when I grow up—more than anything else in the world."

His mother took him to all the concerts she attended, often making trips to larger cities. She was a devoted musician and, apparently, a good teacher. Van once said: "I loved being taught by my mother because she never treated me like a child. She never flattered me or patronized me."

Van Cliburn's biographer, Abram Chasins, emphasizes the fact that in this boy's home the spirit was one of love and loyalty, of faith and enthusiasm.

From the time he was a small child, Van Cliburn was treated as a full member of the family, and the feeling was implanted in him that he was a "wished for" child and that what he did was important and valuable.

The reader will recall from earlier chapters that psychology has recognized this feeling of being valued by the parents as one of the principal bases for an emotionally healthy development.

In this boy's case we have the unusually fortunate situation of a child prodigy being brought up to become a healthy, happy, modest, and warmhearted human being.

At first, Van's father was not enthusiastic about the prospect of his son's entering upon a musical career. He tried to talk him out of this exhausting future and hoped to get the boy interested in being a medical missionary—a career that he had once ardently desired for himself. Van refused. "Daddy," he cried, "please don't say things like that! I'm going to be a concert pianist!"

Van had a great many friends. His performance at school was excellent. He was well liked for his fine character. His teacher said of him: "Ordinarily you take somebody that's a genius, and you'll find there's something peculiar about him. You know, something different. But not Van. He was a good, solid boy."

When he was eighteen, in 1952, Van Cliburn won his first big scholarship award in New York. One of the members of the jury said that she didn't know why he should want to do any more studying—he was already a finished artist; all he needed was experience. When he was twenty, he played in Carnegie Hall with Mitropoulos conducting, and in 1958 he had his famous great success in Moscow, where he was enthusiastically acclaimed.

The case of Van Cliburn shows a life favored from the start by enormous talent, and one in which self-determination at the age of five came about in the most natural way. At the same time, it also shows the blossoming of this talent in an environment that, through admirable guidance and direction, brought not only the musician but the human being to full unfolding.

Problems of Instinctive Sexual Development

Despite the extensive educational work of two generations, there is still a lack of clarity with respect to what constitutes successful sexual development in adolescence. By "successful," we mean it in the sense of preparing a *disposition toward sexuality and love* in such a way as to achieve fulfillment of this important area of life.

Parental ignorance is still a large problem in sex education. Frequently, parents combine with this ignorance a disinclination to discuss sex with their children. We still find children and adolescents who were shamed or humiliated when they were discovered masturbating. The resultant guilt or anxiety had unfavorable effects on their later sexual development. We still come upon many individuals for whom sexuality has been forever spoiled because of unfavorable early sex experiences that no one helped them understand.

On the other hand, there is sometimes a thoughtless tolerance of extensive sex play that, in certain circumstances, degenerates into promiscuity. Without thinking some parents stubbornly hold fast to principles through which they hope to protect their children from any kind of sexual experience. The result is either obedience—the adolescent suppresses all his instincts and curiosity and anticipates his marital sexual experiences with fear and dread; or the opposite—he enters upon secret relationships, which are accompanied by guilt feelings and possibly end in unwanted pregnancies.

In Western society, preparation for vocational and social maturity continues far beyond the period in which sexual needs have matured and are pressing for satisfaction. However, no generally acceptable solution has yet been found to serve both ends during this difficult period. Early marriage, to which today's youth often makes recourse, is only in exceptional cases the right thing, as one can see from the great many divorces that end teen-age marriages. The results of Alfred Kinsey's interview-studies of some 20,000 persons have aroused a great deal of attention, and, despite their controversial nature, have thrown new light on many facts that were not clear before.

Worthy of note is his finding that the beginning of sexual activity corresponds closely with the beginning of sexual maturity. That means that the sexually awakened adolescent seeks satisfaction regardless of the fact that parents and teachers expect him to suppress them.

The problem of the best attitude toward youthful sexuality will not be solved soon. Satisfactory solutions are the exception rather than the rule, because uncertainty in this regard is still so universal. Half a century of psychoanalytic practice has shown that the inability of so many adolescents, and also many persons beyond this age group, to cope with their instincts goes back to early experiences of unfavorable emotional relations with the parents, by which the problem of puberty was exacerbated.

Quite characteristic of this sort of adolescent is Ellie, a girl of seventeen, an only child, who grew up in a home without love. Her father was a government official whose love of order was much disturbed by his wife's lack of orderliness. There was constant quarreling and bickering between the parents. When she was a child, Ellie used to pray to God to reconcile her parents.

Ellie was a very sensitive child, one who very much needed love. All her life she felt lonely. She masturbated a great deal and had a bad conscience about it.

When she was sixteen, in her longing for affection, she entered into an intimate sexual relationship with an older schoolmate. Her opposition to her parents was expressed by her choosing a young man who was socially unacceptable to them. However, he gave her the tenderness and affection that her parents had denied her.

Even when the relationship was discovered, and Ellie sent into psychotherapeutic treatment, she was not ready to give up her boy friend. Only through the trust and confidence that Ellie developed with her therapist, and also through gradual self-understanding, did there come about a change in attitude that made it possible for her to free herself from a relationship that was not very healthy.

It appears that the most advantageous treatment of adolescent sexual problems is provided by group therapy. In the author's opinion, this form of treatment should be incorporated into the educational system, for it provides an opportunity for discussion, with professional help, and for inner clarification, which the adolescent requires today more than ever.

About Divisions into Phases

Before turning from the problems of adolescence to those of life's middle period, it may be well to mention the concept of *life phases* used in this presentation.

The question of life phases is actively debated. Those who take up the question are of the opinion that it ought to be possible to find certain objective viewpoints that would provide a natural principle for dividing life into phases.

On one hand, life changes in a steady flow; on the other, as the result of biological, psychological, and social factors, there are times when one function, type of performance, or form of life stops and is replaced by a new form. How one divides life up into phases will depend upon which changes are held to be most important.

The author sees no reason to change from her division of life into *five phases*. This is based on theoretical as well as practical considerations.

Theoretically, her central concept is *self-determination:* a goal-setting that finds expression in one's own identity. Self-determination, as has been shown, has *forerunners* in childhood, when it is expressed in the form of personal wishes rather than as life objectives.

In adolescence, the second phase, self-determination becomes concrete in relation to life, but it still has a *temporary* and tentative character.

In adulthood, the individual normally becomes established in life, with a *definite* self-determination. Furthermore, the *results* of the goal settings begin to make their appearance. The author tentatively places this phase between twenty-five and forty-five. Biological and psychological factors are taken into consideration: early marriage and early decisions as to vocation can bring this phase on earlier; early climacteric and other disintegrative manifestations can cut it short.

The author's fourth phase—from about forty-five to sixty-five—is determined by the fact that in this period, more than ever before, a *balance* is drawn and life examined with a view to seeing whether it corresponds to one's expectations and, if not, whether it can still be rounded out and developed.

The fifth phase is old age, which, as the result of greater life expectancy today, frequently sets in much later, in the seventies or eighties. This phase is characterized by *retirement,* which comes *after* self-determination, just as childhood comes before it.

From the *practical* standpoint, these five divisions seem particularly useful because they correspond to the periods that are decisive for occupational development and the founding of a family. Thus we have the following periods: period I, preschool and school; period II, preparation for an occupation, the beginnings of a career, and relations with the other sex before marriage; period III, complete occupational activity, marriage, and the founding of a family; period IV, when career successes and results become important (In this period there is sometimes a regression in the occupational field. Furthermore, the children leave the parental home and become independent. They may enlarge the family by founding their own families, or may diminish the family by breaking away); period V, former occupations are replaced by part-time occupations or hobbies, and there is often the loss of the marriage partner.

The Middle Phase of Life

For most people, the middle phase—between the twenty-fifth and forty-fifth years—represents the summit of their lives. Lying between growth and decline, it is the period of highest development and greatest emotional *energy* and *reproductive* powers. For most people it is the time of the greatest mental *elasticity, capacity for work,* and *creativity.*

Bill is from Kentucky. From the structure of his life history, however, he might have come from any country in the Western cultural circle. At the time the study was made he was sixty-seven years old. He received a modest pension and lived with his wife in a pleasant little house. He had a medium-priced automobile in his garage and took good care of it. He also had a neat little garden in which he and his wife raised roses and other flowers.

Bill was very fond of his house; periodically he gave it a fresh coat of paint, both inside and out. He did most of the repairs and odd jobs around the house. He liked to go with his wife to visit his neighbors and relatives. He and his wife were very proud of their two sons and two daughters, all of whom were married and who had enriched their parents' lives by providing them with nine grandchildren.

Bill grew up in simple circumstances in a small town where his father owned a modest farm and a general store. When Bill was twelve he lost his father, whom he loved dearly; when his mother remarried he felt that his stepfather did not like him. By agreement with his mother, he went at age fourteen to live with relatives in a large city, where he worked in a factory. Thanks to this decision he was almost wholly independent at an early age.

From seventeen to twenty he was in the army. When he left, he tried to better himself by going into the transportation field. There he got a certain amount of training. First he worked for a railroad and then for a trucking firm.

In his personal life Bill showed the same decisiveness and straightforwardness as in the development of his vocation. He gave up the girl he wanted to marry because she asked him to change his religion, which was against his convictions. At twenty-six he married a girl who had been a schoolmate in his home town.

After World War I, into which he had been drafted soon after his marriage, he returned to his wife and the son she had borne in his absence. In the following years the family had three more children. Bill spoke of them and of his grandchildren with pride and said: "We were always a closely knit family, and still are."

Despite financial difficulties in the crisis years after 1929 and a severe illness and a kidney operation when he was forty-nine, as a result of which he had to give up his job, Bill looked back upon his life as happy. When he was fifty-three, he acquired a small grocery store, similar to the one his father had owned. At sixty-four he retired from the business and turned it over to his youngest son.

The rise and decline of this man, who can be regarded on the average as healthy and happy, corresponds in its regularity to his biological rise and decline.

The high point of his life came between his twenty-sixth and forty-ninth years—the period of his maturity. After a phase of tentative self-determination, which, as a result of his particular circumstances, began at fourteen, he established himself in his marriage and his vocation at twenty-six. He started a family, he built a house, he attained a certain social position, and advanced in his career. He considered the *high point of his life* a three-month vacation he took at age forty-six, when he and his family traveled all over the United States in their car.

Characteristic of this particular man is the way he reacts to life's problems and makes his decisions. Bill is not a fighter, but he never lets himself be forced into anything that does not suit him or that doesn't appear right to him. From an early age he showed a great *capacity for adaptation*. This is without doubt the principal tendency of his life. Yet his adaptability was not such that he passively submitted to life's disappointments or denials. On the contrary, it skillfully led him away from them. The success of Bill's life rests in his adaptability. He was repeatedly compelled to face disappointments—having to leave his parental home, which was hard for him, having to give up his education; being forced by illness to give up his work at an early age. Despite them, he was able to find increasing fulfillment during and after the middle period of his life.

Bill's life cycle shows clearly how the right decisions—in the sense of a proper and suitable self-determination—contribute to the success of a life.

In comparison with the life of a primarily adaptive person, let us now discuss the life of an unusually creative individual.

In her long, full life, the great Norwegian educator Anna Sethne (1872–1961) contributed substantially to the development of the Norwegian public school system and to Scandinavian education in general.

Anna Sethne was born in a small harbor town. Her father was a Swedish sea captain and her mother came from a Norwegian peasant family. When Anna was four her parents were divorced. The mother, too proud to accept alimony or allow anyone to help her, supported herself and her child by working as a seamstress.

Anna reacted strongly to this situation. By inventiveness and initiative, she tried to compensate for her lack of toys and other childhood pleasures. Thus she learned to read early.

She was very ambitious and became such an excellent student that her pastor helped her obtain a scholarship to a secondary school that was normally accessible only to the children of well-to-do families.

The experiences that she had in this early environment provided the basis for her later social-democratic attitude; also, her mother's fate contributed to making her a believer in women's rights.

Anna's main interests, however, were education and her love for children. She taught from the time she was seventeen. When she was twenty-two she married one of her colleagues, and their marriage was a happy one until his death in 1946.

With limited means Anna created a lovely home for herself and her family. She was a loving mother, interested in everything that went on in the family, but she also demanded obedience and competence. These same qualities characterized her as a teacher and later as the head of a school.

Anna began her activity as Norway's school reformer at about the age of forty, when she founded the Norwegian Teachers Association and a professional journal, *Our Schools,* on which she frequently worked all night.

She was an excellent organizer and was famous for her teaching schedules and curriculums. Her school soon had visitors from all over the world, and she was held in high regard far beyond the borders of Norway.

In addition to her countless positions and honorary positions, she participated in social and political affairs. During the political suppression of her country by the Nazis she took an active and energetic part in the resistance movement. With great courage she spoke up against the denial of people's freedoms, and she saved the lives of a great many people. Among her many publications, the one considered most important is her book *The Standard Plan for the Norwegian Public School* (1935–38).

One of the most unusual things about Anna was her broad outlook and wide horizon. To bring new stimulation to Norway's teachers, she sought out famous educators and psychologists from other countries and invited them to congresses and lectures. At the same time she was a solidly integrated personality, deeply rooted in her beloved homeland.

When we observe this great life in connection with our examination of success in life, we can designate it as uniquely fulfilled. It is an explicit example of complete self-realization.

This life is characterized by *creative expansion*. But it also comprises the satisfaction of needs, adaptability to circumstances, and an extraordinary inner organization and orderliness. Anna's accomplishment, which extends over many years, finds its high point relatively late, in her fifties. In her personal life, the high point may well fall within her twenties and thirties, when she started her family and created her home.

The final, definitive results of a life cannot be determined until that life nears its end. However, the middle phase is very decisive for final success. Lives in which self-determination, marriage and the founding of a family, professional and social anchoring, have failed to develop during this critical period face great difficulties in achieving any final success.

Hesiod said: "At the right time, lead a wife into your home, when you are not far from your thirtieth year. For four years let the woman thrive, and have the wedding in the fifth!" From the psychological point of view, this ancient Greek's wisdom would still be applicable. It is, however, no longer widely followed.

Girls' concern about not getting a man if they wait too long is just as great as it has always been. Young girls in psychotherapy repeat this theme again and again. This means that marriage, despite frequent criticism of the institution, is generally considered the most desirable form of life.

The impetus to marriage, especially to early marriage, can be seen as resulting from pressure toward marriage and from the removal of former barriers to marriage. The former consists primarily of social and psychological factors, whereas the latter is essentially economic in nature. The extensive changes in both stimuli is reflected in statistics: in 1890 only 63.1 percent of all adults in the United States were ever married, whereas now 80 percent of those over eighteen years of age are married and living with their spouses.

The stimuli toward marriage are products of social change, although they may act upon the individual psychologically. The general loosening of family relationships, the isolation of small family units no longer in continuous interaction with the extended family, the widening of interests beyond the home, and the increase in family breakdown through divorce and social disorganization leave the young adult in an emotionally isolated position, and he seeks to find through marriage new emotional ties to replace the old traditional ones.

The open attitudes toward sex and the abundance of sexual stimuli in the cultural milieu, coupled with persisting moral values that sanction sex only within marriage, constitute another push toward the marriage relationship.

In addition, there has also been a shift in emphasis from achievement and "good character" to "happiness." The marriage relationship has been romanticized, with the result that it is seen as the royal road to happiness. Marriage has come to be something of a social necessity. A normal sex relationship is believed to constitute one of the hallmarks of "normality," and marriage constitutes official endorsement of such normality. Furthermore, there is often a social stigma attached to being unmarried. The degree to which a young woman is free to choose whether or not to marry is less than in Victorian days, when a spinster aunt was afforded her share of respect and a place in the family circle. To be married today is part of the popularity cult that has engulfed the younger generation. In *The Pyramid Climbers,* Vance Packard points out that to be married is one of the prerequisites for advancement in corporate organizations.

On the other hand, some former barriers to marriage no longer exist. Economic prosperity and the many social welfare measures reduce the economic hazards of life and thereby remove some of a young man's fears about taking on family responsibilities. The fact that the wife can also work often makes marriage more economically feasible. Increasing awareness that they can limit the size of their families through contraception, thus removing the fear of being encumbered beyond their ability to provide, also encourages many young people to marry. Many young people postpone having children and, for such couples, marriage provides the opportunity for both companionship and the pleasures of shared interests and activities.

Then, too, the shift from the old patriarchal, institutional family to the modern democratic family has freed the young adults to make their own decisions, facilitating marriage plans.

The modern democratic family is characterized as having a high degree of self-expression yet united by bonds of affection, congeniality, and common interests. These characteristics can be seen as positive motivational pulls toward entering into marriage.

It is possibly a consequence of the high expectations regarding *companionship* and lasting affection that *divorce* rates are increasingly high. The over-all divorce rate in the United States is 25 percent of all marriages, but higher among marriages with partners under twenty years of age.

In the material gathered by William Goode, 82 percent of the divorced women questioned are convinced that the decision to divorce was right. And, of those who remarried—more than half—87 percent considered their second marriage better than the first.

In general, the children are the ones that suffer most from divorce. Every psychological clinician has observed heartrending examples of this distress. Yet Goode provides figures that show that, in problems observed in school, there is little difference among children of divorced, separated, or living-together parents. However, there may be deep-lying problems beneath the surface.

Concerning Homosexuality

In connection with our observations of the role that marriage and the family play in life success, let us briefly consider another interpersonal relationship, *homosexuality,* which seems to be on the increase again. We say "again" because at various periods in history the turn toward homosexuality has increased and then subsided.

Kinsey found that male homosexuality, which usually develops between the ages of eight and seventeen, occurred in almost 40 percent of the male population examined. He found that it rises to 50 percent among unmarried males, and that even among married males it constitutes from 20 to almost 40 percent. These figures include, of course, the high percentage of homosexuality among adolescents, which is differently interpreted than later homosexuality. Adolescent homosexuality is generally looked upon as a phenomenon of immaturity.

The figures for homosexuality in the female cross-section of the population examined by Kinsey are lower. Among unmarried females the figure is 28 percent, but even among married women there is still a certain percentage.

A great number of those questioned had only occasional or temporary homosexual episodes, and many were heterosexuals who for various reasons also enjoyed homosexual experiences. The percentage of those who remained exclusively homosexual after adolescence is low among females, but about 4 percent among males.

Since the investigations of Freud and his school, it is generally assumed that only in exceptional cases are constitutional factors responsible for homosexuality. In the majority of cases, psychological factors are the basis for this development. This, however, does not imply that a changeover to heterosexuality can be attained simply by means of analysis or psychotherapy, even when the individual urgently desires this. In certain circumstances, however, "cures," if they can be designated as such, are successful.

The decisive question is whether the homosexual accepts himself or not, and if not, what makes him want to change. In his interesting study on homosexuals in the United States, Donald W. Cory finds that the desire for children and for a permanent family relationship is the most frequent motive that moves the homosexual to make a change and to enter into marriage. Further reasons are the difficulties of continuing relationships between homosexual partners and the fear of loneliness in later life. Added to this there is, naturally, the problem of social censure and the fact that in some areas homosexual activity is punishable by law.

In homosexuality, too, the need for a lasting companion comes to the fore. From her own experience with homosexuals the author knows that the unhappy feeling of being "different" is one of the most frequent motives for wishing to change.

Sally, age twenty-six, is an example. Sally comes from one of the slums of New York. Her father, an unskilled laborer, and her mother, who also worked, were alcoholics and lived in perpetual strife. The children used to get beaten and were sadly neglected. Sally lied and stole even as a very little girl.

Sally's father deserted the family when she was between eight and nine. Her mother took a boy friend into the home. Sally was raped by him, and from then on her hatred of men grew to enormous proportions.

When she was seventeen and had finished school, she succeeded, with the financial assistance of an older sister, in moving to another city. There she was able to find jobs, and she worked her way through a state teachers college. It was her ardent wish to become a teacher.

Although she was sufficiently talented and physically strong enough to carry out her plan, she was continually thrown back by her personal problems. These consisted of her instability when it came to learning, her homosexual way of life, which was accompanied by feelings of guilt, and a deep lack of confidence in herself, which had its explanation mostly in her contempt for her past.

Her homosexuality had developed in the course of a friendship with an older woman colleague, who was the first person to meet Sally halfway with any sort of loving understanding. In the course of therapy, Sally realized that in this gentle and tender woman she had experienced for the first time in her life the feeling of being loved and cherished, something she had sought in vain from her real mother. At the same time, her youthful sexual drives were sufficiently awake so that she consented to the love-play initiated by the other. The thought of a male lover aroused only horror in her.

Despite her insight into her behavior, Sally was incapable of resolving the conflict within herself. She not only had feelings of guilt because of this relationship, but also the feeling that her way of life, in the long run, was not what she wanted. Yet Sally could neither accept her way of life, that is, she could not acknowledge herself as a part of it, nor give it up.

Her bitter conflicts and her failure in the teachers' examinations, from which she repeatedly shrank back in anticipation of failure, gave her the despairing feeling that in this decisive period she was missing the meaning of her life.

The problem of time, incidentally, became clear to Sally: When would she find her way out of all this? And when would she attain to a way of life that would seem worthy to her?

The Problem of Time

Different people, at different periods in their lives, become aware of the significance of *time*. Very ambitious, goal-conscious young people sometimes, even very early in life, make a sort of timetable and get impatient when, through unexpected circumstances, they fall behind schedule. In general, however, time, and with it aging, is a significant factor only during and after the middle phase of life.

The awareness of *getting older* is felt earliest in those people engaged in occupations demanding physical exertion, for example, certain manual workers and most professional sports figures. Next, people become aware of age in connection with establishing a family. Not only does the end of the capacity to procreate set relatively early limits, but conscientious parents also take into consideration whether they may not be getting too old to live with growing children.

The *passing of time* is experienced in a different way at different ages. There are also considerable individual differences in people's feelings about time.

Several authors find that while in childhood time passes slowly, in old age it seems to accelerate rapidly, except in depressive individuals. For them, time seems to flow slowly. Creative people feel they have work to finish before they die. Others hope for a few years of quiet contemplation at the end. And many feel that they have been forced to retire too soon.

Particularly in the middle phase of life, many people are conscious of what A. Maslow has termed "peak experiences." They feel that they are standing at the summit or that they are having a unique experience that they will recall all their lives as the high point. This is particularly the case with certain experiences of love or of creativeness, which usually occur in the middle phase of life.

A tragic sense of time is found in *Streetwalker,* an autobiography of an anonymous prostitute. The author of this book, which gives the impression of being authentic, is an English girl who left her parents' home, in which rather good circumstances prevailed, to make her way in the world. This woman's experience of time is related to her *rootlessness.* She writes:

> Strangely enough, though, this rootlessness of day as well as night, engendered by possessing only the contents of two suitcases and living as a self-contained unit within four impersonal and alien walls, is in itself an antidote to dwelling on how time is, was, and will be spent. For I am afraid to look clearly on the passing of time. I fear to look forward lest I perceive nothing. I shut my eyes to all but the most immediate realities, lest I find in today, too, nothing. And I dare not look back, lest all I have lost should confront and confound me. I must see no more than the little, present moment, lest I perceive that there is nothing for me in the stars and nothing in the clock-bound passing of each day.

When we compare this woman's tragic outlook at the loss of time in her rootless existence with the pulsating experience of time of Anna Sethne's "Every day is wonderful because of my work, only the day does not have hours enough," we see the extremes that human existence can encompass.

Activity and a life goal, the sense of being firmly rooted, and the sense of time are all closely related. Allport, Bruner, and Jandorf (1941), who studied the personality characteristics of ninety refugees during the Nazi period, found a general tendency to hold on obstinately to earlier goals and activities, despite the dangers connected with them and the hopelessness of it all. The reason for such tenacity is that, to a large extent, we see in our goals our innermost selves.

Occupational and Leisure-time Activity

The problems of time and aging are today being studied intensively in connection with questions of *occupational* and *leisure-time activity*. The problem of meaningful utilization of leisure time is particularly important, since the average industrial worker finds little satisfaction in his work.

Anne Roe, who has occupied herself intensively with questions of occupational psychology, reports on studies of the desire for *occupational changes*. The results of the studies agree: some two thirds of workers would choose some other occupation if they could begin all over again. However, among those belonging to the so-called better occupations, less than a third express a similar dissatisfaction.

It is a generally recognized fact that work and occupation are unsatisfying to many. Closely connected with this problem is the need for satisfying utilization of leisure, itself a problem. Added to all this is the problem of demoralizing *unemployment,* which threatens workers mainly toward the end of the third phase of life, and in the fourth phase, from forty-five to sixty.

For a clear idea of the amount of time that work occupies in the life of modern man, we may find useful a simplified diagram that Sebastian de Grazia made in 1954 on the basis of questions directed at a representative group of Americans. Questions are published in more complete form in the book *Aging and Leisure*, edited by Robert Kleemeier. Although these figures perhaps do not tell much that is new, they clearly demonstrate an important problem: that during the major portion of their lives the majority of people spend half their waking hours at work. After attending to all the other things necessary for living, most people have only a few hours of leisure.

How can it be possible to see one's life as a success if one's work offers no satisfaction? To the author, it seems improbable that leisure-time activities alone can provide a sense of fulfillment. It is this question that recent studies of motivation attempt to answer.

Among the many works in this field, one that strikes the author as particularly interesting is an intensive study by Herzberg, Mausner, and Snyderman, *The Motivation for Work.* In interviews with bookkeepers

ACTIVITIES of an Average 17-hour Working Day	MEN		WOMEN	
	Ages 20-49	Ages 50 and over	Ages 20-49	Ages 50 and over

I. OUTSIDE THE HOME

At work or in school	7.1	5.2	2.0	1.3 hours
In transit	1.5	0.9	0.6	0.4 "
Purchasing	0.1	0.1	0.4	0.3 "
Hairdresser, visits to friends and relatives	0.8	0.6	0.5	0.4 "
Church, sports, amusement	0.3	0.2	0.4	0.4 "

II. AT HOME

Housework or work in and around the house	0.8	1.2	4.2	4.0 "
Eating or preparing meals	1.2	1.4	2.5	2.3 "
Dressing, bathing, etc.	0.6	0.6	0.9	0.6 "
Leisure activities, including reading	2.8	4.6	3.3	4.8 "
Sleeping (in addition to 7 hours of sleep)	1.8	2.2	1.8	2.2 "

Fig. 34

Activities of American men and women in two age groups during an average 17-hour day (after Sebastian de Grazia).

and engineers, the authors questioned their subjects about what factors give them satisfaction or dissatisfaction. They then compared these factors with individual morale, which was also established during the interviews.

By this method they came to the following conclusions.

, Those who are strongly motivated in their work point out that the *work itself* and *what it accomplishes* satisfies them, that they value the *responsibility* placed on them, and that *recognition* and *getting ahead* are important to them.

On the other hand, those who are little motivated in their work mention quite different factors as being responsible for their satisfaction. For them *salary* and *management policy* are of prime importance, followed by the way *supervision* is carried out, by *personal relationships* that have been formed, and finally, by the physical *working conditions.*

When we think through these findings in connection with our theory as to life's four basic tendencies, we reach the following conclusions. In the first group are found those whose major tendencies are either creative expansion or a conscience-satisfying attitude toward inner order and organization. People with these basic tendencies are usually strongly motivated toward work. In work they find their self-realization. We can call this *primary motivation.*

In the second group are those people whose personal or adaptive needs must be satisfied, directly or indirectly, by their work. Good wages and good working conditions serve to satisfy these needs when the activity does not provide them with any pleasure. Favorable social and management-political conditions furnish them with the satisfying personal relationships that make their work endurable. Their motivation for work is thus determined by *secondary* factors. For these people, money for the purchase of comforts and social relationships to provide security and a sense of belonging are important. At higher-income levels, the desire for status and influence becomes important. Self-realization here comes about in a different way—not by *doing the work* but by the material and social gains that are the by-products of the work.

Several modern studies on the conditions under which those employed in industry can be made satisfied have reached conclusions that correspond to these ideas. Good salaries, and also some sort of participation in management, are common practice today.

The Climacteric and Assessment of Life

From a very early age man evaluates himself critically, and at no time more harshly than during the climacteric.

The word "climacteric," taken in its exact meaning, applies only to the female sex. The end of male reproductive capacity usually comes much later and without the side effects characteristic of the female menopause. In spite of this fact, many psychiatrists speak of the "male climacteric," a period that does not necessarily signal the end of the ability to procreate but does bring about many of the emotional characteristics that, in a woman, would be called typical for the climacteric.

The expression should therefore be used symbolically rather than actually, especially since the period is much longer than the true change-of-life years. The climacteric is an appropriate symbol since, in this period, the important life dimension of reproductive capacity is, if not wholly lost, at least diminished. This and other manifestations indicating the deterioration of capacities that were formerly fully developed warn of the reality of approaching death.

After the age of fifty, most physical, mental, and emotional functions suffer deterioration. This is, of course, only a general rule and may not apply to every case; for, with today's longer lifespans, functions are better preserved and productive and performance capacity prolonged.

Roughly the period between twenty-five and forty-five is considered the middle phase of life; in it the adult normally establishes himself on the basis of a definitive self-determination. It is the phase of adult maturity, regardless of the fact that, in so many early marriages and early vocational achievement, maturity is hastened or forestalled. In our time, most life experiences belong to the thirties and forties.

This situation is different from what it was even one generation ago. At forty, today's woman feels herself to be at the high point of her life. Her sexuality and participation in life sometimes arrive at their full development only at this point. In the previous generation, a woman of forty thought of herself as getting old, and if we go back still another generation, a woman of forty was actually considered old—"an honorable matron." As Erich Stern has said, the word "aging" has a negative flavor. Formerly, one spoke of the "gracious" days of youth; today youth is generally regarded as a period laden with problems, and not a very happy time. The word "young" in our day has a new meaning, and not only for a woman. A man is considered young until forty and, for the most part, only in his forties does he begin to achieve success in his field of endeavor.

After this feeling of peak achievement at thirty or forty, a turning point comes gradually or suddenly in the forties or fifties. It may make itself felt either as weariness and giving out or as a *life crisis* like that experienced at puberty. Just as newly throbbing drives and new life problems may bring about in puberty a personal crisis, so in the climacteric the loss or diminution of potentialities may create similar problems.

The number of *suicides* begins to rise sharply. More than half of the women and almost two thirds of the men who commit suicide are forty-five or older. In female suicides, according to some American statistics, the suicide curve reaches its highest point in the age group between forty-five and fifty-five. In men, the curve rises steadily to higher ages.

Norman Farberow and Edwin Schneidman made intensive studies of suicides and in doing so investigated the motives that lead to suicide. They concurred with Karl Menninger who in *Man Against Himself* named hate, guilt, and hopelessness as the most probable principal motives. Farberow and Schneidman analyzed letters and notes left by suicides, and found that the majority of these suicides were forty to sixty years old. What these, as well as the younger suicides, report about their motives discloses primarily hate and guilt.

Hate and guilt feelings because of omissions and mistakes that cannot be reversed assume a lethal character in this period because they coincide in time with the depression that comes from the diminution of strength and capabilities. Hate and guilt are the principal motives for suicide. With advancing age, hopelessness becomes a motive.

In women, the loss of the reproductive power is a particularly drastic experience. The *menopause years,* as a number of statistical studies show, fall mainly between forty and fifty-five, with the greatest number occurring around forty-seven to forty-nine.

This ending of the reproductive power, however, *does not necessarily* mean the end, or even an ebbing, of sexual interest. But many women are distressed that they can no longer have children.

After the age of forty-five there occurs a considerable increase in severe, and frequently chronic, *illnesses,* which often seriously affect a person's capacity to work and his sense of well-being. A rapid rise in fatal illnesses appears after the age of forty-five, among which heart disease, cancer, and arteriosclerosis play the principal role. The incidence of certain fatal accidents, such as burns and falls, also increases greatly at this time. Heart trouble, today the most frequent cause of death, is responsible for one death in ten among those aged fifteen to twenty-four. The curve then rises steadily. Between ages twenty-five and forty-four, 25 percent of deaths are due to heart conditions; between forty-five and sixty-four the percentage rises to 50; among those over sixty-five it is 65 percent.

Edward Stieglitz says that in the *illnesses of old age,* unlike those of younger years, there is not usually a single cause, such as an infection or trauma. Rather, there is often a series of disturbances, even when there is an acute illness and specific symptoms, which Stieglitz calls the "multiple etiology" of old age.

Occasionally even young people occupy themselves with the thought of *death,* but generally only when deterioration begins to set in does one face

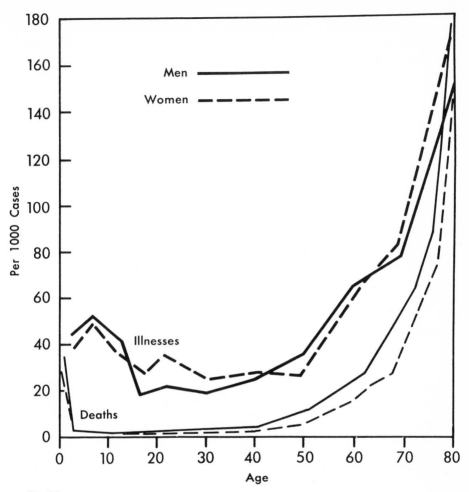

Fig. 35

Number of persons in the U.S.A. ill on a particular payday in 1950 (Public Health Reports).

the fact of the impending end. Jesse Stuart, a contemporary poet, remarked after an almost fatal heart attack: "No one really begins to live until he has come close to death."

Happy is he who in the fourth phase—the one before the last—suffers from nothing more than the wish to complete his life's work. At fifty-six, Albert Schweitzer wrote of his work in Lambaréné:

How much of the work which I have planned and have in mind shall I be able to complete?

My hair is beginning to turn. My body is beginning to show traces of the exertions I have demanded of it and of the passage of the years.

I look back gratefully to the time when, without needing to husband my strength, I could get through an uninterrupted course of physical and mental work. With calmness and humility I look forward to the future, so that I may not be unprepared for renunciation if it be required of me.

In this phase of life, more than in any other, the paths of those who still have a future diverge from the paths of those who are unable to think of the future with any hope. For many who bear a heavy burden of regret and guilt over missed opportunities, of wasted time, of wrong decisions, or of wrong modes of life, it is too late to start anything new and make good the errors of the past.

Goethe, that great student of mankind, remarked on two separate occasions: "We live on the past" and "We are ruined by the past." He meant that, while we get sustenance from what we have built up for ourselves in the past, our past also destroys us.

The individual must cope with both his past and his future. The problem of coping with the future becomes more difficult the older a person gets. To lose sight of the future completely means to die. But absorption in a future that gets progressively shorter and less meaningful can become unrealistic and hectic.

Still more difficult is the *transition* period, in which one's own life poses problems for the future. There are great individual differences in how far into the future the transition period stretches. For example, the creative person is always oriented toward the future because, as Albert Schweitzer says, he hopes that his life work will have an impact in the future. Strong preoccupation with the past is partly conditioned by culture, for example, in connection with the cherishing of tradition and customs.

The aging person normally spends much time in retrospection, but in the neurotic the past becomes an almost intolerable burden. Ben is an example of someone being destroyed by the past.

Ben, a childless businessman who had been divorced twice after very short marriages, was fifty when he came into psychotherapy. He was severely depressed, was suffering from fatigue and headaches, and had recently been impotent. His life was lonely and unsocial. He was intelligent enough to realize that his depression was the result of his meaningless existence, for which he felt guilty. He felt that he had spent his life striving for what was unworthy and that he had done many things he did not believe in. He had begun several enterprises, but, because of his lack of conviction or serious commitment, they led to nothing. To his two wives he was bound by neither love nor understanding. He married his first wife because of her physical charms and the second one for her supposed business acumen, which soon turned out to be nonexistent.

The only thing that Ben would really have liked to do was to write fiction, but he considered his talent insufficient and had never pursued this goal in earnest. Yet he admitted that two of his short stories had been published at once and had been very well received.

When coming into psychotherapy, one of his half-admitted hopes was that through it he might achieve his longed-for writing career. However, he realized it would be a rather late beginning.

Ben had a long unfavorable history. His childhood had been made unhappy by a harsh and unloving father and his adolescence spoiled by rebellion, early dropping out of school, and running away from home. Ben's whole life remained set on rebellion. One of the real gains of his treatment was that it freed him from hating his father and enabled him to love.

A happy result was that he entered into a successful relationship with a woman he loved. However, in the field of creative writing, it appeared to be too late for this restless and tired man to make the necessary efforts. Perhaps the automobile accident that killed Ben at the age of fifty-two was less of an accident than it appeared to be. It provided a merciful ending to a life that had become hopeless.

In the case of a neurosis like Ben's, a high degree of rigidity and inflexibility prevents further development. The primary requirement for successful development in and after the transition period of the climacteric is *flexibility*. Helmut von Bracken refers to a phenomenon that he calls *restructuring*. By this he means that, in the aging, performance is attained in a different way and through different functions than in younger people. Speed of reaction, memory, and other functions deteriorate, but experience and responsibility increase. Many years ago, William Stern defined *intelligence* as general mental adaptability to new life tasks and conditions. Mental flexibility (and, under certain circumstances, great physical flexibility) characterizes those still capable of good performance at an advanced age.

The Problem of Fulfillment in Old Age, and Death

Today, almost universally, retirement comes at sixty-five. Because the law so wills it, at this age people enter the stage of retirement and begin drawing their pensions or Social Security payments. Then the period commonly regarded as old age commences.

It was not so long ago that the work phase of life continued past this age. The pushing forward of this point in time means that retirement comes prematurely for the majority of people who are still hale and hearty in their mid-sixties. In this respect, the law is obviously more justifiable from a social-political standpoint than from a psychological one. In a certain way it is even absurd, for it was instituted at a time when, thanks to progress in hygiene and medicine, both life expectancy and creative activity had been extended. As a result, one hears frequent expressions of dissatisfaction about enforced retirement, primarily from those who are not in a position to find a rewarding supplementary occupation.

A comprehensive interview study that B. D. Kutner and co-workers made of retired Americans in 1956 found that loss of morale was common. In a culture as strongly oriented toward action and activity as ours, the person who is shut out from competition and from earning money frequently sees himself as superfluous and a burden to others. It is hard to maintain self-esteem, which was formerly connected with earning money and having a stable position, unless perhaps one holds other positions of prestige or receives honors of some importance. In so-called primitive societies, these are frequently accorded to the aged. In our society, too, there are certain honorary positions for the elderly. But now that many former voluntary activities, such as charity, social work, care of the sick, and the like, have become professional vocations, opportunities for such work are limited.

More and more people are coming to recognize the importance of suitable occupations for older people. However, recent scientific studies have not provided any solution on a comprehensive scale.

One of the principal psychological problems of the aging person with no definite tasks before him is to *organize his time* satisfactorily. The working day has a natural rhythm; the day of the retired person does not. In general, pursuits of hobbies and amateur interests does not follow a set rhythm. It is difficult to free oneself from the discipline of one's working life. For housewives, who continue to run their households as usual, the change is less upsetting than for the man or for the professional woman.

Despite all the complaints they once voiced about the trials and tribulations of their jobs, many people experience the end of their occupational life as a rejection.

"I always used to look forward to my retirement," says a government employee whom A. L. Vischer quotes in his sensitive book *Emotional Changes in the Aging.* "But when my last working day came along and I said good-bye to my colleagues, I felt an unknown emptiness inside me and all around me. The question: 'Now, what?' suddenly began to gnaw inside me. Only too well do I recall how, with mixed feelings, I left the administration building and started on my way home. Everything seemed to be different, the streets and the houses I used to know so well, all the people—everything appeared strange to me."

The man quoted here has overcome the anxieties that assailed him. He helps his wife in the house, goes marketing, helps out in the bank, goes to lodge meetings, reads, writes poetry, and goes to the theater. Never again has he wished to return to his former work at the office.

"But," as the head of personnel of a large plant said to Vischer, "you can't create hobbies. You can only perfect and refine those that already exist." That is why those people who formerly did gardening, odd jobs, or little things on the side are the best off. Bill, for example, whose life we discussed (pp. 145–47), is happily retired. He and his wife raise roses; he continues to make improvements in his house, repairs toys and bicycles for his nine grandchildren, goes to his lodge, and visits his friends and relatives.

An important fact emphasized by Vischer is that among those drawing pensions a part of the *social ego,* as William James called it, is lost. A major role in the world is given up with a concomitant loss of social significance.

Here is what a retired factory manager said to Vischer: "What hurts me the most since my retirement is that I have become so unimportant. Six months ago I was number two man in my firm. People used to look up to me; I had a deciding word to say as to how the business was to be managed. They came to me with a lot of problems. How different that all is now. When I had to go to see my successor at the plant recently, my former secretary, who had worked devotedly for me for a good many years and for whom my opinion used to be the last word, scarcely paid any attention to me or noticed me. Even the doorman gave me only the most perfunctory 'Good morning.' "

Since retired couples spend so much time with each other, arguments and disagreements that had formerly been avoided may arise. After retirement, deterioration often sets in and leads to an early end.

Happy are those who, through their many *interests* or *creative activities,* are able to live fulfilling lives to the very end because they see themselves as useful and integral parts of their environment.

Of all the creative older people of our time, the lovable figure of Grandma Moses has aroused the most interest and admiration. This country woman died in 1961 at the age of 101. From childhood she had painted little pictures for her own pleasure. She painted her first important picture when she was sixty-seven, just a few weeks before the death of her beloved husband. The most remarkable thing about her life history is how, after a healthy, useful, and happy life, she awakened in her late sixties to an exceptional creativity in which no problems are expressed, but only joy in life and love for her fellow men.

"Even now I am not old," she wrote. "I never think of it, yet I am a grandmother and have eleven grandchildren. I also have seventeen great-grandchildren, that's a-plenty!

"I look back on my life like a good day's work, it was done and I feel satisfied with it. I was happy and contented, I knew nothing better and made the best out of what life offered. And life is what we make it, always has been, always will be."

The extraordinary flexibility of this personality is expressed in a sentence she uttered at 101. She told of a little accident that had come about through her own carelessness. With a wink she added: "I guess I'll have to mend my ways."

In 1958, *Time* magazine showed a gallery of people between eighty and one hundred, all of whom were still active in some field of endeavor and many of whom were still in public life. Perhaps the most noteworthy of these was ninety-five-year-old Theodore F. Green, the oldest U. S. Senator, who swam and played handball and, up to his eighty-eighth year, tennis.

By contrast, others in this life phase occupy themselves with the question of life's end, in which fear of death, apparent indifference or stoic resignation to the inevitable, or religious subjection to fate can be met in the most varied forms. Herman Feifel, in *The Attitude Toward Death*, distinguishes two principal attitudes toward death, the religious and the naturalistic. The religious person, who believes in a hereafter, does not suffer from the depression frequently found in nonbelievers. The belief in the immortality of the soul is a comfort. Waiting for nothing is a disconsolate situation.

As Paul Tillich has said: "One strives ahead valiantly, particularly at the beginning of life. But this feeling is always in a schism with fear and dread of what the future may bring. . . . Finally, the nearer we get to the inescapable end, [the more] we experience the impenetrable darkness and the threat that our entire existence ultimately may be judged a failure."

Although it is occasionally denied, *fear of death* among human beings is universal. From those who felt used up and useless, Feifel often heard: "One has lived one's life and one submits to the fate of having to die" or "One no longer has anything worthwhile to live for." Naturally, this attitude was especially marked in those who are incurably ill.

The question of death has occupied the poets and thinkers of all times.

How is it possible in this last phase, they ask, to hold on to the consciousness of a life that has been fulfilled?

At forty-five, Wilhelm von Humboldt said: "We must not let the end of life now sink down upon us." This friend of Goethe's and Schiller's, as great a statesman as he was an intellectual, gave much thought to questions of the soul and fate. He often wrote and spoke about death as the possible fulfillment of life.

Like him, Carl Jung, in his thoughtful observations in *Reality of the Soul,* sees in death the fulfillment of life's meaning.

"O Lord, give to each one his own death," is the prayer of Rainer Maria Rilke, in which he, like Humboldt, expressed the idea of the *readiness for death.* "O Lord, give to each his own death, his dying, which departs from that life in which he had love, meaning, and distress." Unfortunately, this fate, as benevolent as it is great, is probably granted to only a few.

PART II

SOCIETY

CHAPTER 6

THE INDIVIDUAL AND SOCIETY

When Wilhelm Wundt founded modern scientific psychology, he had be-
fore him the idea that there is a "psychology of peoples," as he termed it,
parallel to the psychology of the individual. In other words, he recognized
that human psychology viewed solely from the standpoint of the individual can be understood only incompletely. Man is not only an individual,
he is also a member of a group and generally of a number of groups.

The particular groups to which he belongs is an essential characteristic
of an individual, for only in the group can the highest performances of
which a man is capable be accomplished. Indeed, *human culture* represents a group creation.

Today's enormously developed social psychology and cultural anthropology are, in the main, American creations. They had their origin for the
most part in the practical problems presented by the mixture of races and
nationalities in the United States. Since it is our aim to explore the significance of psychology for daily life, an understanding of psychological
processes may help us gain useful insights into our "human situation"
inasmuch as it is conditioned by our association with others.

Our subject matter is vast and complex, and we shall have to be selective in our treatment of it. The headings of the sections that follow provide a guide to the major themes.

Social Conditioning and the Social Needs of the Individual

No man lives in isolation; men live together with others. Human society is a structure found everywhere on earth, a structure that is as complex as it is varied. It also has all sorts of subgroupings. From birth the

169

child is a member of society. Normally, he is born into a family; this is true of all races and peoples. This means that from the very beginning of his life, an individual's existence is socially conditioned, that many of his needs can be satisfied only by the group, and that he always has group membership.

The individual, of course, has no choice; his membership in any group results from his birth. Each individual's fate, as is stressed by social psychologists, is already conditioned to a great extent by his group membership before he has the slightest opportunity to assume any position with respect to it or to express his individuality without inhibition.

Normally a child reacts favorably to an environment that is helpful to him. In this reaction the same motives are involved as those on which human society rests.

The question of how human society came into being has occupied thinkers for thousands of years. Mutual needs have been primarily responsible for its development. These needs were at first frequently considered *instincts.* Today, caution is applied in the use of the word "instinct," and one speaks more generally of a "drive component in social behavior" with respect to the love, care, and attention that the infant, even unconsciously, requires from his environment.

In the early stages of an infant's life the mother or the mother surrogate plays an exclusive role, and she continues to play a decisive one for a long time afterward. According to varying social needs, more people important to the child are soon added: father, brothers and sisters, other members of the household, and playmates are a part of the life of even the preschool child.

The efforts of even a one- or two-month-old infant to enter into *communication* with his environment were described in Chapter 3. Smiling, imitation of sounds, and gestures—all as early as the last months of the first year—are efforts at reciprocal expression and appeal. In these linguistically imperfect communications a so-called conversation of gestures occurs. Gestures always play an important role in contact, for they supplement speech. Once a child masters speech, he may develop an enormous need for communication. Children who have grown up in a friendly, trusting environment will talk to any stranger they meet. This is documented in two true stories about unusually sociable children.

After a trip to town, one mother tells her neighbor: "My three-year-old Tommy always calls out to everybody from the car window. Today I said to him: 'Tommy, why do you talk to all those people you don't even know?' He answered: 'Mommy, I like people.' I just hope it will always stay that way."

Another child, four-year-old Freddy, is a storehouse of information for his family. It is his special pleasure to walk up and down in front of the house for half an hour at a time and talk to everybody who goes by. He stops the neighbors coming home from work or going marketing or visiting, and asks them: "What's in that package?" or "Where are you going?" As all those who live in the neighborhood are fond of the charming little blond boy, they generally stop for a moment or two to chat with him. Later Freddy runs into the house and relates all the news while he's having his supper.

This child's social world is very large at a very early age, and his *capacity for communication* is unusually well developed. Later Freddy was president of his school class, and he grew up to become a very successful businessman.

Other children, from perhaps the eighth to the tenth month on, are shy in the presence of strangers and, in certain circumstances, develop definite anxiety reactions when they are spoken to by someone they don't know. René Spitz calls this phenomenon "the eighth-month anxiety."

Jean Piaget, whose extensive investigations of children have frequently been referred to here, is of the opinion that before the seventh or eighth year children speak *egocentrically.* In other words, they listen to others less than they listen to themselves, and they don't want to let others be the center of attention. Not until school age, according to Piaget, does a child develop *socialized* speech that actually serves mutual exchange.

Young children are very preoccupied with themselves. But the author believes that it depends to a great extent on the situation whether a child shows an egocentric or a social attitude. Some four- and five-year-olds are quite capable of conducting a real conversation.

They are also capable of *sympathy* and of participating in the joys and sorrows of others. This capacity for *empathy,* which consists of identifying with the experiences of others, is often developed in even very young children. We need only recall the "contagious" effect as a child joins in with the yelling of other infants. In social studies of infants at play, "comforting" of another child was observed as early as eight and twelve months in three different children.

The ability to put oneself into the place of another—many research workers see in this the basis for empathy—is usually not developed before the third year of life. Before then the "I" and the "you" are not yet definitely differentiated in the child's consciousness.

The social world into which the infant grows is for the most part limited to the *family* and the *play group.* These effective face-to-face groups are the major forces for socialization.

Socialization

Today the word *socialization* refers to the entire *process of incorporating the individual into group life.* The socialization process, which goes on for years, is given extraordinary attention by social psychologists, for it has become increasingly clear that the favorable or unfavorable course of this process determines the fate of the individual as well as that of society.

When we speak of a favorable course, we mean a form of social incorporation of the individual into the group that is fruitful and constructive for both parties. For the individual this means that he can express his individuality in relative freedom and realize himself without having to submit blindly to authority and suppress his true self. It also means that the group contains members who, by voluntarily coming together, cooperate enthusiastically toward the realization of the group's goals and their own development.

This process does not always proceed absolutely smoothly. Normally a child is willing to let himself be guided and to learn, and he lays value on belonging to the group. But he also has needs and individual peculiarities that are contrary to group goals.

The question of how the *conflicts* between individual and group can be resolved is one of the principal problems for those in favor of proceeding carefully toward socialization. They condemn both *authoritarian behavior that is lacking in understanding* on the part of adults and superiors and impulsive *self-indulgence* on the part of the individual. Somewhere between these two extremes they see the possibility of psychologically suitable leadership and development.

Socialization is then understood to be a process by which the individual learns the ways of living and of thinking of the society or group to which he belongs so that he may be able to function within that society or group. This is the definition that Frederick Elkin gives to the socialization process in *Child and Society.* What he describes as "ways of living and of thinking" is generally called "ways" in the American literature. "Ways of mankind" is an expression frequently used, and will be used here in this sense.

The means of socialization are social relationships: the *interaction* between human beings. The growing human being enters into this interaction with a *behavior system* based on his inborn dispositions, which have been modified by his experience. It is in this *behavior system* that more or less definite *attitudes* gradually develop.

The foundations are laid by the newborn infant's experiences in the "emotional climate" of his home and in his first interactions with his parents. The development of *aggression* and *dependence*, two of the most important variables in the socialization process, is determined to a great extent by these first experiences. In certain circumstances the variable *performance* might develop with less dependence on emotional and social experiences.

One of the most difficult and obscure themes of psychology is *aggression*, for many different meanings are ascribed to the word and the origin of the phenomenon is disputed.

Let us first discuss aggressiveness only in the sense of *hostility* or destructiveness. Leaving out Freud's controversial theory of a destructive or death instinct, it is generally accepted today that aggressiveness has its source primarily in early *frustrations;* that is why we refer to "frustration aggressiveness."

Thus, as there are frustrations from the beginning of life, so there are, from the beginning, causes and reasons for hostility. In what circumstances this hostility develops to the extent that it becomes a danger to its possessor and to others is still largely unknown.

There is no simple answer to the question of what conditions are responsible for the development of aggressiveness, nor is there one that applies in every instance. Many consider parental rejection of the child, lack of harmony between the parents, and oversolicitousness and spoiling the principal causes. Others deny this. Robert Sears believes that the reaction of the parents to the child's first aggressions decisively affects his further development. Dollard and Miller are of the opinion that the *type of punishment* plays a decisive role in the socialization of the aggressive child. They hold that *fear* of certain punishments generally prevents further outbreaks of aggressiveness and thereby contributes to the child's socialization. However, punishments do not prevent hostility from increasing.

How the child can be given an opportunity to express his frustrations and get over them without developing hostility is another unsolved problem.

It has been learned from psychotherapy that individuals who, as a result of years of suppression of their hostile impulses, have amassed an enormous amount of resentment are gradually able to rid themselves of their pent-up hate if they are given an opportunity to talk it out and are met with understanding. It is often necessary to permit children and adolescents to express their anger in aggressive play, which may even culminate in the symbolic killing of people they hate. In *Children Who Hate*, Fritz Redl discussed the methods used in his educational institution to provide an opportunity for these partly criminal but mostly neglected adolescents to relieve their hatred without becoming dangerous to themselves or others.

In the daily life of the family it is naturally difficult to manage this in a constructive way. Anna Freud, who is greatly concerned with these matters, concludes that the child who is going through frustrations and conflicts tends to react with fear to both very strict and very permissive parents; the main difficulty lies in finding the golden mean between excessive strictness and permissiveness.

Many modern mothers have heard that children are helped in conquering their negative feelings if they are occasionally permitted to give free expression to these feelings. These mothers encourage their children now and then "to pour their hearts out." Thus Eve's mother tells her friend: "When my little Eve says 'I hate you, Mommy!' I tell her, 'That's all right; sometimes we all have feelings like that.'"

Her friend is outraged; she simply can't understand it. "I really think you pay too much attention to all this modern stuff. A little psychology is all right in its way, but this is going too far!"

Eve's mother replies, "Frieda, be honest with me now. Which of us has the more difficult daughter?"

Frieda responds in disgust, "Oh, but what has that got to do with it?"

But the fact is that the possibilities for expression given to a child has a great deal to do with it. A. L. Baldwin studied child behavior in connection with the control, whether authoritarian or democratic, with which parents handle their children. In psychology, "control" is the technical expression for the behavioral limitations placed on a person.

Baldwin found that the strict discipline of authoritarian parents, who will not stand for any resistance and who insist on strict obedience to their orders, results in obedient children. But at the same time such an upbringing suppresses important positive qualities such as initiative, fearlessness, and independent planning.

Children whose parents were generally tolerant, who explained to their children the reasons for the measures they took and who gave them an opportunity to raise objections, show much more initiative, independence, fearlessness, and ability to plan. These children developed a greate. ~na-city to be "aggressive" in the *positive* sense. In other words, they had the enterprise to go out into the world and to cope with problems independently and without hostility.

Here Baldwin uses the word "aggressive" to mean the ability to take hold of things, a meaning that must be distinguished from the aggressiveness of hostility.

Aggressiveness in the sense of destructive hostility was observed by Kurt Lewin and his co-workers, especially Ronald Lippitt, as a result of authoritarian leadership. Lewin is particularly interested in group structures. He and Lippitt carried on experiments with boys, placing one group under *authoritarian leadership* and another group under *democratic leadership*. The result was that authoritarian leadership reached performance more quickly and that boys felt safe under such leadership. But it also released a great deal of aggression. The democratic leadership, which appealed to the boys' sense of responsibility, at first set the group into a state of uncertainty and confusion, but gradually brought about initiative, independence, and a spirit of cooperation based on freedom.

Frustrations that are meaningful or that are made meaningful by being explained can usually be borne, so long as the individual can assimilate them. Parents who make it possible for their children to identify with them in a good mutual understanding provide the best support for the ability to bear losses and frustrations. On the other hand, a father who, when his son asks him the reason for an order, gives the answer "You'll do it because I tell you to," gives a double burden to the child—he must not only put up with a disappointment or an inconvenience, but also suffers an indignity and a rejection.

Dependency, which is a necessity to the infant, can also develop into a behavior detrimental to socialization. Most frequently the circumstances responsible for this have to do with the feeding situation. Babies who are treated with rigidity and strictness while being fed and are weaned without regard for their needs develop insecurity and dependency. Lack of love and interest in the infant also increase insecurity and dependency. Later, punishment and frustrations continue the pattern. As Sears, Whiting, and others have shown, the same factors that are responsible for the development of excessive dependency can also bring about aggressiveness. Frequently both are observed simultaneously.

Perhaps the most important factor in the socialization of the individual is his readiness *to perform and to work*. While society can get along with all sorts of personality problems, it cannot maintain itself without the individual's work contribution. Work and performance can be understood only in the relation of the individual to society. High demands and discipline that is not authoritarian are the best prerequisites for high performance.

The hypothesis for socialization is the existence of an organized society that has different structures in the various cultures. Society in Western culture consists of various, increasingly mixed *ethnic* groups. This society is more or less definitely divided into *classes* and comprises a great many institutions such as the family, school, church, the law, community, the state, and so on. It lends a certain *status* to those who belong to it, giving them their "position" and certain *roles*. It sets up *values* and *norms* by which the individual is to be guided. In some respects it is rigid and tradition bound; in others, it is flexible and capable of change. The individual has got to come to terms with the rigidity as well as the *flexibility of social institutions.*

The Concept of Role

The concept of social *role* is considered by many to be one of the most fundamental concepts in social psychology. But just what is this role? Its origin, of course, is in the theater; the actor plays a role. And this is what occurs: he is given a particular part to play, that is, he has to represent something, but, he must, to a certain extent, be suited to this role.

Sociologists define the individual's social role primarily from the point of view of the group. In social interaction every individual is accorded a role—an organized sector of behavior. Society defines this sector as certain duties and certain rights. In other words, for the roles of child, parent, husband, wife, there are certain rules within the family, which may vary in the various cultures and social groups but which generally are known to those involved.

In contrast to sociologists, social psychologists emphasize that the role must also be looked upon from the point of view of the individual. A person approaches his social role with definite individual characteristics. The role of the obedient child may have more appeal for one, less for another. One person may have been born to the role of leader before he has been named to that role.

Let us look again at the case of Allen (pp. 36–37, 43, 46–47, 132–33, 135). Allen's mother was strict, and she set extraordinary store by obedience and good behavior. Even at the age of four, Allen did not like to be reprimanded, and so he played the role of a *model boy.* He sought perfection and was an extremely amenable child.

Sociologically speaking, the role that Allen played vis-à-vis his mother was that of son. He played it "in the style" of a model boy. In his relations with his friends, however, Allen's role was that of a playmate. At this early stage he played it "in the style" of the leader. He was able to play a leadership role because he had many good ideas and the other children were glad to have him suggest games. This sufficed for the informal type of leadership role that is characteristic for this particular age group. Whether Allen's qualifications will still stand him in such good stead at a later age is a question for the future.

In a way, the two roles that Allen played are opposed to each other. In his relation to his mother he is subservient; in his relation to his friends he is superior. It is noteworthy that even a child of four can play two roles and keep them separate.

In each of these roles, one might say, the child is a different person. He makes a *choice* of the various ways of behavior that are at his disposal and *organizes* them with a view to certain *goals* that he pursues in the various social relationships. In one case he wants praise from his mother; in the other, he wants recognition from his friends. In each role, Allen *operates* in a different *system of relationships*. The two roles do not stand in conflict with each other, as might appear at first glance. Both are so constituted that a social *distinction* or a higher *status* is reached.

In other cases, however, an inner split may result. This occurs when the roles a person plays bring him into conflict with himself.

Steven is a sixteen-year-old whose mother spoils him and saves him a lot of trouble and exertion.

Outside his home, Steven is completely set on great independence, both personally and in business. He is already an employer: he distributes several periodicals for a firm that permits him to work with a number of younger boys whom he has hired and whom he supervises. Thus, although at home he plays the role of baby, he is an employer; this brings him into great inner conflict.

His conflict is in part the result of a characteristic of our culture that Ruth Benedict designates *discontinuity*. By this she means that in our culture children are frequently allowed to get accustomed to a role that, later in life, they have to unlearn completely.

For years they are treated as too young, too inexperienced, incapable of dealing with certain things independently. Then, as young adults they are suddenly expected to take on great responsibilities. In contrast to this, Ruth Benedict showed how there is a *continuity* in certain other cultures, for example, that of the North American Indians. From an early age the children are guided to take responsibilities, which are increased as the child grows.

There is still no scientifically determined yardstick for what should be the level of responsibility of a person at various ages and in various situations. Obviously, however, a child has got to learn two social truths: that there are various roles in social life, some of which are dealt out to one, and that in various groups, entirely different demands are made regarding roles that may be chosen or must be taken over. With this, we arrive at a discussion of the basic significance of *social values*.

Roles and Values

Many groups participate in the socialization of young people. The most important are, of course, the family, the school, and the child's peers. There are also the neighborhood, the parents' friends, and the cultural group in which the young person grows up and which has its effect on him mainly through such mass media as radio and television. Of later importance are his vocational groups, his activity groups, and his interest groups.

These groups can become meaningful to the individual in two ways: he can belong to them as a *member* or he can make use of the group as a *reference group*. The important role of the reference group is that it provides certain value standards for the individual who wants to be accepted and acknowledged by this group.

Membership groups and reference groups can, of course, coincide; for example, a child who believes in his family uses the values and norms of his relatives as his standard.

Membership and reference groups, however, often represent a conflict to the individual. Adolescents in particular are in conflict because the values of their peers differ from those of their parents. In these days it seems much more important for a child to be accepted by his schoolmates and friends than to be guided by the values of his parents. It is not unusual to hear stories like Kenny's.

Kenny is five years old and goes to kindergarten. One day Nick, an aggressive youngster, begins hitting him. Kenny, not knowing what to do, runs away. A number of children run after him laughing and making fun of him. Kenny is in despair. He is not a coward, but his mother has forbidden him to fight with other children because she is convinced that world peace could be assured if children would stop fighting with one another.

Up to this moment Kenny has always done what his mother told him to do without opposition. Now, however, he loses faith in her principles, at least insofar as they deal with self-defense. Suddenly he turns around and with his little fists lashes out at the surprised Nick, who had been triumphant up to this point, and gives him a licking amid general yells of approval of the whole kindergarten.

Probably everyone has experienced similar incidents in which the faith of the child in his parents was put to a test because the values of other people seemed more important to him. The "others" may be a reference group, such as a school class, or may be individual people. These important "others" can become decisive in one's *self-evaluation* and in the *evaluation* of others; finally, they may even become *models*.

As David Riesman and Talcott Parsons emphasize, today's young people have a tendency to seek their value-orientation and their models among their peers more frequently than was the case in the older generation.

The values of reference groups are of great importance to people seeking to assimilate, or fit into, a new social or cultural environment, and into new social *and* cultural conditions. This process of *assimilation* is a special prob-

lem for immigrants, who often have ambivalent—at once positive and negative—feelings about the customs and values of their new environment.
Their children, on the other hand, are generally eager to become assimi-
lated. Occasionally this leads to internal and external conflicts.

An amusing example of an assimilation that proceeded smoothly is reported by Ernest Burgess. On a visit to a Russian immigrant community
of the Malakanen sect in Los Angeles, he noticed that the women of the
older generation who were admired as handsome were plump and sturdy.
Quite different, however, were their daughters who had been born in the
United States. They were slim, wore modern hair-dos and make-up—they
sought their models in the Hollywood movie stars.

On the other hand, Pauline V. Young, who in 1932 published a sociological study of this particular sect, reported to the author that in a recent
visit to one of the young couples she found exactly the same eating habits,
food preparation, blessings of the meal, religious ideology, and attitudes
toward life as among the older generation. In other words, new reference
groups were only partly accepted.

The problem of belonging to membership and reference groups becomes
particularly complicated when we discuss the role of the two sexes. Wholly
inappropriate value-aspects often come to the fore in these discussions.

Up to this point the author has carefully avoided the theme of *masculinity* and *femininity* because it is one of the most controversial in psychology. The question is what effects *sex differences* have on development and
personality. Many opinions have been expressed, but only a few incontest-
able facts have been contributed. Among these the findings of Torman
and Miles are still valid.

Men are more aggressive, more self-conscious, tougher, more fearless, and
somewhat rougher in their conduct, speech, and sentiments.

Women are more sympathetic, reticent, more sensitive, more moralizing,
more emotional, and more inclined to succumb to their emotions.

The interests of men are more in the direction of daring and adventure,
of physical activity with tools and machinery; they are more interested in
science and technology, in work and business.

Women tend more to domestic affairs and the arts; they prefer sedentary
occupations and occupations that deal with helping and healing, with phil-
anthropy and humanitarian goals.

Concerning *differences in intelligence,* it was formerly assumed that
women were intellectually inferior to men. This view, however, can no
longer be maintained, although—as Georgene Sevard showed convincingly
in her summary—men show a certain superiority in tests dealing with
words and speech.

Various cultures at various periods in their history have prescribed explicit roles for the two sexes. Often roles are forbidden or permitted with no reference to natural abilities, but are value judgments. One need think only of forbidding women to attend college or to vote—two prohibitions lifted only recently. A woman was often forbidden to train for certain occupations and could not practice many of those which were theoretically open to her without arousing opposition, that is, without going against her reference groups.

This is not to be understood as a rejection of all natural roles. Measures that take into account physical differences between the sexes are more meaningful than regulations regarding admission or nonadmission to cultural occupations and institutions. An example is the Soviet law of 1943, under which boys are prepared for service in the armed forces and women for motherhood.

Role restrictions seem more often to be based on value judgments than physical reasons. In varying degrees this is the case in all cultures.

The Development of Prejudices and Opinion Formation

Reference groups, "important others," and models determine the world pictures of the growing individual. *Prejudices* often prevail over healthy value judgments. Unfortunately, Karl Gutzkow's remark is still valid: "Custom, you have got to realize, does not follow judgment; it follows prejudice."

Modern experimental and questionnaire studies about the origin of prejudices have thrown light on the development and dynamics of these processes. Especially in the United States, research studies have been made on the origin and dissemination of prejudices against racial and national *minority groups,* such as the Negroes, Japanese, Chinese, Mexicans, and Jews.

We shall mention a few examples of the many significant results of these studies. The conclusions reached by Horowitz and by E. L. and R. E. Hartley in their investigations of the origin of prejudice against Negroes are still valid, especially in the Southern states.

In 1938 Horowitz showed a group of New York children a series of pictures of youngsters of different racial and national groups. The children were asked to mark the pictures of those they would choose as playmates. In this test, children as young as five gave expression to prejudice against Negroes.

The Hartleys asked the parents how their children could have developed such prejudicial attitudes. A common answer was "inborn instinct."

In contrast to this, Allport and Kramer studied a student group and found that in a high percentage of those questioned their attitude toward other races could be traced to early parental influence.

The insights gained from these and many other investigations make us realize that from a very early age every individual *unconsciously takes on attitudes* and prejudices from his environment. Even where prejudice is not systematically taught to the growing child, where there is no "indoctrination," there exists what today is called *inculcation*—an unconscious imprint or transference of prejudices from the environment that gradually forms a person's image of the world.

The process, as the Hartleys have shown, consists of three phases, which are dependent on one another. First, at a very early age attention is directed toward certain conspicuous characteristics of the "others," for example, the dark skin and kinky hair of a Negro. Thus a *differentiation* is made between those characteristics and the peculiarities characteristic of one's own group, for example, light skin and smooth or curly hair. In this *identification* the ego experiences a strengthening—it has now been taken into an in-group, that is, a community inwardly bound together in certain respects and more or less closed off externally. Finally, *values* are introduced by declarations of the superiority of one's own group and of the inferiority of the other group, for example, that light skin and gently curling or straight hair are beautiful.

As a result of this process there develop *stereotype* images of certain groups. These prevent people from having an unprejudiced, objective perception and judgment; they know only *the* Frenchman, *the* Italian, *the* Jew, *the* Negro.

The first pioneering investigation in this field was undertaken in 1930 by Katz and Braly with 100 Princeton University students. This study showed how consistently stereotypic and schematic were the value-attributes ascribed by these young people to ten different nationalities.

Almost twenty years later, Gilbert worked with the same group and found that the stereotypic attitudes had undergone almost no change. The only difference was that in 1950 the subjects were a little more skeptical of their attitudes than they had been twenty years earlier.

Thus, a certain loosening up had come about; today in many places people are less prejudiced about races and race differences.

Prejudices are directed at not only national or racial differences, but at many other group characteristics, such as religious, cultural, social, and class affiliations. Even the sportsman may occasionally express himself in a prejudiced way about a rival ball club. This can be seen in the fanaticism occurring at championship football games. Many investigations have shown how difficult it is not to allow oneself to be influenced by the attitudes of an in-group or a majority.

Gordon Allport, who has been concerned with the problems of the in-group, urges his readers to ask themselves to what extent their various attitudes agree with those of their family, social class, occupational group, or church. Allport belives that answers would run from "very extensive" to "total." It thus becomes unavoidable that out-groups are in many respects regarded as "enemies."

Even in relatively unimportant matters, the individual allows himself to be influenced by majorities. This was demonstrated in the well-known experiments of Asch and Sherif, in which simple estimates as to the length of lines and the speed of movements were at issue. Even here, where one would not expect prejudices or value judgments, the subjects largely let themselves be influenced by the judgment of the majority.

Dependent and *insecure* persons are especially under the influence of group leaders and *authorities*. Dependency begins in the relationship of the child to his parents. Erich Fromm points out that the young child is naturally dependent on his parents, but that later, if the parents suppress the spontaneity and independence of their child, the growing individual will be incapable of standing on his own feet.

The detrimental effect of *authoritarian* upbringing was examined in great detail in *The Authoritarian Personality,* by T. W. Adorno, Else Frenkel-Brunswik, R. N. Sanford, and D. J. Levinson. This comprehensive study, based on interviews and projective tests, shows a correlation between authoritarian upbringing, inner dependency, prejudice (in this instance mainly anti-Semitism), and belief in authority. External social suppression and inner suppression of impulses together bring about what Horkheimer and Adorno call the *authoritarian syndrome,* defined as a complex of characteristics in which the various components mutually condition one another and always appear together.

In further analysis of this syndrome, the authors found that inner insecurity and fear, particularly the fear of uncertainty, unconsciously dispose the individual to cling to authority. At the same time there is, in the background, an animosity toward possible attackers of one's person and group. Thus, the whole syndrome is basically one of self-defense.

Since this particular work on the authoritarian personality was laid out on a broad scale, and for the first time attempted to correlate political attitudes with personality structures, it aroused great interest. Critical of the methodology of this work, Richard Christie and Marie Jahoda showed that the generalized conclusions drawn by the authors are questionable. Christie, Jahoda, and their co-workers demonstrated that certain facts, by the very nature of the way the material was gathered and worked over, were seen too one-sidedly. These critics point out that there are entirely different ways of being subservient to authority, as can even be seen from the material that was presented. They emphasize that there can be conservatism, and beyond that, even subservience to authority, without neurotic bases and that generally the correlation between personality and political attitude is more complicated than would appear from the work of Adorno, Frenkel-Brunswik, Sanford, and Levinson.

Despite some objections, however, the statement remains valid that the person who believes in authoritarianism lives in a closed system. Because of the isolation of this system, he is not in a position to be open to different possibilities and to admit that many questions are unresolved; the authority to which he is foresworn has answered them for him. He pays for the anchoring of his convictions with a loss of freedom.

Mass Media and Their Influence on Social Attitudes

Up to this point we have discussed attitudes and formations of opinion as they originate in the individual under the influence of his immediate environment. This influence is meant to be educational.

However, influences other than educational ones are also at work. These are the partly conscious, partly unconscious efforts of the broader environment to draw the individual into a group ideology. The family, school, social, vocational, religious, and political groups all want their members to acknowledge and adhere to the views and attitudes of their particular group.

Beyond these more or less openly manipulated influences are others that are much less clear in their origin and effectiveness, but that are nonetheless very effective. By this we mean the suggestive power of *public opinion* and *mass media,* which disseminate public opinion.

Mass media disseminate news and opinion; they are directed at the masses, not to the individual. They comprise the press, with its newspapers and magazines, radio, moving pictures, and television. They are planned with the utmost sophistication, produced with the most modern techniques, and utilize all the tricks of advertising addressed to the "man in the street." They are far removed from former methods of disseminating news and rumors, which reached only a small circle of interested people.

The Gallup Poll has become famous throughout the world. Since the 1930's it has not only played an authoritative role in public opinion research in the United States, but has become famous for its forecasts in elections and other important events.

In addition to the above-mentioned mass media, there is still another method of mass influence: solicitation, or advertising. In its practical application as well as in its theoretical illumination, advertising employs scientific methods known as propaganda and includes all measures purposefully aimed at the dissemination of opinions for a certain, clearly circumscribed purpose.

Scientific procedures utilized in the formation of public opinion and advertising—from information services to the "hidden persuaders," those advertising methods that have their effect on the individual subliminally, so that he does not consciously recognize the influence—result in the continual guidance and manipulation of the public.

Few people are willing to admit that they are uninformed in any field. And, as has already been mentioned, many people cannot endure uncertainty. These people are often only too ready to permit themselves to be influenced by anyone who asserts that he is certain about this or that. In many cases this is the way opinion is formed about things of which no one, by the nature of the case, could have any definite opinion at all.

An interesting example of this is P. Hofstätter's study of 100 recruits of the Austrian army. They were asked about the influence of the stars on the lives of human beings. The sentence on which they were to give their opinions read: "The position of the stars at the instant of birth has an influence on the rest of a person's life." This is a remark, the proof of which no one has yet succeeded in finding; as Hofstätter says, the only rational answer would be: "I don't know."

The majority of those questioned declared that the correctness of the statements was "probable"; some even gave a definite "Yes" or "No."

Based on this small inquiry, it would appear that the public has quite a belief in astrology, a fact confirmed by a great many other investigations. Hofstätter reports that in the United States not less than 162 newspapers publish horoscopes daily and that 25,000 people are active astrologists and 80,000 are card readers and fortune tellers. The same holds true for central Europe.

In the matter of the influence of the stars on human life we are dealing with a *question of fact.* In other cases, we are dealing with *convictions,* which are based on *values.*

Here public opinion exercises the role of *censor;* in many instances it even plays the role of *fate.* This applies not only to the individual whose life is affected by public opinion, but also to the nations whose leaders are elected under the influence of public opinion. Here the mass media and the propaganda directly or indirectly transmitted by these mass media play a decisive role.

Experiments conducted in connection with political matters give us a certain insight into how mass media operate.

P. F. Lazarsfeld, B. Berelson, and H. Gaudet studied the effectiveness of various media in connection with the Presidential election in 1940. They found that the radio was considered by the voters to be the most important source of information. This, however, was the case with Democrats to a greater degree than with Republicans, who depended more on the press. In addition, it was also brought out that the majority of voters had already made up their minds before the election campaign—a result of American party loyalty. Had it been a matter of decisions on other matters, different results would probably have been shown.

In 1940, radio still played the leading role as a mass medium in elections. Today television has a greater influence. In the United States today 93 percent of all households have television sets.

Besides television, moving pictures are still extraordinarily important in the creation of public opinion. Experimental investigations have shown how prejudices in favor of or against a race, a nation, or other group are changed through seeing a film with a different point of view. And to what degree movies provide models and ideas (or ideals) can be observed at every turn. Everybody knows teen-agers who copy a Hollywood idol; and, regrettably, we also know how frequently a scene in a movie has provided the model for a burglary or a holdup.

What operates in all the various kinds of opinion formation has been studied in great detail. Two studies by Paul Lazarsfeld and his co-workers at the Bureau of Applied Research reveal two particularly important processes.

The first is the study of so-called *selective exposition*. Lazarsfeld begins with the fact that our attention is selective, meaning we pay more attention to things that are interesting or appealing to us. Lazarsfeld, Berelson, and Gaudet studied this process in elections. According to their investigations, selective attention begins with the fact a person does not listen to every speaker, but only to certain ones. In addition, he understands certain arguments better than others and remembers them better because they *appeal to him more.*

Another illustration of this process of seeing the world selectively— screening out unwanted information—appears in competitive sports, for example, in watching football games. How adherents of the opposing teams perceived the events of a particular Princeton vs. Dartmouth game some years ago was intensively studied by Albert Hastorf and Hadley Cantril. Their findings clearly show that, without any conscious attempt to distort reality, the expectations, hopes, and needs of each side drastically influenced what they were ready to "see" in the game and in its controversial aftermath.

The second interesting process found by P. Lazarsfeld and E. Katz is the "two-step communication": the peculiar fact that the mass distribution of views, ideas, and opinions proceeds in two steps, in such a way that *leaders of public opinion* are interpolated between those interested in disseminating an opinion and those supposed to make the opinion their own. The opinion leaders, who are assigned their role by other people for the most diverse reasons, are asked for advice, and the public is guided by them. It is expected that they have the necessary information or are able to get it, in order to tell people what they should do or not do.

This procedure in the formation of public opinion has been found in matters of *style, marketing counseling,* and *political events.* It is likely that similar processes may take place in the formation of opinions on other matters, for instance, one's attitude to court cases that arouse public interest or one's judgment of an artist, writer, new movie, or book.

The decisive factors that make it possible for a person to attain the influential role of opinion leader are personality (he must "be somebody"), competence (he must "know something"), and a definite social position (he must "have contacts").

Those who let themselves be influenced are frequently people who like to identify with the influential ones. That is why the *personality* of the leader of public opinion is an important factor.

But *competence* is also necessary: one asks advice about shopping from older women because of their experience in this area; one asks a physician about a new drug.

The *social activity* and the position of the opinion leader are important because he must have a great many contacts and must get around a good deal in order to hear and to disseminate views and opinions.

The opinion leaders subject themselves to "selective exposition" through the mass media. They read newspapers and other reports, go to concerts, the theater, movies, and art exhibitions, and study the advertisements. By virtue of their information and influence, they are not only transmitters of information; they are also in a position to exert pressure on other people's opinions, and thereby significantly further this or that particular issue.

CHAPTER 7

THE GROUP AND THE INDIVIDUAL

Society represents an organization with goals that are set forth in laws, regulations, and precepts, and that serve the *common welfare.* "Welfare" is interpreted differently in different societies, but it always deals with protecting and furthering the interests of the individual and the community. The community represents a hierarchy of organizations. Every person belongs to many *groups,* some on the same level as others and some above or below others. These may be *formal* structures, such as family, community, or state, or they may be informally constituted, such as youth groups, friendship groups, and labor groups. These in turn can assume more definite forms as clubs, organizations, and societies.

The concepts of a "group" and of the individual's *role* in the group are of considerable importance, not only in the theories of such formal disciplines as sociology and social psychology, but from the practical standpoint, since groups influence many aspects of our daily lives.

What Is a Group?

It is difficult to define exactly what the characteristics of a group are. A number of people who come together by chance are not, in the sociological sense, considered a group; they are a gathering or a crowd. An example: A small crowd gathers in front of a store window in which the newest model of a television set has been turned on. It is possible that one or the other of those present may make some remark, yet there is no connection between the viewers. The arrangement in which they happen to come together has no significance.

Suddenly someone exclaims, loud enough for a number of people to hear him, "Here they go again. Always advertising."

"I don't think so at all," a stout housewife replies. "It's very interesting. You see something new."

"Nonsense," the first speaker grumbles. "All it's supposed to do is to get you to buy something."

Now others enter the conversation, and, if it continues, it generally develops some sort of order; perhaps the first two speakers will emerge as "leaders" of the discussion. It is even possible that regular parties or sides will begin to form.

Here beginnings of an organization can be seen. In the sociological sense, however, it is not yet a true group because the gathering has neither goal nor cohesion.

A gathering acquires a certain measure of group structure when a *mutual relationship* arises among those present. Through this interrelationship the individuals soon come to play certain definite *roles*. The stout woman in our example gradually becomes a spokesman for the firm that is doing the advertising, while the man plays the part of someone who attacks advertising.

The "group" that has been described is a product of chance and came into being just for the moment. The fact that people, wherever they come together, have the tendency to enter into mutual relationships with one another, and to influence one another, is being intensively studied today. It is also being widely used in educational and therapeutic procedures.

The "group" was not only conditioned by chance, but was also loose and unstructured. Before the group can be thought of as a true structure, it must have *members* who stand in mutual relationships to one another, and it must have an organization and a well-defined *goal*. Members of a group are mutually dependent on each other. The foundation for a group is laid when the members feel themselves as "we."

To grasp fully the concepts involved, it would be instructive to use an example from everyday life. Suppose Mr. and Mrs. Leeson are about to give a party. They have a large circle of acquaintances, and they want to make up the group in such a way that all the guests have a good time.

"Well, to begin with," says Mrs. Leeson, "I certainly want to ask the Baldwins and the Kings. They will set the right tone. They're very pleasant people, and very entertaining. They've always been to see or to hear the latest thing. As a matter of fact, Lena Baldwin just got back from a trip to Europe."

"That's fine," says Mr. Leeson, "but I really must ask Bill McDonald. He did me such a good turn at the office that I'm really indebted to him."

But Mrs. Leeson cries out unhappily, "Bill McDonald would spoil the whole thing. He goes on talking without let-up, and he always wants to take over the whole conversation. Why don't we ask him and his wife for dinner sometime, instead of running the risk of having the party spoiled by him. Please, Art, you must understand."

"Yes, I know you're right," Mr. Leeson replies, "but I've got to think it over a little more. If we don't invite him, then we can't invite anyone else from the office this time. Let me see, who else do we owe an invitation to?"

"Well, there are the Allisons. But then, Lena Baldwin and Millie Allison can't stand each other."

"You pay much too much attention to Lena, Betty. She's just a spoiled child. If she doesn't like Millie, she can perfectly well talk to other people. The party will be big enough so that those two don't have to step on each other's toes."

"What I want most of all," says Betty, "is for everybody to have a good time and enjoy himself. If people don't get along, the way it was the other night at the Thompsons', it all sort of falls apart. Now let's see, who else shall we invite . . ."

In this fragment of a conversation, important aspects of the structure of a planned group can be recognized. In making up the guest list for a party, the couple has various goals—good conversation, good atmosphere, congeniality. All these things are important fundamentals for the evening's success. Although the group formation in this particular instance is only temporary, it is nonetheless desirable that all the members of the group have a good time. At the same time, the Leesons must give thought to their obligations. They are aware, from earlier parties, that the effects of the participants on each other are remembered. The *dynamics*—the interplay of forces—at such an occasion is seldom of much consequence, but in certain circumstances words might be spoken that could actually be helpful or harmful to one participant or another.

The group that has just been described represents a more planned and more goal-seeking gathering than the one described earlier, which came together by chance. Yet, from the sociological point of view, this is not a true group either.

A true group is defined, first and foremost, by a *common goal,* and then by a number of other indications: the group's *cohesion,* its *standards,* its *leadership,* and the *assignment of roles.*

Cohesion is more important than anything else for it ensures the continuance of the group. The degree of cohesion depends on two factors: the reciprocal attraction that the *members* exert on one another and the interest that the group's activities arouse.

In this connection, Stanley Schachter conducted the following experiment with students at the University of Michigan. He formed four *clubs,* which he called the Radio Club, the Movie Club, the Editorial Club, and the Club for Juridical Studies.

The Juridical Club was ostensibly formed because some judges and lawyers wanted to have the opinion of a student group concerning certain law cases.

The formation of the Editorial Club was ostensibly the result of the suggestion of a new nationwide publication that wanted advice as to the type of articles it should publish.

The Film Club was ostensibly set up by a motion picture theater to help select films. The Radio Club was supposed to examine how successful a certain radio station was.

The clubs were then told about a fictitious "Johnny Rocco case," which was the story of a youthful criminal. The story was then given to the four clubs to be worked on in accordance with the particular goal of each: as a juridical problem, as the subject of a newspaper article, as a film, and as a radio script.

The experiment was so arranged that the most varied factors could be examined. For example, the director of the experiment selected for the legal and film clubs only those members who on an earlier questionnaire had expressed enthusiasm for the contemplated activity; the editorial and radio clubs were made up of less interested members.

When cohesion in the various clubs was measured with the help of certain questions, it was found to be almost twice as great in the first two clubs as in the second two. Besides cohesion, several other factors were measured and manipulated.

This kind of experiment shows that the course of group processes follows definite internal laws. Anyone who is experienced and skillful can apparently *manipulate* them extensively. The degree to which this can be done depends on how closely knit a group is, how important its activities and goals are, and with what degree of conviction the members of the group work together.

Stable groups, such as municipal or state administrations, large organizations, and political parties, generally have their basis in statutes, by-laws, or regulations—that is, in some form of constitution. Keeping these rules and regulations is guaranteed by the members, especially by those selected as directors. These *functionaries* maintain the body politic. The *roles* of the rest of the members can be more or less explicitly set down. In any case, all the members of the group are bound together by the fact that they are *working together* toward common goals. And from the goals there arise the rights and duties of each member of the group.

The Origin and Continuance of Small Groups

Many groups originate by the spontaneous coming together of a number of individuals voluntarily working together in a definite direction. For example, women may come together with the intention of holding a public demonstration for the preservation of world peace. If there is only a single demonstration, the group structure is temporary. If, however, some of the participants should decide to form an organization that would systematically continue working in the interests of world peace, then the form of the organization, its goals, and the tasks of the members—their roles—must be formulated and set down in regulations or by-laws.

As long ago as the turn of the century, Georg Simmel occupied himself with the problem of group structures by studying small groups to determine their basic characteristics. Simmel held, for example, that groups of three are not stable because two of the three will always unite or conspire against the third. In recent experimental investigations, Simmel's assumption has been corroborated in its essentials. However, the third member can be important as an arbitrator. Also, under certain circumstances, the third member—the only child of a couple, for instance—can contribute materially to the unity of a couple (the couple, of course, representing the smallest possible group).

The *number of members* and the *size* of a group are important factors when the group has to prove itself—that is, when it has to solve a problem. J. James, a sociologist, recently discovered that Congressional committees have, on the average, six members when they are designed to act and fourteen members when they have advisory functions. He also found that *informal groups* that may develop for such purposes as hiking trips, marketing, entertainment, and studying contain an average of two or three members.

Such small groups, in which we spend the greater part of our lives, are *primary groups,* or "face-to-face" groups. In other words, they are groups whose members know each other and must be distinguished from *secondary groups,* whose members do not necessarily know each other. A large club is just as much a secondary group as, let us say, all the workers of a large plant or the inhabitants of a city. For differentiating broader or narrower groups, still other terms of classification, such as "community" and "society," have been suggested. In the opinion of the writer, the separation into primary and secondary groups appears particularly plausible.

Simmel considered small groups such as the *family* and the *play group* miniature social systems that should be studied for an understanding of social structures. As a matter of fact, small groups are today among the most important subjects for sociological research.

Through rivalry, tension, and conflict—as many of us know from experience with lunch clubs, card groups, office cliques, political parties—group processes are often undermined. Crises—situations in which the collapse of individuals or of groups is threatened—may result. Crises that endanger the continuance of a group or the relationship between two or more groups and that do not find a solution through *compromises* or common goal-setting may, in extreme cases, lead to ruptures, hostile actions, and, among nations, *war*.

In all groups, the members are the components that bear the responsibility. According to the goal and the make-up of the group, different *tasks* fall to different individuals, that is, there are certain expectations with respect to the members' abilities and corresponding roles are assigned to them.

The more rigidly a group is structured, the stronger is its influence on the roles its members are expected to play. In certain circumstances, *pressure* is exerted by the group on those who do not fulfill their role according to expectations. This is as true of small organizations as it is of society as a whole.

Many roles in the group are determined by *consensus,* that is, by a common understanding. The role of the woman in the home, for example, came about this way.

With a view to the maintenance of a consensus and other social regulations, there exist in various groups varying degrees of freedom—in other words, a *variable* degree of conformity is expected of the individual. However, some consensus and conformity is essential for the continuance of a group, or of a society. The fact that, in daily increasing measure, human society is engaged in revolt against existing regulations leads one to the conclusion that a completely new social order is coming into being—unless, perhaps, social disintegration is approaching.

The *order* that exists in strictly regulated organizations usually rests on a conformity that is so widespread that it can be counted on. One study of conformity was the observation of Catholics as they entered a church. In such a situation a Catholic is expected to touch himself with holy water and make the sign of the Cross. Almost to a man, they performed this ritual.

Important for the course of group activity is the *frame of mind* or *atmosphere.* Suppose we go back to the party being planned by Mr. and Mrs. Leeson (pp. 188f). If the hosts were to succeed in choosing their guests so as to make the evening pleasurable for everyone, then as a result of the conversation, behavior, expressed or suppressed feelings and ideas, a pleasant frame of mind or atmosphere would develop.

We use the expression *sentiment* to describe those reactions that are partly emotional and partly based on fact. Sentiment is one of the most important indications in the determination of group structure. The group as a whole, as well as the relations of individual members to one another, is governed by the development of a particular sentiment.

If, for example, at the Leesons' party, Lena Baldwin and Millie Allison become annoyed with each other—if Millie begins to talk about cats with her neighbor, Mr. King, while Lena tries to direct the group's attention to her trip to Europe—there can ensue a temporary or extended discord, with reciprocal negative sentiments on the part of the various guests.

If, however, Lena and Millie should unexpectedly arrive at a good understanding on this particular evening—Lena may admire Millie's dress or hairdo, for example, and Lena might talk charmingly and amusingly about her trip—a good atmosphere might develop, with friendly feelings all around. It is even possible that Lena would go up a step on the ladder of popularity.

The fact that children—and adults, too—arrange the members of their groups into a certain ranking order is due to a number of different reasons. The most important are *popularity* and *competence*. Such ranking demands· a certain degree of mutual acquaintanceship. But even complete strangers evaluate one another according to looks, behavior, way of speaking, and other characteristics.

In every group the members assume a *sociometric rank,* that is, a place assigned to them on the basis of certain criteria. The assignment of a place in the ranking order proceeds with extraordinary ease, without much thinking about it. It is therefore not at all surprising that friends who value each other and have certain values in common are inclined in such selections to support each other.

Sociometry, as developed by J. L. Moreno, can help an individual acquire a certain *insight into himself.* From an early age, everyone carries within himself a *self-image* as well as an image of others. The origin of the self-image is, naturally, in the family.

Pretty little Tina, prepared for her later role as a juvenile star by adoring parents and admiring relatives, was so conscious of her charms that she was distraught at being rejected by a young man who called her a "spoiled kid." Later she admitted to her psychotherapist that she had wept bitterly when she placed near the bottom of the list in a popularity contest in her class.

Thus a sociometric finding can show a person how much his self-image corresponds to the image others have of him.

Today courses called *sensitivity training* are gaining ground, particularly among business executives who have become aware of how important it is to know what effect one's behavior has on others. In this training of management, however, more refined methods than sociometry are being used.

Sensitivity training proceeds in the form of group-therapy sessions in which young business people find out how their manner of talking and behavior affects their subordinates and colleagues. By the reproduction of actual interviews and in dramatic presentations of business conversations it makes the subjects aware of the impression they make, and how others react to it.

The awareness of a ranking order seems to be present in the individual's social perception from an early age. Experiences of superiority can be observed in children in the second year, and sometimes even earlier. These experiences are possibly fundamental in man and animals, for they relate to the competition necessary for the preservation of life. Even in animals, ranking order of behavior has been observed in feeding situations and in sexual competition. Well known is the "pecking order" in chickens. At the top of the rank order is one chicken who pecks all the others, while the lowest-ranking chicken is pecked by all the others.

In some groups that are maintained exclusively by a few leading persons who pursue questionable goals and endanger the members of the group the rules of the rank order are very strictly enforced. Of particular interest in this respect is F. Whyte's *Street Corner Society* (1955), a study of adolescents in the slums of Boston. Whyte found in this society an extremely rigid social structure.

Whyte made friends with the leaders of these groups existing on the fringe of society and so managed to obtain a clear picture of what takes place within them. Their structure shows a hierarchy of personal relationships based on a system of reciprocal duties. The boy who belongs to one of these groups receives training that sometimes prepares him for a real political career, but more frequently for a career in the ranks of political gangsters and racketeers.

The demands made on the individual member correspond to this goal. His position in the gang depends very much on how full of ideas he is, how far his ideas, interests, and capabilities correspond to the present interests of the group, how adaptable he is, how much he can be depended on, and how ready he is to share what he has with others.

The leader of one group, Doc (all the gang had nicknames), worked in the Norton Street Settlement and was considered an intelligent and talented fellow. He was the youngest son of a large family that came from the Abruzzi region in Italy. He had lost his father when a very young boy.

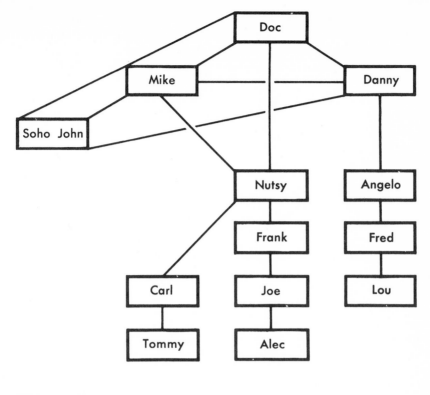

Members of the Norton gang

———————— Exerts influence on

The arrangement of names from top to bottom shows the relative rank of each member

Fig. 36

The order of rank of the thirteen members of Doc's gang (after W. F. Whyte).

From about the age of twelve he was convinced that the only way to gain respect from others was by winning fights. So he began, successfully, to take on larger boys. However, he owed his position as the leader, which he had been building up since about his thirteenth year, to the fact that he not only was strong but was helpful to those weaker than he and who had been attacked unjustly. Also, he was intelligent, imaginative, and reliable. To Dr. Whyte he said, "They trust me, Bill."

In the structure of the gang, which lasted for about two years before falling apart, Doc was the undisputed leader. He chose his own subordinates and assigned them places in the ranking order. When anything—for example, a bowling contest with another group—was planned, Doc discussed it with his subordinates, who then mobilized the group.

If someone in the lower ranks wanted to undertake anything that concerned the gang, he had to get permission from his superiors. Once, Alec, who occupied the lowest rank, had the idea of selling beer to the other members, thereby hoping to make a certain profit. The plan was favored by Doc and then approved; however, Alec had to agree to changes in his original plan suggested by Danny, who was above him in rank.

The gang had a definite code of honor, and there was punishment for breaking it.

When, for example, Nutsy, who occupied a high rank, wanted to marry a girl who was looked upon by the group as inferior, he lost his rank.

The "Nortons" then, provide an example of a group structure that is extraordinarily firmly structured and held together by a complex of rules and norms.

The principle of leadership is evident in Doc's case. Even in a group held together by dubious motives the leader can maintain himself only on the basis of certain qualities that are considered valuable by the members. He must be intelligent and full of ideas, he must show the capacity to make decisions, and his decisions must prove successful for the group. He must be reliable and fair, must be helpful in word and deed, must be magnanimous, and, even if he is not the best in everything, he must make a good showing in any of the fields that are important to the group.

Group and Mass Leadership

The development, the types, and the *processes of leadership* have been studied in the last few decades perhaps more than any other social process —obviously with the realization that the world would be much better off if it were possible to train people for leadership roles.

In all circumstances, a leader is someone whose effectiveness makes itself felt in a social situation. This influence may arise as a matter of course from the given circumstances, in some cases without anything being done specifically toward it by the particular individual, or it can be sought for by someone who feels himself *called* to the leadership role. And finally, a person can quite simply be *named* as the leader.

The influence of the great intellectual leaders of mankind is based on their *ideas* rather than action. However, their influence is often proved only in the course of time.

The other extreme is represented by those who are *named* as leaders—those who have been raised to their positions without necessarily being suited for them. The reasons for their elevation to positions of leadership may be historical or may be occasioned by a particular purpose. The hereditary monarch falls into the first category; political appointments comprise a large part of the second.

Midway between these extremes is the leadership of the person who feels a *calling*. The extent and effectiveness of this type of leader depends on a number of factors: his *personality,* the *situation* in which he tries to exert his influence, the *followers* that he seeks to win over, and the *goals* he pursues. Only in this real leadership do the dynamics of the leader find full expression. Essential to true leadership is the *intention* to influence others, for the effectiveness of the leader comes from the way his personality and goals impress his potential followers. In the United States, the military and big business organizations feel that in the future leading positions should be occupied by real leaders, not by routinely promoted executives.

Studies have been made of what characterizes a leadership personality. Originally, it was held that the leader represents a particular personality or that he was marked by having particular *qualities*. The studies confirm that, in general, leaders possess greater energy, intelligence (but not *too* much), self-confidence, social ambition, general ambition, and desire to rule than the average person. Yet all these qualities are found in nonleaders as well. No two studies name the same traits as characteristic for a leader. It is more widely believed that the leader personality as such is less responsible for the development of leadership capacity than the working together of the above-named qualities. Experiments show that elected leaders are distinguished by the fact that their judgment of group attitudes is much more precise than that of the others. In other words, they possess greater "social sensitivity."

What *motivates* people to strive for the role of leader? In general, the closely related needs for *power, respect,* and *holding a pre-eminent position* are looked upon as the most important motives. Added to these there is, in varying degrees, the need for activating such *creative proclivities* as find their expression in the guiding of human affairs.

According to R. F. Bales, one of the best known among the sociologists working in this field, those leaders who combine the capacity to lead with the gift of contributing constructive ideas are the most successful. Those leaders who realize the goals or tasks of the groups they lead are in the long run more influential than those who enjoy general popularity.

The manner in which a leader pursues his goals may be *gentle* or *harsh, democratic* or *autocratic.*

The type of leadership that develops in a particular situation depends not only on the leader, but also on the needs of the *followers*. In the previous chapter we mentioned the studies made by Kurt Lewin's group on authoritarian and democratic leadership and the preference the followers showed for one or the other.

In R. Lippitt and R. K. White's experiment with a boys' club of eleven-year-olds, the members were exposed to three kinds of leadership. For periods of seven weeks at a time, they had an authoritarian leader, then a democratic leader, then a "laissez faire" leader—a passive one, who pretty much left the group to itself. The principal results were as follows.

The authoritarian leader is distinguished, first of all, by the fact that he makes rulings and gives orders that interrupt the regular work. He engages in more nonconstructive criticism than the other leaders, but also gives his followers more praise and approval. The average authoritarian leader spends 60 percent of his time at these activities, while in the other leaders it amounts to only 5 percent.

The democratic leader gives useful suggestions and spurs his followers to do things by themselves. He is kindly and gets along nicely with them. At other times he is cool and factual. He frequently passes on information to his followers.

The laissez-faire leader is largely inactive, except for passing on information; to a certain extent he too gives helpful suggestions.

The reactions of the club members to the authoritarian leader are dependency on the leader (either aggressive or apathetic), dissatisfied criticism, and demands for attention. In addition there is also a good deal of work-minded discussion and a good deal of asking for information.

The democratic leader's followers react to him primarily with group-oriented suggestions, with friendly and trusting behavior, and with conversations that deal both with the work and with other matters.

The reactions to the laissez-faire leader are, primarily, questions for information; in additon, there is conversation and friendly behavior.

R. N. Sanford dealt particularly with the types of leadership favored by the different followers. He found that those who believe in authoritarianism prefer authoritarian leaders who prescribe the path to be pursued. On the other hand, "equalitarians" are capable of acknowledging strong leadership when it seems essential, but they would otherwise prefer a less forceful hand. They tend to judge their leaders with respect to their human qualities. Goal achievement is less important to them than the success of the group process. Those who believe in authoritarianism are more concerned that the leader guide the individual members, as well as the group, toward the goal. Under a leader who does not unequivocally point out the direction to them, they feel uncomfortable, and it is not long before they consider him weak. When the "equalitarians" are exposed to strict leadership, they are apt to let up on their performance.

In *Escape from Freedom,* Erich Fromm examined the problems of power, authority, dependence, and subservience. Fromm is of the opinion that there exist well-intentioned autocrats but that the use of power often serves to satisfy sadistic needs, as the Nazi leaders so clearly demonstrated.

Harold Lasswell, in his extensive studies of *political leaders,* comes to the conclusion that in this type of leadership the need for *power* is preeminent.

What seems especially important to the author is whether a political leader would rather deal with *well-organized groups* or with the *másses*. As N. E. Miller and J. Dollard observed, influence over the masses has always carried a certain prestige, and always in some way seems to be right. Probably no leader is competely free from the fascination of influencing the masses and winning them over. However, it is only the *demagogue* who prefers stirring up the masses to having a well-reasoned effect on organized groups. While such groups function rationally, the masses react emotionally and irrationally. G. Le Bon's explanation—that in the influencing of masses suggestion and "contagion" are at work—does not seem to be sufficient, since these factors are also at work in rational and cooperative group influences. However, another of Le Bon's assumptions is generally recognized as correct. He assumes that in mass action there is a release of urgent impulses, at which the consciousness of responsibility is lost through submergence of the individual into the anonymity of the masses.

Totalitarian leaders apparently prefer to operate with masses of people, as Hitler did and as others are doing.

Seymour M. Lipset makes the hypothesis that the stability of a democratic regime depends on the *legitimacy* and *effectiveness* of the government in power and that governments break down when they are ineffective or illegitimate, or both. According to him the Weimar and the Austrian republics were, in the eyes of many people, not really legitimate and, finally, ineffective. Lipset then asks why some societies are so healthy and stable that they never fall a prey to *mass movements,* even when the governments fall. Like de Tocqueville, he sees the collapse of a society under a revolt of the masses. Disintegration of a traditional *elite* is a prime danger to the maintenance of freedom and creative civilization.

Not all mass movements are bound up with political leadership. Lynching, for example, has its origins in the religious and racial fanaticism of certain groups. The same is true of the persecution of minorities.

Sociologists make distinctions among various forms of *collective* behavior, the most significant differences being those between the crowd, the masses, and the public.

The *crowd* is a physically close association of people who are temporarily in unorganized contact with one another and have common values or emotions.

The scene of an auto accident provides an example. Quickly, a number of people gather. If it is a big accident, the numbers can grow into a crowd. Excitement holds them together. Another example is a football game, which brings together a multitude of spectators whose common interest is the game. Once the game is over, the crowd disperses.

For a common action, such as a lynching, the crowd generally needs a leader. The crowd thereby becomes a *mob.*

The *mass* is differentiated from the mob by the fact that it is made up of individuals who do not necessarily meet physically, as they would in a crowd. The people composing a mass react separately to some things and together to others.

For example, a mass reaction occurs when a song, enthusiasm for an actor or a speaker, or outrage at a crime carries away the mass. Here communications play an important role. The madness that seizes adolescents when a new dance appears or certain fashion crazes to which women fall prey are spread mainly by radio, television, and the press.

The masses can also be swept toward *common action.* Here rumors, speeches, discussion meetings, or propaganda literature can serve as the trigger. To influence the mass of people, *leadership* is needed. The influence can be created by individual leaders or by mass media. Or the influence of a leader of public opinion can spread from one *strategic point.*

The human group is never simply an aggregate (aside from crowds that happen to congregate by chance), but a structure in which there are mutual roles and dependencies.

In most matters of *public life,* the masses are less involved than the *public.* The public deal with *opinion formation,* they create opinions and are influenced by other opinions. Here *leaders of public opinion* play a role.

Women's fashions are an interesting example of the *disseminating process.* Fashions are decided mainly in London, Paris, and New York. Leading stores take them up, and they soon begin to spread. From being the most exclusive and expensive, the styles gradually reach the medium- and lower-price stores. By the time the new fashions reach the very bottom, something different and quite new is already being shown on the uppermost level.

Organization, Motivation, and Control

Groups can be divided into two categories. The first is made up of those clubs, organizations, societies, and the like whose purpose is human activity. Such organizations serve the entertainment, health, education, development, or special interests of individuals. We may call these groups *interest groups*. The second group comprises institutions that serve *production* and product distribution, like plants and factories, or serve the *general welfare*. These groups include local governments, public facilities, and the military establishments. These may be called *duty groups*.

In the first category, the needs of the individual come first; in the second, individual needs are secondary to the objective purposes of the group. The necessity for a "fusion" between the individual and the group in the second category makes great demands on the individual's readiness to sacrifice.

This constraint, which the individual must place on himself in the interest of purposes that transcend him, necessitates measures that are not called for in the interest group. In the duty group category, two principal arrangements, the creation of motivation and the introduction of controls, become necessary.

The *motives* that are natural in the interest groups have to be created *artificially* in duty groups. This is because the duties do not, as in free creativity, arise from natural needs. For this reason the activities in the duty groups appeal more to outer-directed than to inner-directed persons, to use a distinction introduced by David Riesman. Most people have little freedom of choice in duty groups. Not infrequently, a person who feels he was born to be an artist has to earn his living in a factory or office. And usually there is no choice regarding participation in military service.

Artificially introduced motivations take the form, primarily, of *rewards*. Among these are wage raises, promotions, and gains in prestige. Recently, however, there has been what may be termed an *awakening of secondary interests*. Two types of secondary interests that increase readiness for performance are personally satisfying stages in the work process and workers' participation in management.

The problem of motivating all those who, beginning with school, spend the greater part of their lives in duty groups is engaging ever wider circles of research workers. The stultifying effect of assembly-line work and the countless monotonous repetitions of the same motion are prime subjects of discussion.

Originally, the solution to this problem was thought to lie outside the work process, such as extension courses and recreational activity for workers, but recently there has been more emphasis on how satisfaction can be built into the work itself.

Such satisfaction is necessary, for the less power the worker possesses in his organization, the less his personality develops. The result of such immaturity is regressive or aggressive behavior. Therefore, the information of small informal work groups, counseling of workers among themselves, and the development of personal relationships have been suggested so that work in office and factory can be made more *personally satisfying*.

One of the purposes of these measures is to give the worker a *feeling of being a part of the plant*. Although this has been declared impossible by some sociologists, it does succeed in many instances. The more an employee feels he is a part of management, the more his work satisfaction and productivity increase. A skillful management will see to it that feelings of belonging and pride in performance are given a chance to develop. Through measures of this sort, the dull mechanism of impersonal work is pushed somewhat into the background and the unrelated crowd becomes a *community* with personal relationships. The *atmosphere* of the plant improves.

A second type of secondary interests, the motivating effect of which seems particularly effective, is *participation of the worker in management*. Among the many descriptions of this arrangement, Keith Davis's short essay seems especially clear and interesting.

Davis defines three grades of participation of workers in management: *mutual understanding* of all those who work in the plant; *advisory participation* on the part of all workers; and *authoritative participation,* in which the workers are granted certain rights in decision making.

The means by which participation is accomplished are group gatherings in informal sessions or committees, conferences of managers and foremen with workers, production committees, and measures that stimulate workers to make suggestions for management improvements. The last measure requires particularly careful handling. In general, all these innovations succeed best among employers and managers who have taken courses in the psychology of plant management.

For effectiveness in such measures, the worker must be interested in participating in management and be prepared to do so. Workers who have been brought up in an authoritarian way and who do not know how to express themselves to their superiors cannot contribute much to this arrangement. That is why, hand in hand with greater empathy on the part of the employer, there must be better communication on the part of the worker. Both require special psychological training.

Amusing and at the same time revealing as to the strong psychological orientation of modern management is Davis's description of how one can make constructive use of the "grapevine" to bring about an improvement in the atmosphere of a plant. The grapevine is the stream of gossip and rumors continually being passed on by word of mouth. Davis cites an article by Joseph K. Shepard in the *Indianapolis Star* magazine in which the circulation of rumors behind people's backs is poetically described.

> With the rapidity of a burning powder train, information flows like magic out of the woodwork, past the water fountain, past the manager's door and the janitor's mop closet. As elusive as a summer zephyr, it filters through steel walls, bulkheads, or construction glass partitions, from the sub-basement to the rafters, from office boy to executive. . . . It carries good news and bad, fact as well as fancy, without discrimination. It cares nothing about reputation, nothing about civil rights; it has no respect for persons or for prerogatives of management; it will carve up and serve the big brass, the shop fore-man, and the stenographer with fine impartiality.

Davis then goes on to show how skillful use of the grapevine not only transmits a good deal of information to management, but also permits it to steer information to the working force. Gossip and rumors in a plant can thus be used in a definitely constructive way.

All this means that in the most modern group—a thoroughly organized plant—the system of *controls* is changed in accordance with psychological principles.

Control is a fundamental concept that embraces supervision and re-striction of behavior and procedure. Everyone knows how parents, teach-ers, and supervisors exert controls on the basis of, and with the help of, the authority at their disposal. The concept of *social* control is, however, more complicated and thus more difficult to grasp. In the author's view Parsons and Shils come nearest to an inclusive definition in *The General Theory of Action,* in which they systematically examine a number of sociological phenomena. According to them, the function of "control mechanisms" is to keep the prevailing social system in equilibrium.

This means, then, that pressure on an individual is not exerted pri-marily in his interest; nor is punishment meted out with the goal of im-proving him. Rather, these serve to maintain the equilibrium of the family or plant, and thus keep it functioning well.

In certain circumstances these controls may not be factually distinguish-able from those that serve the interests of education or improvement. Social control can, however, consist of a kind of pressure that runs com-pletely counter to the interests of the individual.

Social control is practiced with an eye to the social role assigned to an individual. If someone behaves in a manner that does not correspond to the role assigned to him, he is *punished* or *rewarded,* or *pressure* is put on him. The individual can be changed by punishment or reward. But pressure, which can be exerted by opinions or behavior of others, can also influence him strongly: he temporarily or permanently lets himself be coerced by the opinion of others. In extreme cases, he can be expelled from the group. In a factory or office he can be forced out of his job. In the case of criminals or psychotics, *isolation* is an additional method of control.

The simplest form of control is, naturally, *authoritarian.* The child is under this form of control both at home and at school. However, he also experiences control through his play group, which exerts pressure on its members. Especially in early childhood, it often lightly and thoughtlessly inflicts expulsions from the group.

The *control of opinions* by majority groups was demonstrated by the experiments of Muzafer Sherif, who showed just how extensively individuals submit to majority opinions, often against their better knowledge and judgment. The majority rules through the fact that the members of a group tend to converge toward a *norm.* In other words, they strive toward consensus in an authoritative opinion.

The pressure that certain *labor groups* exert on individual members is well known. In 1908, Max Weber used the expression "braking" to describe the control that a group of workers can exert on a particularly energetic, quick, or skillful co-worker if his superior performance threatens the rate of work maintained by them.

In their Hawthorne Plant study, Roethlisberger and Dickson show that the workers in an assembly plant had a social code, according to which they gave disparaging nicknames to members of their group. Those who performed too much work were called "wage depressors"; anyone who produced too little was termed a "cheat"; and anyone who reported to the foreman or bosses anything that was unfavorable to the group was a "tattletale."

While the groups try to control their members in this way, management exerts its own controls so that proper performances may be achieved.

The pressure of *responsibility,* which weighs on all who hold leading positions in factories and offices, has recently been the theme of a great many studies. These men must control the workers under them, but they are also under the control of superiors. The term "cyclist" is often used to describe these people: their backs are bent in subservience to their superiors while, at the same time, they push or kick those beneath them.

The work of J. and R. Useem shows the social pressure to which so-called middle management is exposed. Their study is concerned with the psychological structure of people of this middle rank. The authors studied how the individual copes with the demands made on him and with the problem of how to get ahead under the prevailing conditions.

J. and R. Useem describe a phenomenon called "anticipatory socialization"—that anyone who is interested in rising in the social scale feels his way into the psychology of the higher positions open to him, and through this anticipation, grows into his later tasks with greater ease. In other words, successful professional as well as social ascent presuppose flexibility, adaptability, and anticipatory learning.

Finally, there is the so-called *total institution,* a particularly extreme type of duty group. By this term is meant institutions under the direction of a single authority and whose members must spend a considerable part of their lives in one place. Examples of total institutions are prisons, mental hospitals, military installations, and convents.

The total institution represents the most radical form of fusion between the individual and the group. Here, complete subservience of the individual to group rules and group norms is demanded. This almost always invites opposition, since the individual is deprived of his freedom to a very great extent. That is the reason why so many people refuse to enter old people's homes or similar institutions.

Social Stratification, Mobility, and Change

Wherever they may be living and in whatever social forms, people hold various and diverse *social positions.* In different societies, different roles are assigned according to age, sex, family, occupation, property, and other distinctions; but everywhere there are certain positions that set those who hold them apart from the others. Some social positions are officially determined and recognized; others are more nebulous and unexpressed. However, most people are conscious of their own and others' positions, and they know that every position demands a specific *role.* There can, however, be errors and misunderstandings when the actual role does not coincide with the nominal one.

Consider, for example, the head of an authoritarian household, Mr. Hart. He considers himself the boss and plays the part of a ruler. But Mrs. Hart, an attractive person much given to flattery, knows how to circumvent her husband's rules and regulations and how she can get him to change his mind. Thus, it is actually Mrs. Hart who plays the decisive role, although she permits her husband the prestige of holding the top rank.

The more complicated a society, the more manifold and diverse the kinds of group formations become and the more varied the ranks that an individual can occupy. Every individual lives in a unique structure of group-belongingness with varied ranks.

The same Mr. Hart who enjoys playing the "big shot" in his family may have only limited prestige in his office or his community. However, in his bowling club he may enjoy great respect because he is an excellent bowler.

Psychologically, it is noteworthy that people regard the phenomenon of social rank with extraordinarily different *evaluations*. They range from those who simply deny the existence of rank and to whom the mere thought of it is a horror, to those who regard everyone according to what rank they belong to and who are deeply convinced of the significance of the position a person holds.

A series of interesting studies on this subject is presented in Sargent and Williamson's *Social Psychology*.

For example, in a small Western town with a population of 275, J. West found such a specialized class organization that every individual, on the basis of his belonging to a particular family, clique, lodge, church, or other organization, held a rank that was recognized by all the others. Yet, the inhabitants of the town declared firmly and proudly: "Our village—now, there you have a place where everyone is equal! We don't have any classes here."

When it was observed carefully, the community was found to be made up of two main classes: the "good, decent, respectable people, who work all the time" and "the lower-class people," who may be either "good, decent, and religious" or "bad elements, without any religion." In addition, there are also low people, "who live like animals," and a few who constitute "the upper crust."

In general, as Warner and Lunt show in a *Yankee City,* six classes can be distinguished today. The distribution in a New England town was as follows:

1.44 percent	Upper upper
1.56 percent	Lower upper
10.22 percent	Upper middle
28.12 percent	Lower middle
32.60 percent	Upper lower
0.84 percent	Unknown

This distribution was arrived at on the basis of reports from the inhabitants showing how they placed their fellow citizens in order of rank.

There were a great many different criteria. The most important were economic circumstances, occupation, social relationships, neighborhood, descent, and moral reputation.

A further important question concerns, then, the actual results these ranking divisions have with respect to people's living together. One thing is definite: up to a certain point rank determines the access an individual has or does not have to certain things. However, there are two factors that act against this.

One factor is the great *social mobility* of society today, and the other is *social equality,* the subject of a brilliant study by Granville Hicks on social life in a small town.

Hicks says that despite all classes of rank, of which everyone is conscious, people do live with one another in relationships in which rank does not count. They come together in stores, at the hairdresser's or barber's, in restaurants, in church, at political meetings, and in a great many other places. Such social equality probably exists only in certain smaller communities or in particular circumstances. In larger cities there are relatively few informal contacts, and only under certain conditions— carnival time, for example.

Hicks' observation, if it is correct, points to a conflict in American feeling on the subject of equality versus prominence. While there is universal allegiance to the ideal of *human equality,* there is also a tremendous striving for *status* and *prestige.* Since theoretically there are no classes in American society, the definitions of various types of prominence are subtle and complicated. Apart from the traditional prestige of certain occupations—doctor, lawyer, minister—there are no generally applicable rules by which to interpret what constitutes prominence.

In one sector of society, money may be considered the criterion; in another, belonging to a certain social set may be significant; public acclaim may matter most to a third group; and in a fourth personal influence may count. In any of these sectors, many struggle to get to the "top," whatever the "top" is.

In *Industrial Sociology,* by D. C. Miller and W. H. Form (1964), two aphorisms express the frustrations of struggling industrial workers at not getting ahead: "You've got to have money to make money" and "To get to the top you've got to act like the top."

Two cases illustrate the problem. Joe Doaks carries a sack lunch to work. No matter how good a lunch it is, he thinks he would "get further" if he could afford to eat in the cafeteria, or perhaps in the "exclusive" restaurant a few blocks away. He feels that he cannot associate with people of greater influence if he eats his lunch in the department. He would gain prestige and a greater chance for advancement if he could eat with "higher-ups" in the cafeteria or restaurant. But his income is not high enough to permit him to do this.

Managers and staff personnel often stop for a cocktail on the way home. Participating in this ritual calls for economic power. To belong to the same social organization as "the men of influence" in the plant likewise demands economic power.

On the other hand, there are strong pressures toward uniformity in the American industrial society that counteract the individual's striving toward prominence. Several sociologists have explained these pressures. Asch reasons that people tend to accept other people's views even without pressure. Festinger proposes that the pressures toward uniformity among members of a group may occur because uniformity is considered desirable or necessary for the group to achieve its goal. The acceptance of group goals as opposed to the individual's personal motivation has been studied by a number of researchers. Many factors influence individual members' acceptance of group goals. Important is the "fitting" of members' motives and group goals. (M. Horowitz)

The individual's participation in the goals of various groups depends on his *needs* and *values*.

A. H. Maslow presented a theory of motivation based on the idea that human needs arrange themselves in hierarchies of predominance. On the lowest level are physiological needs. As these are satisfied, higher and higher needs emerge. Maslow sees five sets of needs in this hierarchy: physiological, safety, social, self-esteem, and self-actualization. He finds that none of these needs is ever completely satisfied, but that in our society the lower needs have a greater chance of being satisfied than the higher ones.

The author's studies on life goals do not corroborate the assumption that everybody has to satisfy these needs in this hierarchical order. In addition, the list is incomplete. Creative or adventurous people do not want safety as much as they want to create or accomplish something. In Maslow's set of needs there is no category for this important objective. Safety-oriented persons, on the other hand, may place this goal above all others; it may stand at the very top of their list. In other words, the way an individual organizes his goals depends on his *values*. Besides the pressure of needs, a selective process is at work that may lead an individual to choose a certain goal, even though pressures are counter to that particular choice. An example is the artist who prefers to go hungry rather than give in to the public's demands for a more popular product.

In *Industrial Sociology*, Miller and Form feel that in our "affluent" society "increasing numbers of workers at all levels of the labor force are achieving high satisfaction of their physiological and safety needs."

While this may be true of a large portion of the American labor force, other categories of people all over the world find that there is more *insecurity* at the present time than there ever has been. Political upheavals, migrations, war, the inflation of monetary values and unemployment resulting from the increasing need for higher educational and technical qualifications cause insecurities that previous generations did not have to face.

These facts correspond to a sad truth noted by Karl Mannheim: "Just as Nature was incomprehensible to primitive man and his deepest anxieties arose from the incalculability of natural forms, for modern industrialized man, this system under which he lives, with its social crises, its inflation and so on, has become a source of deeply rooted anxiety."

The pressure to rise on the social scale, which was referred to in connection with social stratification, is a part of what is termed *social mobility.*

Social mobility is made up of "horizontal" and "vertical" movements. Horizontal mobility means migrations, changes of locality or residence, changes of employment, conversion to another religion, a switch in political allegiance, etc. "Vertical" mobility refers to ascent or descent of individuals on the social scale and to social strata.

Horizontal mobility is so great today that one is tempted to speak of a new "migration." And hand in hand with the extensive overthrow of traditional conditions and the lessened importance of class systems goes an increased vertical mobility.

In the many refugees and emigrants from all countries one can clearly observe the upward movements and the even more frequent downward ones.

In other respects, too, mobility in industrial societies is much greater than in the earlier mercantile society, whose closed class system made upward movement much more difficult. The increased mobility in our day demands great flexibility, motility, and adaptability in the individual. Americans have always tended strongly toward an upward movement, and they count on it for their children. The great mobility of the United States has brought to fruition a readiness to help one's neighbors. This differs somewhat from friendship, for friendship is a more personal form of relationship and presupposes a longer acquaintance and a mingling of roots.

Social mobility is the phenomenon of movements that break up and change the social relationships in which individuals and groups have lived together. In certain conditions, strong social mobility changes the existing social stratification.

However, social stratification is more decisively affected by what is called *social change*. Pitirim Sorokin pulls together all these changes in his concept of *social evolution,* which may be correct if we consider only the movement as a whole, for there are regressions, that is, steps backward, and changes in structure that cannot come under the heading of evolution. The continued changes in women's hairdos and fashions are neither progressive nor regressive; they are merely expressions of taste. However, if short skirts and short hair are introduced as being more practical, especially for the professional woman, progress is being made—at least in the eyes of those who believe in women's working.

Social change can proceed gradually as well as suddenly. Gradual change comes about in continuous minor changes, and sudden change as the result of decisions or some forceful activity.

Gradual or sudden changes may develop *within a group,* or they may be introduced or forced on the group from the *outside.*

Furthermore, these changes can be *small* changes or they can represent *great* and important upheavals. A few examples may make these distinctions clear.

A small, internally conditioned change is described by Bales in *Change in Rank*. Groups that had elected the most popular member as their leader changed their minds after only four meetings. The most popular member increasingly steps behind the one who has the best ideas, even though he may not be generally popular.

Small changes brought about from the outside were investigated by Kurt Lewin. He found that despite the various ways in which foodstuffs get into the home, it was finally the housewife who determined what the family's food habits were to be. He terms her the "gatekeeper," who can open up the gate for new foods or can keep it shut against them.

Together with Alex Bavelas, Lewin thought up experiments for the purpose of changing certain habits so that, for example, the consumption of otherwise unpopular kinds of meats and milk drinks would be increased. It turned out that this could be accomplished more easily through group discussions than through individual instruction, because a group is more influential in decision making.

This can be corroborated by group therapists, who know that certain changes in patients can be brought about more easily through group therapy than in private sessions.

The psychological implications of social change as it takes place in *political movements and upheavals* is very difficult to understand. One of the main questions is whether there are general attitudes toward social change. Obviously, there are various attitudes among different groups; for example, the system of organized and consolidated *political parties,* reflects the various attitudes of large groups toward social change.

Talcott Parsons has drawn up detailed theoretical observations on the problem of social change. He distinguishes between *two change processes,* which one might say are superimposed one upon the other—an *autonomous* process (having its own laws) and a *politically generated* one.

The autonomous process is a change in the social structure (in the United States caused mainly by economic factors), whereas the politically generated process comes from the interaction of radical and conservative groups.

In addition to the economic factors, many others bring with them an autonomous change in the social structure. For example, education is a very important factor. Better education and increased knowledge change not only the cultural but the social structure of a country.

Factors such as wealth, upbringing, education, religion, and social and international relations are all values for which political parties stand.

A fourth variant of social change—that is, for the radical, externally caused overthrow of an economic and cultural order—occurred among the Tanala tribe on the island of Madagascar when the tribe transferred from dry to wet rice cultivation, as reported by Abraham Kardiner and Ralph Linton.

The dry cultivation of rice was performed by family groups who lived together in independent, self-contained villages. After a period of cultivation, the dry rice field became unusable, was returned to community ownership in exchange for another loaned by the community. Thus, nobody owned any land. The organization of the village was democratic. When the entire region that had been cultivated became infertile, the community moved elsewhere.

Once the fields were irrigated, the rice field became a valuable property. Now the community no longer had to wander about in search of flat land to be cultivated. Steadily cultivated rice fields led to the building of permanent village settlements. These became organized in hierarchical fashion, and land ownership and other differences in economic conditions played a role. A king reigned with unlimited power, and a strictly regulated caste system developed.

With the organization of the tribe, the family also changed: the father of the family now began to hold a position that corresponded to the powerful position of a king.

Kardiner emphasized that the safety and equality that the individual possessed in the old system disappeared completely and that in the new system anxiety and hostility increased extraordinarily.

The examples that have been used to throw light on the phenomena of social change show how closely it goes hand in hand with cultural change.

CHAPTER 8

EXAMPLES OF SOCIAL STRUCTURES

Natural and Artificial Groups

One of the most interesting questions in sociology has always been how the various forms of organization of human society (groups) come about. Very early it was recognized that two factors play a role: *natural* needs and *rational* viewpoints.

The organization most strongly based on *natural factors* is obviously the *family,* where the ties between the members rest on a blood relationship.

The classic example of an organization based on *rational factors* is a modern industrial enterprise, a factory or any other kind of plant.

Seymour Lipset sees the family as the group that does more than any other to hold society together. The opposite, according to him, is true of institutions that are built on purely economic principles, for they—from the purely theoretical point of view—must be guided by the demands of the marketplace regardless of the results for individuals and other groups. However, even in the most rational organization some nonrational factors are involved.

Efforts are being made to incorporate the factor of "man" into the industrial plant in a way that is psychologically appropriate for human beings. Things are no longer the way they were in 1930 when S. Kracauer noted with considerable bitterness in his brochure, *Employees*: "In the definition of the [German] National Ministry for Industry, the word man is absent. Apparently it has been forgotten, because it no longer plays an important role." He was telling the truth; for the National Ministry gave the following definition: "Rationalization is the utilization of all the means provided by technical development and well-planned organization, to raise the economy and thereby to increase the production of goods, to lower their cost, and also to improve their quality."

Despite improvement in corporate attitudes, the fact remains that, in principle, the existence of the institution does not depend on the fact that certain persons belong to it. The family, however, arises as a social structure because of the individuals who founded it.

The Family, a Natural Group

It is often said that today's family is disintegrating. There is a certain truth in this remark, but only a partial truth. Whole traditions are indeed disappearing, and new customs and methods of behavior are taking their place. Furthermore, great changes have taken place in the relations of family members to one another, and as a result there has been a loosening of family ties that would not have been permitted or even thought of in earlier times. But, as Ruth Benedict has said, the family has maintained itself in all human societies and it will continue to maintain itself even though its structure and its functions may undergo changes.

In the United States, where there has been a great deal of experimenting with bringing up children in boarding schools, a return to bringing up children in the family can be noted. And in the Soviet Union, recent legislation tends toward a strengthening of the family, an idea that was strongly combated in the early postrevolutionary years.

Thus, rather than speaking of the disintegration of the family, we will limit ourselves to stating that, in structure and function, the family today is undergoing wide-ranging changes. These can be observed not only in Western culture, but in other cultures as well.

Burgess and Locke, whose *The Family* is one of the best-known studies in this field, consider the basic change to be the development of the family from an *institutional* group to a "companionship" group, that is, to a group of people who feel that they belong together—a "fellowship in living." This sense of belonging together is, according to Fröhmer, Stackelberg, and Eser in *Family and Marriage,* the principal mark of today's family, which earlier was thought of as a "fellowship of those living together in the same house."

The family is characterized by Burgess and Locke as follows:

1. The family is made up of persons who are tied to each other by marriage, blood relationship, or adoption.

2. The members of a family live together under the same roof, consti-

tuting a single household. If they live apart from one another, they still consider one household as their home.

3. The family is a unit of people who stand in specific relationships to each other in the roles of father, mother, son, daughter, sister, brother, and in reciprocal relationships among themselves.

4. The family represents a cultural entity that comes into being through the mingling of the cultural structures contributed by the two marriage partners and through participation in the culture in which the family lives.

George P. Murdock, one of the leaders in the field of family research, distinguishes between the nuclear family, consisting of the two parents and their children, the polygamous family, which originates from multiple marriages of one of the marriage partners, and the extended family, which results from the living together of various family members.

The *extended family,* also called the *patriarchal family,* is historically the oldest form. It prevailed in China, Japan, and India, and even today is frequently found in those countries. Ancient Roman families were also of this type. The family in Europe during the Middle Ages is termed a "small patriarchal family." In this type of family only a few relatives live together in the same household. Common to all patriarchal families is the male head, the father or grandfather, who has absolute authority over all family members.

Both the polygamous and the patriarchal family have an institutional character. Today, in our culture and in many others, there is a tendency to give up these institutional forms of family. In their place the nuclear family that developed in Western culture is increasingly coming to prevail.

In *The Family, Its Function, and Its Fate,* edited by Ruth N. Anshen, various authors describe the changes that have taken place in the family traditions of Moslem countries, China, India, Russia, and North and South America. Particularly striking are the Western concepts being introduced in Islamic families and in China and Latin South America. The change in the Chinese family is the most radical. Here, particularly in educated circles, there is an insistence on freedom of choice of the marriage partner and on equality of the sexes.

In China, India, and the Moslem countries, the institutional regulation of family life was formerly extremely rigid. In Moslem families, for example, engagements were arranged by the parents when the couple were still children. The age, personality, and preference of the couple were not decisive. Rather, the partners had to be of suitable rank, religion, and occupation.

Such institutional regulation demanded subservience from the woman, who had to be obedient and could be punished and beaten. Like the entire household, she was completely subject to the authority of her husband. Her only right was that she could expect to be supported in accordance with her position; she also remained in full possession of her dowry.

The right of divorce was completely the husband's, and he could obtain one with very little cause. He could also legally marry several women. This was even recommended. The children "belong to the bed." Even illegitimate children were, as a general rule, drawn into the family.

One can begin to measure the extent of the change in the growing resemblance of the Moslem family to the Western family. The battle for this assimilation is led by the young people who demand modern education and more freedom and by the feminist movement, which is in revolt against the harem. Those involved in these cultural changes and penetrations are faced with particularly difficult problems.

Tomi is a young Japanese girl whose family emigrated to the United States but whose father still held to the old customs and views. He demanded complete authority in the home, expected the submission of all family members to his will, and insisted on being waited on by the female members of the family. Tomi, who frequently saw her mother beaten, was outraged when she compared these conditions with those in the families of her American schoolmates.

She married an American Chinese, Fred, who, in complete contrast to her father, gave in to all her wishes and even helped with the housework. This degree of submission on her husband's part, however, led to serious conflicts in Tomi. While she was grateful for Fred's kindness, she also had guilt feelings when she allowed herself to be spoiled in this way. Sometimes she caught herself criticizing his devotion as a lack of manliness. At such moments it seemed to her that the authoritarian personality of her father corresponded more to her idea of masculinity than her husband's kind and gentle manner.

In the structural change from the institutional family to life companionship and the nuclear family, which William Goode presents in *The Structure of the Family*, the factors on which the nuclear family rests are clearly brought out.

The first important factor is the free choice of mate, based in principle on *love*. Each partner's right to divorce is a logical outcome of the postulate of marriage based on love.

A second important point concerns woman's place. In the modern family the wife has the same rights as the husband. Thus, both her role in the household and her social position are changed.

Another important factor is birth control practiced by mutual consent. Today many families plan the number of children and the intervals between births.

The dynamics of family life constitute the fourth important factor. In the institutional family the relationships of the members to one another are legally and traditionally regulated; they are usually relationships of *authority* and *dependency*. In the modern family, the principle of authority, according to M. Horkheimer, assumes an "irrational aspect." Control by the father no longer has any legal support, and economically the family is no longer solely dependent on him.

What takes precedence in the dynamics are the *emotional relationships* among family members. According to Goode, every member has the "duty to love all the others—paradoxical as such duty may appear to be. The children are supposed to love their brothers and sisters, and they are punished if they admit that they hate a younger sibling who is being spoiled. The children have got to love their parents, and vice versa."

Goode points out that people in Western culture often have intensive emotional relations with other members of the family, especially with the mother. She is the symbol of sacrificial love, and frequent difficulties and problems arise from this situation.

Psychoanalysts have concerned themselves with the dynamic problems in modern family life. Nathan Ackerman in his *Family Psychodynamics* discusses the burden of responsibility that society places on the modern family. According to him, it is expected that the family give the individual the *security* and *warmth* he no longer finds in the society from which he has become alienated. This "alienation," as Erich Fromm terms it, results from the fact that in our industrialized society the individual often feels *lost* and *lonely*.

Institutionalized forms of behavior in modern business and professional life, as Talcott Parsons explains in his discussion of the social structure of the family, contrast sharply with man's deepest needs and motivations; for example, the need for relationships in which personal feelings, friendship, trust, and readiness to help play a role. To function in business and professional life, today's man must exercise strict *discipline*. This is a work-discipline motivated by the desire to turn out a good performance; it is maintained by not giving in to one's personal feelings.

According to Ackerman, the sense of being forsaken in this system puts an unbearable burden on the family. Thus, "togetherness" has become a widespread goal. But Sunday arrangements for the purpose of building togetherness frequently have something artificial about them. It might well be said that they practically create a "Sunday neurosis," because the people who *gather* together frequently really don't *belong* together.

In the author's collection of the diaries of several generations of one family the difference in attitudes toward life is especially marked. In the naïve chatter of an adolescent of the 1870's and 1880's a thousand trivial family matters play a pre-eminent role. They are described with an obvious feeling of participation and a sense of belonging. The adolescents of the present generation, on the other hand, appear through their diaries as *isolated individuals;* they also show their family members and friends in much the same isolation.

Today, says Ackerman, nobody knows exactly what his family stands for, what its goals, norms, and values are or ought to be. Mother, father, and children have the most diverse views. The parents are insecure; their roles have not been precisely assigned; their various authorities are not clear. The father, who is mostly absent, is continually admonished to pay more attention to his family and to take on more responsibility in the home. The mother must take many duties upon herself and must act with a sense of assurance and strength she does not possess. The children either seek security in conformist adaptation or soon become independent and frequently tend to asocial behavior if not to actual criminality. Max Lerner calls them "the unenthusiastic youth."

A particularly acute problem of family dynamics, especially in the United States, is the woman's ambivalent role. She is supposed to be a good housewife and a "glamor girl" of charm and elegance. She must also be the understanding helpmate of her husband. When, added to all this, she has to take care of young children or has a job outside the home, she is daily faced with the question of how to do justice to all these roles.

Often the husband is not clear as to what his wife's primary role should be. But for him, too, the role he is to assume in the home is not clearly defined.

The multiplicity of the problems that have been briefly touched upon here shows that the modern family is exposed to strong attacks and great demands. It seems remarkable that despite all these difficulties there are families that not only preserve their solidarity but actually serve as a haven of rest and relaxation for their members and offer them a firm support in the whirl of modern life.

The family structure is, as Parson explains, in sharp contrast to the structure of vocational groups. It is based on blood relationship. The rights and duties of the members are defined by age, sex, and relationship, and the dynamics of the relationship are emotional. Vocational groups are built up on impersonal relationships and performances that have to be supported by proof of qualifications; emotions play no part.

The Factory, an Artificial Group

Just as, at one end of the natural groups, there is the family, so, at one end of the artificial groups, there is the factory or plant. In between, there are many transitional forms, such as the adolescent society or associations and clubs with diverse goals and with more or less close relationships among the members.

The plant is a product of modern industrial society. In the broadest sense, it is a total sociotechnical system in which men, machines, and material work together to effect a definite purpose. In this general definition, then, a business enterprise is also a plant, as is a transportation system, a farm, a workshop, a theater, or a hotel.

Originally, the plant was primarily "the location of the technical production of goods," but today it is considered a "technical-economic-social-human structure."

F. Fürstenberg quotes a remark of Alfred Krupp's as characteristic of the earlier attitude among industrialists: "What I am striving to achieve is that nothing should be dependent on the life or existence of a particular person, and that no knowledge and no function should cease with him . . . that one should be able to survey the past of the factory as well as its probable future, at the main office, without having to ask a question of a single person."

From this one can clearly see that a completely *impersonal character* was considered necessary for optimum *performance* and *profit*.

Today this concept has been entirely changed as a result of the pressure that workers have exerted. Human beings justifiably object to being treated as cogs in a machine. As this more humane viewpoint has found acceptance, the purely technical and economic aspects have been supplemented by humanitarian ones. Now the question is: "How can the worker be incorporated into the huge modern plant so that he inwardly has a positive attitude toward his work and its side effects, without thereby having to give up the idea of any independent further development?"

From the modern standpoint, the factory or plant is an institution, the main characteristics of which are *division of labor, delegation of authority, communication arrangements,* and *forms of behavior.* The last two must be so arranged that they bring about the cooperation of the workers.

Let us look at the Chicago meat-packing plant of Swift and Company in 1957.* This plant is one of fifty-seven meat-canning plants run by the firm. In 1957 it had 2,954 workers and 254 foremen, managers, and division heads. The organization is complicated. There are eleven specialized divisions; which are in turn divided into specialized subdivisions. The four main divisions correspond to the most important work done in the plant: slaughtering and treating meats; processing the meat into ready-to-

* These data were graciously provided by Dr. Harvey Locke. They were taken from a report on the structure of various plants that he had made for a work in progress.

eat canned food; processing soap, glycerin, and other by-products; the machine shop.

In all these divisions there are a number of highly specialized skilled workers. Their roles in the work process are carefully delineated, and their relations to one another are definitely fixed. This division of labor is referred to as the "horizontal dimension," as opposed to the vertical dimension of the various ranks and levels of authority.

Authority Levels in the Chicago plant of Swift & Co., 1957

Director	1
Assistant Director	1
Division Heads	9
Plant Managers	
Assistant Plant Managers	245
Foremen	
Workers	2,954
Total	3,210

T. V. Purcell, who studied this plant, says that to the individual worker his particular division represents "the firm." There are workers in the "East End" of the plant who have never been in the "West End" and who would not be able to find their way there.

The following characteristics were demonstrated in this plant: organization of all parts of the plant into specialized fields; a hierarchical structure with horizontal and vertical dimensions; delegation of power with respect to authority and responsibility; communication limited to assigned channels; impersonal relations with members of other parts of the plant.

It is interesting to note that the twenty largest U. S. plants—having an annual production of between $2 and $11 billion—are those of the automobile, oil, steel, electrical equipment, aircraft, and data-processing industries.

These huge organizations comprise a great many specialized functions; their directives for all in-plant processes are issued in printed form; and they require a large management apparatus.

Despite their great size, these plants attempt to maintain and increase their productivity by arousing in their personell subjective attitudes of a constructive kind, especially a sense of *belonging*. This goal is realized when the worker has a positive attitude toward team work and a high evaluation of his own work group. Contributing to the feeling of belonging and to the readiness to work is a personal interest in the individual worker on the part of management. Exemplary work and behavior on the part of superiors is also necessary.

Despite all efforts to bring about a good plant climate, there are always tensions and conflicts. Today there are a great many carefully thought-out measures to lessen or eliminate them—from *negotiations* to *strikes.*

Many plants give their workers a chance to make suggestions for technical, management, and welfare improvements. Generally, the suggestions are placed in a letterbox anonymously. There are differences of opinion regarding the value of this arrangement. Many factory managers believe that it is better to hold open but confidential discussions with workers than to pay attention to anonymous criticism.

Negotiation is increasingly used to settle both internal conflicts between management and labor and conflicts between groups of whole industrial branches. Unions represent the interests of labor.

According to Harvey Locke, the conflicts that come into the open in negotiations and strikes are sociologically interpreted as having useful functions for the following reasons:

1. Open conflicts lead to a clear statement of differences and compel the fighting parties to justify their demands.

2. Conflicts bring controversial questions to the attention of the public and provide an opportunity for it and for the government to take a hand in matters affecting the public interest.

3. Open conflicts between powerful and influential groups necessitate a quick solution; therefore, compromise and adjustment have to be sought for.

4. Open conflict stabilizes the social structure insofar as it leads to clarification and definition of the behavior to be expected. In discussions between worker and management groups—especially with respect to questions of working hours and wages—collective bargaining plays an extraordinarily large role.

Hence, it becomes clear just how the factory represents the greatest contrast to the family group. The family exists as a group before some of its members, the children, have developed fully as individuals. Membership in the group and the roles of the individual members come about naturally. The relations of members to one another are primarily personal. It is demanded that love should bind them together. Each formalization or distancing in the relationships of family members is a major production. It is the purpose of the family to provide life support and the possibilities for development to all its members. Beyond these tasks, the family, in and of itself, has no goal. Values and traditions are a part of the basis of the family; husband and wife establish them when they marry. The children grow up into an already existing value structure.

In the structure of the plant quite the opposite prevails. This group has been artificially created through decisions and agreements. The individuals are not members from the very beginning. Their roles are acquired—assigned to them. The relations of the group members to one another are impersonal. Only through particular measures can the formality and distance in interpersonal relations be lessened or discarded. If loyalty to the plant is demanded from the workers, management must do its part to arouse and maintain such loyalty. The purpose of the plant is to produce goods, which then leave the plant. Only secondarily does the plant accord its members life support and possibilities for development. The creation of traditions and common values within a plant requires special and continuing efforts.

Both the family and the plant are groups in which *conflicts* and *tensions* arise. Both structures can be torn apart by these conflicts. But the fact of belonging to the family is never fully wiped out, even though the group as such may no longer exist, but the plant ceases to exist if the conflicts that tear it apart cannot be settled. For the settling of conflicts, the plant has set up formal regulations, whereas family conflicts often remain unresolved for a long time and are seldom led systematically to their solution.

In the *dynamics* of the plant, the impersonal, rational work structure plays a role that is contrary to human nature. Tensions between management and workers and between employers and unions and emotional resistance against the plant structure by the workers' group provide, as Arthur Mayer says, a sort of "human island."

CHAPTER 9

CULTURES

It is extremely difficult to give an unequivocal definition of "culture."
Kroeber and Kluckhohn have pointed out no fewer than 164 definitions
of the word! No wonder, then, that the concept is not used in the same
sense everywhere or by all authors.

In today's scientific terminology, however, culture is understood as *the
complex of knowledge, morality, law, usage, custom, and other capabilities and habits that man has acquired.* Frequently, culture is described as
that part of the environment that is *artificially created.* Other researchers
prefer to consider, apart from created objects, culturally determined *behavior.* Walter Goldschmidt speaks of culture as *ways of mankind.* Here
the word "ways" is used in the sense of a way of life. The philosopher
Charles Morris speaks of "ways of life" as meaning the different life
philosophies by which men are guided.

The important question is: *How does the factor of culture become effective in our lives?* To be able to take a stand on this question, we must
first undertake a survey of the facts. We must make a choice among
them that will help us find the aspects that are most important for our
own lives.

Universal Indications of Culture

First of all, some of the general and specific indications of culture must
be clarified. It is generally known that all cultures have certain traits in
common, which are termed *universal.*

Similarities occur among various cultures because the life and fate of all human beings is similar in respects. All human beings are born of a mother, and all die. Growth and development, capacity to reproduce, ability to communicate, needs, feelings, perception, thinking, language, movement—are common to all men.

The universal aspects of culture that men have developed with the help of their mental and physical equipment have, since Malinowski, been investigated by many research scientists. It appears, however, that no system finds universal acceptance.

Melville Herskovitz suggested a model which, with some modification, is as follows:

I. Material Culture
    Economy
    Technical development
II. Social Institutions
    Communication, social organization
    Education, political structure
III. Arts and Sciences
    Graphic and plastic arts
    Music, dance, customs, and usages
    Language and literature
    Intellectual organization and science
IV. Man and the Universe
    System of beliefs
    Value system
    Philosophy

All cultures are concerned in varying degrees with the above-mentioned aspects. The means and methods by which they are realized vary greatly, and when we hear of the customs of primitive races we are struck by the great differences between these people and ourselves. And who in the Western world does not look with astonishment at the faces and bodies of natives distorted by tattooing and ornamentation? Who does not shudder at the thought of cannibals, scalping, and child murder?

The following modes of behavior and customs are found among all peoples and races: family life, marriage and burial customs, separation according to age groups, education, play and work, music, dance, and art. In addition, there are everywhere calendars, interpretation of dreams, regulated modes of human intercourse, exchange of visits, gift giving, joke telling, division of labor, differences of rank and position, laws, and regulation of inheritance.

More significant than a comparison of modes of behavior according to content is a comparison on the basis of fundamental points of view. Five categories have universal significance: *organization, values, integration, tradition,* and *change.*

Organization

All cultures develop in social groups that set up institutions for the *organization* of human relationships. According to Robert McIver, *"a system of organized relationships* is, on every level, a primary life-requisite" and it is pure fantasy to speak of "lawless barbarians." The "wild man" is never a man without laws. Quite the contrary: he adheres to the regulations that are valid in his group.

Besides the legal regulation of relationships in the group there is a codification of positions and roles. Ralph Linton here distinguishes between the rank that is *assigned* to a person and the one that he *achieves* through performance. In all societies, *biological factors* such as age and sex receive consideration in the assignment of roles. As Linton explains, there are regulations everywhere for how children are to be treated. To carry out these regulations is the duty partly of the family, partly of other groups. And everywhere there is education and upbringing.

Everywhere there are measures for caring for the aged. Both the family and group or community have certain duties in this respect. True, in some societies the aged are killed off in the interest of the old person and his soul, which are thus spared ultimate deterioration.

Next to age, the most important aspect in the assignment of roles is sex.

In all societies there are regulations for relations between the sexes in puberty, and before, during, and after marriage, although particular prohibitions and taboos differ and there are various attitudes with regard to incest.

Everywhere there are certain assignments of rank, rights, and duties connected with sex. These are so contradictory that—contrary to frequent assertions—the physiological basis plays practically no role at all. As Linton says, cultural caprice or arbitrariness brings about these regulations. Here are a few examples:

Arapesh women regularly carry heavier loads than men "because their heads are so much harder and stronger." In some societies women do most of the manual labor; in others, as in the Marquesas, even cooking, housekeeping, and baby tending are proper male occupations, and women spend most of their time primping. There are many exceptions even to the general rule that women's handicap through pregnancy and nursing precludes their performing strenuous activities. Thus, among the Tasmanians, seal hunting is women's work. They swim out to the seal rocks, stalk the animals, and club them. Tasmanian women also hunt opossums, which requires them to climb large trees.

In almost all societies, men and women are assigned definite occupations. But even when both sexes work together in a single activity, their roles are different. Thus, in Madagascan rice culture, the men make the seed beds and terraces and prepare the fields for transplanting. The women do the back-breaking work of transplanting. The women weed the crop, but the men harvest it. The women carry it to the threshing floors, where the men thresh it while the women winnow it. The women pound the grain in mortars and cook it.

The assignment of certain functions follows on the basis of sex, age, and position in the family. In many societies, however, purely *social factors* are decisive in such assignment.

According to Linton, in most societies there is a tendency to divide individuals into groups or categories and to ascribe varying *social importance* to these categories. The origins of these *class differences* are manifold. In certain instances, they may come from particular qualifications, such as technical skills or warlike courage, or may be seen in the formation of league organizations. One need only look to the war leagues of the North American tribes or the priestly castes of many cultures. The *conquest* of one society by another can provide the occasion for the formation of classes.

Europe in feudal times is a good example of the assignment of roles on the basis of class. Whether someone was brought up to be a knight or a peasant was based solely on what particular class he belonged to.

In practically all societies, Linton says, there is the tendency to assign roles and to prohibit competition from other classes. Linton wrote in 1936 that no woman, Negro, or Indian could become President of the United States, and that only with great difficulty could a Catholic or Jew achieve that position. But now one of these barriers has fallen: in 1961, a Catholic, John F. Kennedy, was elected President of the United States. Generally speaking, society in the United States is competitive.

Values

In all cultures, certain *guidelines* as to how life is to be lived are decisive. They are expressed not only in regulations and prohibitions, in religions and philosophical systems, but in everyday life. Certain principles are expressed in the relations with one's fellow men and in the treatment of problems as they arise day by day.

The researcher in the field of culture must consider an individual's values in a larger context than his motivation and identification, for, although the values that an individual builds up for himself are arrived at by coming to an understanding with his immediate environment, in the last analysis they have their origins in the mass of *ideas of a cultural group.*

Here is a clear example of this from two groups in Western culture:

Martha Wolfenstein describes the difference between the ways French and American children behave in public parks.

A French girl of about two has picked up a leather strap from a neighboring group. Her nurse reproves her, takes her by the hand, and returns the strap. A little later a French boy of about the same age, belonging to the neighboring group, plays with the little girl, picks up her pail, and keeps it while the little girl is fed by her nurse. The boy's grandmother becomes aware that he has the pail, hits him on the buttocks, scolds, and, taking him by the hand, returns the pail to the girl's nurse. In front of the nurse she repeatedly hits the boy about the head and ears.

A three-year-old French boy is playing with a borrowed scooter, and his mother notices that he has torn the handlebar grip. She takes hold of the scooter with one hand and the child with the other, goes over to the mother to whom the scooter belongs, apologizes, and scolds the boy in front of her.

Wolfenstein explains that in contrast to the French notion that a toy is the private property of a child and his family, American children are taught that they should let others take part in their play and games and share their toys. In this way a lively, reciprocal social relationship is promoted, while the French children in the park are kept apart from one another.

This observation may appear unimportant when we think about the great differences in basic life values among men, especially when we compare Western society and Communism. Then it does not seem very important whether children share their toys or not. Yet, if we look more carefully, we see that there are internal connections in the ideas and values of cultural groups. In other words—to come back to our example— in the American children's lack of restraint there is a reflection of an *outlook*.

Difference of outlook in daily behavior was observed by Florence Kluckhohn in five different cultures: two Indian groups, the Navajo and the Zuni; a Spanish-American village (Atrisco); a Mormon village (Rimrock); and a recent settlement of Texas farmers (Homestead). All five communities were located in the American Southwest, and none was more than fifty miles from the next.

Kluckhohn starts with a series of theoretical considerations. First, she makes three assumptions: that there are only a limited number of common human problems for which all human beings have to find a solution;

that the number of possible solutions is limited; and that all sorts of solutions are tried in all societies but that different societies prefer different solutions.

Everywhere in the world, men have ideas about *human nature*: either that it is bad, that it is good and bad at the same time, or that it is naturally good. Everywhere, human beings have ideas as to the *relation of man to nature*. Man is thought of as inferior to nature, in harmony with it, or in command of it. Everywhere a relation to *time* can be found. That is, men live more in the past, in the present, or in the future. Furthermore, everywhere there are ideas as to man's relations to *life activity*. People either live more in the feeling of existing, that is, in the enjoyment and acceptance of what is provided; or of becoming, that is, in continuous striving for development; or of acting, that is, in continuous readiness to act and to bring about something definite. Finally, all men have ideas about their *relation to others*: that they either are committed to remaining individually separate, to being a part of a community, or to following others.

A few examples will make this deep-searching theory somewhat clearer: the American middle class is individualistic, it is future oriented, it sees in man the ruler over nature; it believes in active dealings and regards man's nature as bad or at the same time bad and good.

In the tradition-bound Spanish-American society, it is believed that one should be guided by others, that one lives in the present, that man is subject to nature, that life is being—not doing—and that man is by nature both good and bad at the same time.

The remarks of Spanish-Americans reveal their belief in man's subjection to nature:

"If it is the Lord's will that I die, I shall die," is the explanation for why no doctor is called.

Or a shepherd says, "There's not much to be done to save the sheep if a wild storm comes up."

The typical American has quite an opposite attitude:

"God helps those that help themselves": nature can be altered; it is not admitted that there may be natural obstacles to achievement.

In their relations to their fellows, the Navajo Indians are entirely committed to being community oriented.

"You can't just have one leader in a family. This wouldn't be fair to the rest. You should get together and discuss."

"It is easy to vote, but it doesn't turn out. The only way for the people would be discussing."

"The community gets together in a group to decide."

"And another thing is for the group to work through together."

"Those in a group make a choice."

"They could decide the matter by themselves and by discussing it so it would work out all right with everyone."

"The best thing is to get together in a group and make an agreement."

With regard to an inheritance, Navajos say: "If brothers and sisters would all pull together on the same rope, they wouldn't have any difficulties."

In their relation to time, there is an orientation toward the present:

"When you bring up children, the first thing is to teach them for the present, then you teach them about the old ways."

"The past was good, but we don't know much about it anymore."

"The first is the present. This is true about us. If we try to think back to olden days, it's no use. Now things are changing and we are right in the middle."

In his relation to nature, the Navajo believes in harmony with it. He holds that the equilibrium in nature can be disturbed by man:

"If a person doesn't live right, you can't expect to have protection for your horse or sheep."

"If we try to do our best to live the right way, we will have harmony for our crops."

["It's true about doctors and vaccinations, because I've had experience that way, and also] if you do something bad, it affects your life, and if you are good, you don't worry."

With respect to activity or passivity, the Navajo tends to be active:

["The ones that are doing something,] if you think about good results and work for it, that is it."

"If you do the right things and work hard, then you are happy."

He believes that man's nature is good as well as bad and that it doesn't change:

"I never heard of anything that changed human nature. Even old people said this."

Florence Kluckhohn's concept of the values of a particular culture comprises the life philosophy prevailing in that culture. Generally, ethics is among the decisive values in a culture. Kluckhohn holds that, in the last analysis, the entire *ideology* of a culture rests on values.

Integration

Kluckhohn's presentation confirms better than any previous work the law of *integration*—the inner unity of a culture—which was first propounded by Ruth Benedict. A culture is an integrated whole whose unifying factors must be understood. In *Patterns of Culture,* Benedict shows that a culture cannot be understood by collecting and listing separate facts. Rather, like a human being, it must be understood from the point of view of central motives. Only when one sees culture as a living whole —as a community structure whose characteristic features are developed by purposeful goal-striving activity—can one understand it fully.

In her exposition of the central themes working for integration, Benedict reaches different conclusions than Kluckhohn, and her analysis is intuitive rather than systematic. In the Zuni Indians, for example, she sees an "Apollo-like" principle of moderation; she considers the self-extinction of the individual in the face of society a basic characteristic of this culture.

Conversely, she describes the Kwakiutl Indians of Vancouver Island as "Dionysiac" in individualistic rivalry and ecstasy, with a tendency to paranoiac and megalomanic delusions.

The Dobu of Melanesia she regards as secretive, spiteful, treasonable; they feel themselves in conflict against a harsh environment. They are afraid of nature and full of distrust of their neighbors.

This type of observation, which aims to bring everything down to a common denominator, is, however, oversimplified. A culture has not one theme but many themes, and many different expressions for these.

Margaret Mead has also worked out certain *basic cultural tendencies* from her observations of *child care* and *the upbringing of the young* among primitive tribes. She was the first anthropologist to formulate *meaningful connections in culture.*

The efforts of modern anthropologists to understand clearly the principles that effect integration in the different cultures have not yet led to any unequivocal conclusions. Their further development will contribute fundamentally to our understanding of ourselves.

Tradition

It may be hard to accept that our feelings of love and hate, and the incentives that these feelings release, are culturally determined. But this is the case. Not only the customs of people who seem strange to us—such as the Balinese, who sing and rejoice at funerals, or the Kapankawa Indians, who shed tears when they greet a friend—but our own ways of thinking and feeling have been trained into us from an early age, without our knowing it. Outstanding researches on culture today maintain that cultural possessions are transmitted through custom and traditions and that, accordingly, they are learned and *can be taught.*

Among those who have provided proof that *cultural factors are independent of biological inheritance* is the German-American anthropologist and ethnologist Franz Boas, who declared that "a critical investigation shows that forms of thinking and acting which we are inclined to understand as based on man's nature are not generally valid, but are characteristic for our specific culture."

It is possible that originally, corresponding to given life conditions, certain guidelines were determined by racial predispositions, tendencies, and talents. But today's cultures are highly complicated structures, to the development of which the most diverse people, races, and groups have contributed. Today it is generally believed that if an individual, of any race or nationality, should be transferred in his early childhood to another cultural community, he would take on the speech, behavior, and mode of thinking of that group and would become completely identified with it.

A report by Amram Scheinfeld is impressive in this connection. In the examples of two young men, he shows the extent of the influences that the cultural environment exerts:

"An American-Chinese, born Joseph Rhinehart . . . became Fung Kwok Keung when, as a baby [this was in 1920], he was adopted by a Chinese restaurateur on Long Island and taken to China to be reared in a small town near Canton with the family of his foster father. Not until he was twenty did he return to the United States, but by then he was so completely Chinese in all but appearance that he had to be given 'Americanization' as well as English lessons to adapt him to his new life."

A completely opposite case in that of a Chinese-American—racially Chinese but culturally American—Paul Fung, Jr., a talented cartoonist with a wide syndication. With American-born parents and Chinese-American grandparents, Paul was educated and had lived among white Americans all his life. His thinking, behavior, speech, outlook, and sense of humor were completely American (and this is nowhere more required than in doing American comic strips). But when World War II broke out and he enlisted for service, he found himself with a Chinese-American unit composed mainly of immigrant Chinese youth or sons of immigrants.

Knowing little of the Chinese language and customs, he was virtually a stranger, and—no small matter to a G. I.—he couldn't adjust to having Chinese food at almost every meal. Because he was regarded by the others as "putting on an act," conflicts ensued and he had to seek companionship among white G. I.'s from a nearby camp. Chance eventually brought him a transfer to a regular army unit, with which he served in the Pacific area as an air-force photographer. (Paul participated in the atomic-bomb flight over Hiroshima.)

What happened during the war with our other man, who looked American but was culturally Chinese? As you may expect, he was placed not in the Chinese-American unit but with white troops, with whom he had little in common save his racial origins. One congenial service he could perform was as an interpreter in Italy when Chinese ships came into port. At the war's end Rhinehart-Fung worked for a while as compositor on a Chinese newspaper (an intricate job almost impossible for anyone not Chinese), but he could never quite find himself and subsequently worked for white firms as a night watchman.

These two examples may seem as simple as they are enlightening, and one is apt to conclude simply that if a person grows up in a particular culture it is not easy for him to change over to another culture. But what takes place in the individual as he attempts to conform to the new culture is highly complicated and still by no means clear.

Pioneer observations on the processes and situational factors by which *cultural characteristics are transmitted to children* were carried out by Margaret Mead and evaluated in her books *Coming of Age in Samoa* (1928) and *Growing Up in New Guinea* (1930). Below we shall discuss details of Mead's more recent works.

In her book *Growth and Culture* (1951), which describes a study made with eight Balinese infants, we see at least one influence that is culturally formative—the *human relationships* the infant has.

During its entire first year, the Balinese baby spends almost all its time in the arms of his mother. Later he is bound fast to the hip of his mother or other person. It is the job of brothers or sisters to care for the new baby. During the day, he is never laid down to sleep. Only when the rest of the family retires for the night is the baby, by now asleep, laid down.

From his second month, such a child sees the world from an upright position on the hip of the person who is carrying him. He has the experience of being firmly tied to another person, which may be a different one at different times. Only from the time he can crawl unaided does he move about by himself. But even then he is always with other people.

Contrast this with a child brought up in a Western country. The newborn infant is laid down in a cradle or a bassinet; here he spends most of his waking and sleeping hours. Only for a fraction of a day is he on the arm or in the lap of his mother.

The baby has no adults around him except his parents, and he is more or less completely dependent on their love and interest—especially his mother's. Accordingly, his relationship with his parents assumes an intensity that it would not attain under the conditions that prevail in Bali, where a baby is dependent on many people.

The infant who grows up in his own cradle spends the greater part of his time without close physical contact with other people and thus enjoys a freedom of movement that the tightly bound Bali baby does not have. Thus, he not only gets independent earlier, but is much more active. He is able to experiment with his bodily movements and with handling things. Here, the foundation is laid not only for greater activity but also for initiative and creative activity.

This comparison provides a good idea of a first group of life conditions that create a specific culture.

In Mead's view the individual is not so completely imprinted by his environment that no possibilities for individual expression and self-realization remain. But further investigations are necessary to distinguish *individual factors* from the effects brought about by the environment.

As has been indicated, the Balinese baby is always among a great many people, participating in everything that the adults are doing. For example, he is taken to all religious ceremonies. He grows up into the *cult,* just as he does into *family life.*

The chapter "Children and Ritual in Bali" in Margaret Mead and M. Wolfenstein's book *Childhood in Contemporary Culture* describes how children of all ages take part in the religious cult. The little ones look at and try on the masks that are used in the ritual. Curiosity, fear, and fascination are evident, but at the same time there is also a perfectly natural sense of being part of the cult activities.

From this kind of *participation in the life of the adults* there results, for example, an entirely different kind of *children's art* than the one with which we are familiar. Drawing and music show fewer childlike signs and more cult characteristics.

In this participation of the children in the adult environment, a further culture-forming factor finds expression—what Ruth Benedict called *continuity* of development, in contrast to the *discontinuity* that exists in our culture. Balinese children gradually assume the behavior patterns of the adults without a break, without any striking cutoffs. The children are allowed to attend and to participate in everything the adults do. Their duties and rights are not separated from those of the adults. Just as they take part in the work to be done, so they are not prevented from taking part in the religious ceremonies, games, or even sexual activities.

In Western culture there is discontinuity in the sense that the activities, rights, and duties of children are different from those of adults and that there is a sharply defined separation between the two groups.

The educational process through which Western parents send their children is carefully arranged step by step, and the things that are placed at the disposal of the children change many times. Thus one can speak of a particular child culture and a particular adolescent culture. In the past few decades adolescent culture has been getting more independent.

Cutural Change

Although customs, habits, and traditions serve to maintain cultural

Fig. 37

Children watch the Barong mask in the cult procession around the village.

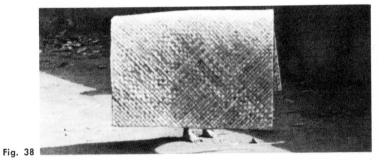

Fig. 38

A child plays "Barong" by holding a mat over his head.

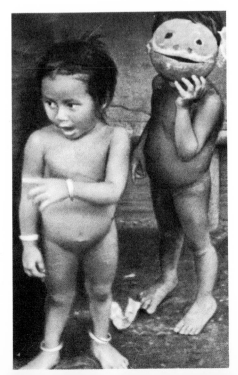

In their play, children use coconut shells to imitate the cult masks.

Through participation in all religious events, the child in Bali grows up into the cult.

Fig. 39

permanency, side by side with these stabilizing influences there are always changes. Culture is acquired and transmitted by learning, but it is absorbed and expressed by each individual in his own particular way.

According to Pitirim Sorokin, a sociocultural system is a living structure, an essential part of which is continual change. Besides this general principle of *imminent change,* there are also special, sometimes drastic, reasons for cultural changes.

Fig. 40

These drawings by five- and six-year-old Balinese children are quite different from those of European children of the same age. The upper drawing shows the god Krishna and the hero Salja from a traditional shadow play. The lower drawing shows "a cow lying down, people, birds, a pig" but there are also figures from the shadow play again (from Mead and Wolfenstein, *Childhood in Contemporary Cultures*).

For example, notable differences can usually be observed in what succeeding *generations* believe in and strive to obtain. These differences can develop into radical transformations.

New ideas—such as Martin Luther's principle of individual responsibility before God and Karl Marx's condemnation of capitalism; *technical progress,* such as the invention of the steam engine, automobile, and airplane; *economic change,* such as modern industry has brought about; *reforms,* such as the enfranchisement of women and the opening up of higher education to them; *new institutions,* such as the United Nations —have completely altered the structure of culture today.

However, except in completely isolated regions, there has always been a reciprocal influencing and interpenetration of culture. There has always been a mutual interchange of new ideas and accomplishments, although, naturally, some cultures offer more resistance to innovation than others.

When we speak of a culture as a living structure, the question arises whether we can speak of its *development* in the same sense as the development of a human organism.

In the course of the victorious progress of the Darwinian theory of evolution, according to which higher forms evolve out of lower ones, the idea of development made its way into culture research. However, the idea of unequivocal progress has been completely discarded. The question of whether, and in what sense, a *trend* can be determined in cultural developments has enlisted the interest of many outstanding historical and cultural philosophers from Auguste Comte, Max Weber, and Oswald Spengler to today's Alfred Kroeber, Arnold Toynbee, and Robert McIver. K. N. Naegele, in editing a selection of writings on the subject, said: "The world has grown smaller, but our skepticism has grown greater since we studied the world as a whole over long periods. Our faith in progress and in continual human betterment has been superseded by more pessimistic ideas."

Cultural values are developed and then are lost, and one cannot resist the idea that there is a kernel of truth in Spengler's concept that a cultural style comes to life, grows, blossoms, matures, and dies off.

On the other hand, neo-evolutionists like Leslie White point out that in certain respects a more or less continuous evolution cannot be denied. It is unfortunately true that on neither ethical nor aesthetic grounds are we in a position to notice "progress." But we can see the steady increase in technical achievements.

Invention and *diffusion* are considered to be the two main principles that further cultural change. *Diffusion* means the dissemination and transference of certain cultural elements from one culture to another.

Kroeber provides a vivid picture of a series of cultural achievements that were acquired by diffusion and that have become an intrinsic part of American life. He cites our Anglo-Saxon version of a Germanic language that contains more words of Latin origin than English ones. Our religion is Palestinian, with specific reformulations developed in Rome, Germany, England, Scotland, and Holland. The Bible is in part translated from the Hebrew, in part from the Greek. We drink coffee, which was first planted in Ethiopia and then in Arabia; tea, which China discovered; beer, which was first brewed in ancient Mesopotamia or Egypt; and spirits, which were invented in Europe during the Middle Ages. Our bread and meats come from plants and animals that were first raised in Asia, while potatoes, corn, tomatoes, and beans were first used by the American Indians, as was tobacco. We write an Etruscan-Roman variation of the Greek alphabet that was invented in or near Phoenicia by a Semitic tribe on the basis of nonalphabetic writings from still older cultures.

This list notwithstanding, many ideas arise *independently* in various places without foreign influence. We are not always dealing with transferrals when we come upon the same ideas and evaluations in different cultures. The Viennese cultural-history school under Father Wilhelm Schmidt emphasized, for example, that the belief in a higher god is universal in human beings, even among the most primitive tribes untouched by missionary teachings.

However, the principle of the mutual interpenetration of cultures retains its significance. If we think of the poorly developed communication and transportation in past centuries, it is surprising that such cultural exchanges could take place over entire continents.

In the immediate future we can expect extensive cultural exchanges as a result of new migrations, the opening up of new regions of the earth, and the advancing conquest over time and space.

Modern migrations, as the mass movements caused by flights and expulsions in our times may well be called, lead to an extended degree of *acculturation*—adaptation to a foreign culture. Acculturation is a burning problem, for almost all the countries of the world contain a large number of refugees and immigrants and their incorporation into already existing groups does not always proceed smoothly.

Cultural Differences

At any particular time in our lives there are a limited *number of possibilities* of behavior. This fact explains the existence of similar customs and skills in different cultures, even where there has been no transmittal from other cultures.

If a man wants a good oar, that oar must not be too long or too short, it must have a flat blade, and it must not be too unwieldly to handle. Just as the fulfillment of these requirements has led to exactly the same form in widely scattered cultures throughout the world, so similar needs and experiences in different cultures give rise to similar modes of behavior. And this the more so as there are only a limited number of possible solutions.

Despite the extensive parallel needs and experience of all men, the various cultures have developed *historically* in differing and occasionally unique ways. Every culture has its own particular stamp and left us with a wealth of cultural differences.

One of the most important human activities, and one in which there is extraordinary variability between different cultures, is *sexual behavior*. All societies and cultures regulate sexual life in some way or another. But they sanction, forbid, or punish quite different things. An interesting summary of various sexual prohibitions was made by Julia S. Brown, who investigated many primitive societies that have no written traditions. Not all societies could be studied for all the behaviors mentioned in the chart; the minimum number was forty-three, the maximum ninety-seven.

TYPES OF BEHAVIOR	Percentage of societies that prohibit or punish
Sex relations between mother and son, brother and sister, father and daughter	100
Abduction of a married woman	100
Rape of a married woman	99
Rape of an unmarried woman	95
Sexual relations immediately after the birth of a child	95
Sexual relations during menstruation	92
Adultery on the part of the wife	87
Infidelity of a male (or female) engaged person	86
Sexual relations during pregnancy	67
Premarital relations by women	44
Premarital relations by men	41
Sexual relations with one's bride before marriage	10

In many respects, the agreement is great; thus, in all cultures incest is abhorred and strictly punished. Yet there are also great differences. For example, a native of the Trobriand Islands (near the east coast of New Guinea) who finds his wife in the arms of a lover may kill him immediately. On the other hand, the Toda of the Nilgiri Mountains in Mar-India do not consider a man moral if he begrudges his wife to other men.

In some societies a man who plays the female role is regarded as a powerful magician. On the other hand, according to Ford and Beach, homosexuality is so detested among the Rivala Bedouins that men and women who disobey the strict prohibition against homosexual activity are condemned to death.

Of interest, too, are the differences in the treatment of the *aged*. Among most primitive peoples the aged have certain rights, duties, privileges, and securities. In others, however, when the aged have become infirm they are exposed to the elements to die.

A chart made by L. W. Simmons from the results of an investigation of seventy-one primitive societies shows both the similarities and the differences in the *treatment of the aged*.

UNIVERSALLY DISTRIBUTED	Percentage
Treatment of the sick by old people	100
Counseling in skills, supervision of work	100
Proclaiming of tribal traditions	100
Celebrated in legends as heroes and magicians	100

ALMOST UNIVERSALLY DISTRIBUTED	
Leaders in festivities, songs, dances	98
Activity as magicians	98
Support assured by the family	97
Honored and feared	97
Members of councils of elders	95
Guardians of propriety and customs, judges	93

VARIABLE	
Rights within the family, inclusive of rights as head of the family	88
Privileges with respect to food prohibitions	79
Support by son-in-law	73
Positions by son-in-law	73
Abandoned to die	32

The universal human feeling of guilt and regret and the conscience that is common to all men have given rise to *beliefs in evil supernatural powers*. However, there are enormous differences among cultures in the rites that men perform to honor and call upon their gods.

Any psychological penetration—even a simple description of the multiplicity of the thoughts and feelings that lie at the basis of men's religions —would be far beyond the scope of this book. The reader is referred to *The World's Great Religions.*

The Individual and His Culture

The interrelationship between the individual and his culture is important in cultural-anthropology research. A continuous dynamic relationship exists between the culture and its individual members. The unsolved problem is, however, *what role the individual plays* and how much influence he has in the matter.

A few researchers who are particularly impressed by the formative influence of culture believe that the individual is completely formed by his culture. Ruth Benedict, who was one of the first anthropologists to establish the unified character and formative power of culture, sees the individual largely as the product of the system of values, ideas, and customs in which he grows up.

To what extent is this true? How far does a person succeed, in a cultural context, in expressing himself as an individual, and how far does he, over and above such self-realization, have the opportunity to influence his environment by what he does and by what he is?

The fact that intellectual leader personalities make their mark on the culture in which they live and point out new paths for the culture can not be seriously doubted by anyone. Other things are much more difficult to understand. First, how can a leader rise from the conditions of his culture and so formulate innovations that the group is able to accept them and make them their own? Second, how does the average person lift himself out of the group and help form the culture process?

A study by T. Gladwin and S. B. Sarasen depicts the development and integration of individual personalities on Truk, an island in the Carolines group in Micronesia.

The group personality of the Truk natives is characterized as follows: weak emotions, little conscience, incapacity for self-evaluation, limited goal settings, and hostility. The need for sufficient food is an important factor in this. The individual is kept in subjection by his family by threats and punishments. Individual initiative is suppressed. Parents are bad tempered and have little love for their children.

However, individual differences are found. First, various degrees of *social adaptation* are apparent. Those who had a friendly and helpful parent of their own sex developed satisfactory relationships with their peers and made their way better in their society. In contrast were individuals who had an unloving, hostile parent of their own sex; even according to Truk norms, they were not adequately adapted socially.

Andy, a Truk youth of nineteen, reports that he was a happy little boy:

"I ran about, sang songs, and visited from house to house. And I was given little gifts. There was always a lot to eat."

Andy mentions with pride his skill and luck in fishing. He identifies with his father in this respect: "My father is the same way. He is number one with the thrown spear while I am number one with the small rubber-propelled spear. I don't know why I can get fish so easily."

"I used to wear a lot of flowers in my hair and give them to girls; I used to tickle their legs with a coconut leaf rib, up their legs as far as I could go."

Only once, when he was six years old, did his father beat him severely. This was because he went swimming, which was forbidden. His feelings were hurt, and he screamed that his father had treated him "like an animal." His mother was sympathetic. She was a loving mother by Truk standards.

On the other hand, Tony, a twenty-three-year-old Truk, had an unhappy childhood. His relationship with his parents was not good. He was bound by rules and prohibitions, was frequently beaten, and often got nothing to eat. As often as he could, he ran away to play with youngsters of his own age. His parents threatened that one day he would come back and find them gone and would not know where they were. This, as a matter of fact, happened a number of times. He fought and argued continually with his many brothers and sisters. In his whole life, there was not a single gleam of love and joy.

Tony's situation was made worse by the fact that his reactions to his situation were extraordinarily foolish and often senseless. For example, he reported the following:

"I would meet my father when he came back from fishing. He would give me the fish to take home, but I would give them to my playmates to eat. When I went home and my parents found out what had happened to the fish they beat me." Why did Tony do this? Was it revenge? Was it thoughtlessness? Or did he want to make himself popular among his friends? His own actions were unconstructive and only contributed to making his situation worse.

When he was an adult, Tony was full of anxiety in his social relationships; he was not able to cope with difficult situations.

These Truk examples have been cited to show how even in the closest, most rigid cultural group individual differences in personality develop. The formative factors are treatment by the parents, identification with one parent, deprivations, punishments, rewards, and relationships with brothers, sisters, and playmates.

There are some traditional skills on Truk, such as the building of huts and boats, spear throwing, and fishing. There are also some customs.

Regular school education was available to some of the natives, but for the most part it was too little and too late. It did not constitute a formative factor in their childhood.

In all cultures there are objective cultural conditions as well as subjectively varying influences of individuals and groups on each other. Today the leading anthropologists who have concerned themselves with the effects of individuals on one another and on their cultural environment seem to agree that the relationships are inextricably interwoven.

In *Culture and Experience,* A. Irving Hallowell discusses the process of the coming into existence of the *self* as it arises from its environment. He goes so far as to explain that the division between "internal" and "external" is irrelevant, and quotes a sentence of Henry Murray's to the effect that "the organism and its milieu are to be considered as a single entity, in other words, they are to be looked upon as one." Hallowell is also of the opinion that motives are acquired, rather than determined by inborn factors.

The author, however, agrees with Ralph Linton when he states in *The Cultural Basis of Personality* that neither inborn capacities nor the environment can be looked upon exclusively as the dominant factor in the making of personality.

Linton, like Kardiner, holds that every society develops a *basic personality type* that is characteristic for that society and that distinguishes it from others. The method by which experiences, internal organization, and capacities work together toward this basic type, or toward variations of it, is not yet known.

The environment may have considerable influence on people of average intelligence. Among creative people, the individual's contribution may be dominant.

Modern research is trying to establish the characteristics of cultural groups and subgroups by means of social and clinical psychology, in which data obtained through questionnaire and interview techniques are processed according to statistical and analytical principles.

Two such studies may be briefly mentioned. One is the investigation by F. L. Strodtbeck, in which the cultural values of two American subcultures, the Italian and the Jewish, are compared. The data were obtained by means of interviews and tests carried out with representative families. The result showed that these two groups recognized quite different values. The Jewish families believed in the individual's control of his destiny, in his responsibility for making his way in life, and in his receiving credit for work accomplished. The Italian families tended to believe that man is subjugated to a destiny, that families should stick together, and that any credit belongs to the family as a whole.

This great difference in values explains to a great extent the different emphasis placed by these groups on achievement and individual worth.

A different type of study is the controversial *Beyond the Melting Pot,* by N. Glazer and D. P. Moynihan. In this fact-finding investigation, several ethnic groups—the Negroes, Puerto Ricans, Jews, Italians, and Irish of New York City—are compared with respect to such items as their jobs, education, family life, politics, culture, and ideology. The idea was to test the theory of America as the "melting pot" in which groups of different national and racial origins, different cultures, and ideologies supposedly grow together into a unity. The authors' conclusion is that, contrary to this theory, the ethnic groups remain distinctly separate and that they represent "new social forms" within the whole of American society. While distinctions of religion and race primarily form this pattern of American subnationalities, the American nationality as a whole is still fluid. "Its processes are mysterious, and the final form, if ever there is to be a final form, is as yet unknown."

Judging from Glazer and Moynihan, the immigrant does not so much aspire to be an American as to join his ethnic group in America, but this is not generally the case. From individual biographies as well as from group studies it has been shown that there are many who, either with pride or apprehension, look forward to becoming Americans. To them, the American culture is stronger than ethnic group ties.

In the acculturation that is today being demanded of millions of uprooted and transplanted people there are extremely varied reactions to be seen. There are those who develop a sense of belonging with ease, and those for whom incorporation into a new mode of life is never possible.

There are many psychological reasons why one person cannot cope with a new environment while someone else adapts easily. Besides variations in flexibility, sensitivity, taste, habits, prejudices and many other things, the particular goals of the individual undoubtedly affect his degree of acculturation.

If he wants to help his fellow man, he can, like Albert Schweitzer, go off to innermost Africa and be happy. On the other hand, a person who finds it hard to get used to anything new and whose functioning is dependent on his living in a structured environment may be thrown out of his equilibrium just by a change of residence.

These are but a few examples of the various responses of the individual to his environment. The many complex problems arising therefrom await their resolutions in research.

PART III

PRACTICE

CHAPTER 10

PSYCHOLOGY IN EDUCATION
AND VOCATIONAL COUNSELING

Education encompasses everything that systematically influences those who are growing up, beginning with the training of infants to be orderly and well behaved to the development of personality and character. In a narrower sense, education is instruction at school.

In the psychology of *education* we must make a distinction between these two concepts of education.

The psychology of *vocational counseling* also has two aspects: a general aspect, the fullest development of the human potential, and a specific one, the choice of a suitable vocation.

The role of educational psychology is limited because of a circumstance of fundamental significance: that there is no unanimous, scientifically based conception of the ultimate goal of education and counseling. Furthermore, we know very little about the educational process and its effects. Worst of all, we have no clear concept of what the ideal image of man should be.

In comparing education goals and processes in different cultures we usually note a one-sided emphasis on certain ideas and neglect of others.

American educators are inclined to view education as a *socialization process* through which the child is introduced to the customs of his society. These social goals of education were emphasized by John Dewey. However, he by no means neglected the development of the individual; as early as 1902 he used the word *self-realization*.

245

By contrast, German educators scarcely mention socialization. One of their most distinguished spokesmen, Eduard Spranger, sees education as guidance toward self-realization, which might be termed an *individualization process*.

A combination of self-realization and socialization would seem the ideal solution, but different societies have different ideas as to how much emphasis should be placed on each aspect. The whole area of education becomes even more complicated when we compare the numerous theories with actual practice.

Theory and Practice in Dealing with Children

When we see how children and adolescents are dealt with at home and in school and hear parents scolding them and teachers warning them, we ask ourselves what they are really trying to do. Often a particular mother is not doing much more than protecting her own skin; or this father does nothing but act out of his own tyranny; and this teacher is trying to make things as easy for herself as possible. In all of this, there is not much education to be seen.

We hear people defend principles that have very little to do with the child's self-realization or socialization, principles that are autocratic rather than democratic, in the sense of consideration for the rights of others.

What are we to say when a father proudly proclaims that his children instantly do exactly what they are ordered to do and that they get punished if the command has to be repeated. In addition, this father is particularly proud of the fact that he never explains his commands, but says "You are to do it because I tell you to." When we hear something like this we cannot but ask: "What higher goal is blind and immediate obedience supposed to serve?"

This type of attitude is obviously left over from the time when the ideals of military autocracies prevailed.

Neither self-realization nor socialization is furthered by blind obedience, for both require thinking human beings who have been taught early in life to understand *why* one kind of behavior is more purposeful or valuable than another.

An authoritarian parent will answer: "But little children don't understand all that. Besides, they get into the habit of contradicting if one gives them explanations. What is important is that they should be trained to have good manners."

All these statements are, of course, completely unproved, and it is easy to bring up cases that demonstrate the opposite. In Chapter 4 there was a report on the happy development of Linda, whose mother explained to her when she was as young as three or four why everyone has certain *duties,* but also certain *rights.*

Many so-called educational measures, however, have their basis in the fact that the parents, at the end of their wits, do not know what else to do.

In the chapter "To Spank or Not To Spank" in *New Ways in Discipline,* Dorothy Baruch tells of the father who assured her: "Nothing is so good as an occasional good old-fashioned spanking." "You think that spanking is necessary?" she asked. "Certainly! It is a necessary evil. I don't know anything better."

Many adults are at their wit's end because they do not know how to approach their children and how to talk to them. Furthermore, parents and teachers seldom think about the reasons for, and the ultimate goals of, the measures they take. Much is forbidden and much ordered merely to achieve something for the moment. Other measures rest on attitudes that come from other authorities or from traditions.

Denny's father (Denny is the seventeen-year-old discussed in Chapter 6) told the author: "I yell at my son exactly the way my father used to yell at me. Just the other day, when my wife reproached me for being as strict with Denny as my father used to be with me, I explained to her that his spankings had done me quite a lot of good. Just imagine that! Actually, I used to hate my father for the lack of understanding he showed when he was bringing me up."

It is obvious that his upbringing had been unfortunate for this man and that he had made a rather poor adaptation to life.

The lack of inner *equanimity and maturity in educators* is a further reason why the course of the disciplining process is often a troubled and unhappy one.

Jean Walker MacFarlane, who directed a comprehensive longitudinal study at the University of California at Berkeley of average families over a number of years, found that parents whose marriages are not happy or who do not agree on how to bring up their children have the greatest number of "difficult" children.

There are still other problems, such as the jealousy a child feels when a new baby is born into the family. More than 80 percent of children in the United States have sisters and brothers, and there is a tendency to have large families.

Jealousy between siblings (sibling rivalry) is normal, particularly among very young children. If the firstborn is four years old before another baby is born there is less jealousy of the newcomer. When there is less age difference—and this is more frequently the case—the older child needs much love and attention to counteract his jealousy.

The fact, first observed by Alfred Adler, that the child's *position in the family* carries with it psychological advantages and disadvantages was for a time denied, but it has since been confirmed by many careful studies. Generally, the older children in a family are insecure and lacking in self-confidence; they form a high percentage of the children whose parents seek educational counseling. On the other hand, the older children in the family are often the models for the younger children, and often they have responsibilities for the younger ones. The younger children are, in general, more self-aware and decidedly better adjusted than the older ones. Middle children—neither the oldest nor the youngest—tend toward sociability and are more easily influenced; they are less secure than the younger children.

Nothing definite is yet known about the effect of family size, that is, the number of children, on upbringing.

The Fels Institute has probably proceeded further than any other investigators in understanding the *total atmosphere in a family* in its quantitative effect. An example of parental behavior in a family with a cordial atmosphere and a nonauthoritarian attitude ("a warm, democratic home") is given below.

The most prevalent behavior is *acceptance*. The child plays a central, not a subsidiary, role, for he is loved; the relations between parents and child are close and intensive. There is a tendency to help; the child receives a great deal of stimulation. His intellectual development is furthered. Understanding of the child is above average; he is always given explanations.

However, there is a certain tendency to be too protective. The discipline—the demands that are made on the child and the punishments meted out—is gentle; the child is relatively free and has a less than average number of rules and regulations to obey. These are not given haphazardly but are considered carefully. The attitude of the parents is not dictatorial; they discuss things "democratically" with the child. Between the parents there are fewer disagreements than average in matters of discipline.

The family "policy"—the principles according to which the family regulates the various interrelationships within it—is successful. There is harmony, agreement in everything that is done, and the measures taken are clearly thought through. The contacts within the family are many; the family members are together a good deal.

While in studies like those of the Fels Institute the *behavioral structure* of the family group in its mutual conditioning is the principal consideration, investigators that are more clinically oriented are concerned mainly with the *motivational structure* of the group. Psychoanalytically oriented research pertaining to education for socialization concerns itself primarily with the *individuals* and their interrelations with one another.

From the psychoanalytic viewpoint, healthy personality development consists of the following progression. The baby, born "amoral" and fully at the mercy of his drives, gradually overcomes this exclusively instinctual existence and adapts himself to reality and to the demands of his social environment. This ego adjustment to reality is especially emphasized today. Ego strengthening and lessening of anxiety are important educational goals. The problem of finding and pursuing the right life values is less important than the problem of the dynamics of the relationships out of which a healthy ego can emerge.

However, a clear and comprehensive picture of how education should proceed is gained neither from these nor from other studies of parent-child relationships. Whatever advice we are able to give is tentative and fragmentary.

School Education and Psychology

Anyone who has lived for any length of time in more than one country of Western culture must have noticed that both the theory and the practice of education show decided differences. This is true of education in the home and, to an even greater degree, education in school.

In the various sorts of home education, the main difference is that *strictness* and *authority* are generally accorded great importance in European countries, whereas in the United States children are brought up *permissively* and with greater freedom. It is important to recognize that these two different *foundations for moral development* create completely different foundations for education in school.

Education based on strictness and authority emphasizes *propriety* and *duty,* instilled through orders and prohibitions, rewards and punishment. It is based on *drilling,* as against learning by *insight*.

Education based on permissiveness and freedom does not develop a concept of duty based on authority. Instead, it works with an appeal—based on an *explanation of duties and rights* in early childhood—to the child's understanding and judgment. This means that, in place of obedience, the capacity for making one's own decisions is furthered from an early age. In place of commands there is guidance toward social perceptiveness. This difficult method naturally is not handled everywhere with the same skill, and as a result a good many failures occur.

A second factor contributing to differences in home education is the less authoritative position of the American father as compared to his European counterpart. In the American family the wife often seems to play the dominant role; she is the one who has the say in the education of the children. However, this might be more of an impression than a fact.

Robert Sears and his co-workers, who made empirical studies of educational methods in the family, found that in the majority of cases (62 percent in the middle class, 59 percent among blue-collar workers) family authority is equally divided between the two parents. If, however, one of the parents is dominant, it is more often the father (29 percent in the middle class, 25 percent among blue-collar workers) than the mother (9 percent in the middle class, 16 percent among blue-collar workers). The author does not know of any European figures that might be used as a comparison.

Much more significant than these differences in education in the home are the differences in the theory and practice of education in school. These differences become clearest when we compare the classic German school education with the typical American school education; other European countries occupy positions midway between the two systems. The main goal of the German upper schools is an *academic* one, while that of American schools is *social*.

In other words, the German school stresses *learning goals*. The personality of the child and his adaptation to the group are considered primarily in the light of his success in learning and his maintenance of order and discipline. The child's interest in learning and a good class spirit are also important. The American school, on the other hand, makes use of the learning situation to train the child for membership in groups and for *social responsibility*. Therefore, the student's social position and role in his class are considered as important as his academic performance. From the first grade the child is assigned roles in which he learns to consider himself a member of the group, to take on responsibility, and to develop independent judgments. Insofar as possible, these roles are not given only to a few leaders; through the skillful assigning of duties, every child is placed in a position to establish his independence.

The idea is impressed on the American child at an early age that, if need be, he must be able to master a situation and assume leadership. The same is stressed in American military training—anyone who happens to be at hand must be able to assume leadership if the officer in charge is killed.

In school the American child is introduced into the *dynamics of social interaction*. The development of a sense of belonging to the class group is not left to the individual as it is in German schools. Rather, he gets drawn in as a member from being constantly called upon to perform various functions. He learns to stand on his own feet and not to hold others responsible for his behavior or to rely on authorities. Since table manners and polite behavior are also taught, this system of education helps make up for any cultural deprivation in the home. Finally, everybody has access to some form of higher education. The result of this education is a society in which everybody is brought to a certain average, and relatively high, level of knowledge.

Academic training in American schools is often neglected, but this is changing. In general, the transmittal of knowledge is less thorough than in German schools, and the average American, although he is informed about a great many more things than the average German, often lacks depth and completeness in his knowledge.

These shortcomings have been recognized, and educators are attempting to place more emphasis on academic training. They still try to further social education, but not at the expense of knowledge. In other words, they are trying to combine the advantages of both systems and thereby develop a perfect school.

A further difference concerns *teacher-pupil relationships.* Where the relationship of the teacher to the student is considered decisive, the effects that individual teachers have on various student types are important. Authority, example, capacity to arouse interest, and other personal qualities play a large part.

A German study reports that 40 percent of the ten- to thirteen-year-olds (among older pupils the percentages are even greater) would like to have a personal relationship with their teacher.

If, however, the teacher is occupied mainly with the learning process and with goal settings on the part of his students, then personal reactions and effects become secondary and the teacher is of less personal importance to a child.

In general, it can be said that among American school children, particularly adolescents, adults play a lesser role than they do in the corresponding German age groups. To the German child, it is important to be *praised* by adults; to the American child it is important to be *accepted,* particularly by his own age group.

Orientation toward one's own age group appears to the author to represent a greater maturity than *orientation toward elders and superiors.* However, the striving for *popularity,* which comes to the fore in the first system, narrows the freedom of personal development more than does *domination* by authority. Popularity can become such a fetish that it becomes more influential than performance.

Incidentally, in central Europe, particularly among lower-class German youth, there is a shifting toward American conditions.

In a movement that reaches far beyond the alternatives of either more academic or more social education, new problems have recently presented themselves. These concern the contribution of education to the education of the human being as a whole. Actually this is an age-old question, which educators in the East and West have aired repeatedly. In *Education and the Idea of Mankind,* R. Ulich collected the ideas of leading experts on this problem of what education can realistically do to help man's moral progress.

The problem has become an acute one in view of the apparent breakdown of many strongholds of our civilization. Tradition, authority, the "establishment" of church, state, and other institutions, are being doubted and attacked. The younger generation especially is in a mood of rebellion against the existing order. Different from previous rebels, the young people of our time appear motivated to express what they don't want more than what they do want. As one of their spokesmen, Daniel Cohn-Bendit, pointed out to Jean-Paul Sartre in an interview, they intentionally avoid pinning themselves down regarding their aims, so that their opponents cannot build a barrier against them. "The only way the movement can flourish is through this disorder which allows people to speak freely and will later result in some form of self-organization."

On the other hand, many educators and psychotherapists with educational interests have positive and constructive ideas about a possible restructuring of human relationships from childhood on. One idea is to introduce *sensitivity training* (a process described in Chapter 7) into the school system, and to train teachers as well as parents in this method of mutual understanding and self-understanding. This new program, on which educational leaders in different parts of the country are working, is still experimental, but it is hoped it will bring about far-reaching changes in human relationships.

As this brief presentation shows, the psychological understanding of educational processes is far from complete. Much more detailed and precise is our psychological knowledge of instruction, learning and teaching, intelligence and talent, school performance, vocational aptitudes, and vocational counseling. As it is impossible to do justice here to the tremendous number of known facts, let us choose two themes that would seem to be of special general interest: first, the *learning performance* from the psychological point of view; second, *counseling and aptitude.*

Psychological Understanding and Evaluation of Performance

While basic knowledge, customs, and manners of a culture are acquired in the home and in the street, it is at school that they are systematically laid down and developed. The school is therefore generally and rightfully looked upon as the most important instrument for the education of the individual as well as for the preservation and continuation of the culture.

The close connection between intellectual knowledge and mastery over man and nature is increasingly recognized. The resulting importance of science leads to the school's becoming increasingly the subject, if not the football, of politics. For the "man in the street," however, who occupies himself with politics only leisurely, knowledge means simply graduation from school and college, admission to a profession, and the road to higher income and living standards. Beyond such a pragmatic view, there is also a natural thirst for knowledge. To the psychologist, the most important role of education is to bring human potentialities to their full development and to an effectiveness that furthers both the individual and society.

For the above-mentioned pragmatic reason as well as for ideal ones, *intellectual performance and intellectual progress* are essential for a nation to participate in what is going on in the world.

Educational psychology does not deal, as it ought to, with learning in the sense of a world orientation and world knowledge. Instead, it moves within the narrow framework of the so-called educational situation, primarily in *school instruction.*

Following the national policy of education for everyone, schools in the United States—at least the more up-to-date ones—attempt to match a child's education with his particular skill or talent. The goal of such specialized education is to enable each child to realize his intellectual potential to its fullest degree.

The *retarded* child is a special educational problem. At one time he was simply left back year after year, with the difference between his age and that of his classmates becoming greater and greater, until he was old enough to be released from school. Today there are special classes for these youngsters: classes for those called the educable retarded and the trainable retarded, with the curriculum geared to the abilities of the child.

At the other extreme are the *gifted,* or high I.Q., children. These children are not adequately challenged by the ordinary school program. They may be grouped together and given an entirely different program of study, sometimes telescoping two years of work into one and sometimes studying subjects in far greater depth.

Another group of children who have long been misunderstood and looked upon as either of low intelligence or as behavior problems are those who have *brain dysfunctions* as the result of impairment of the central nervous system. Such a condition is manifested by a variety of signs and symptoms, such as difficulty in learning to read and behavioral irregularities (hyperactivity or poor impulse control). Such neurologically handicapped children are now put into special classes. Children with more obvious neurological problems, such as cerebral palsy, are also included in such a school setting. Here, special teaching techniques help overcome the neurological handicap and enable the child to use what may be his normal, or even superior, intelligence.

In the more progressive school systems, children who are unable to function in the regular classroom because of severe *emotional problems* are transferred to "special adjustment" classes. The classes are small, and the teacher is trained to deal with emotional crises.

Educational handicaps that result from an impoverished cultural background are also coming to the attention of educators. Special approaches to teaching the "culturally deprived" child are being used in some communities with the goal not only of helping the children make up for their lack of intellectual nourishment, but of motivating them toward learning and education. The best known and most successful is the Head Start program, in which volunteer workers teach young children from underprivileged homes.

Such comprehensive programs designed to meet the needs of all children are still in the utopian stage in some communities, but others have made good starts in all these areas. The resources are never enough to meet all the needs, but at least the problems have been defined and solutions to them are being developed.

In trying to clarify what we can learn from psychological research, one subject stands out. This is the study of *performance,* both in school and in later life. Performance presupposes *maturity* for taking on and completing a task that can be irksome and strenuous. However, for the child of five or six, the task must have the attribute of *interest,* which stimulates a certain tension in the intellectual participation that is conducive to creative performance. A healthy child of this age likes to learn and to accomplish something.

Readiness for performing tasks, which is one of the main criteria of *school readiness,* does not, as was formerly believed, appear automatically at the same time as intellectual maturity or learning ability. From the standpoint of learning ability alone, four-year-olds and even younger children can often be taught to read, and in former days were encouraged to do so. Today we know that learning with understanding, interest, and willingness to perform this task is preferable to impressing knowledge on a young child mechanically. To perform properly, a person needs not only intellectual but also emotional maturity.

School readiness, as defined by general and specific factors, seems least dependent on physical readiness. It is, however, significantly related to the age at school entrance and to the home background. The parents' attitudes toward school and their own education are of the greatest influence. Other relevant factors are sex, since girls show a significantly greater school readiness than boys. Mental and somatic defects are most frequently found in pupils of the lowest level of school readiness. Previous kindergarten attendance correlates highly with school readiness, mainly in terms of social adjustment.

The *school readiness test* is the first of a long series of tests and other procedures with which—from the beginning of school to the beginning of a vocation—the performance of individuals and groups are studied and evaluated.

A test is a standardized method of measuring; that is, it is a procedure by which behavior can be *quantitatively* compared with a given standard. This standard is based on the behavior of a large, statistically representative group. The result obtained by the test is objective.

Suppose we say that all eight-year-old school children know the similarities and differences between a ball and an orange and between an airplane and a paper dragon, or that two thirds of all two-year-olds can identify a cup and a thimble in pictures. These are objective results that lead to objective evaluations of performance. A test that comprises a sufficiently large number of standardized tasks for measuring any sort of performance results in a comprehensive and objective picture of performance in the particular field being tested.

Why do we need all this? Why aren't the report cards and the examinations of former times good enough any longer? Why don't we rely on the judgment of experienced teachers or other examiners?

Aside from the fact that not every teacher is experienced and that not everyone who gives a test is objective, standardized procedures provide a more reliable basis for appropriate introduction into the school and for vocational choice. This is an age of both increasing population and increasing specialization in occupational fields. The cost of training for many jobs is high, and there is increasing competition among those seeking apprenticeships and positions. For all these reasons it has become necessary to determine a person's capacities and suitability for a job as early and as precisely as possible.

The value of tests does not lie exclusively in the fact that they serve *the selective process;* they also provide information for the further *educational treatment* of the individual.

This was the twofold purpose of the French psychologist Alfred Binet. In 1904 the Ministry of Education in Paris assigned a committee to study ways of bringing up retarded children. The immediate problems were how to select these children at an early age and how to give them the proper education.

In the following year Binet, with his colleague Theodore Simon, composed and published the first *intelligence test*. The purpose was to determine, through standardized assignments, if a child was able to solve the thinking and learning problems appropriate for his age. Binet's assumption—that with increasing age there is a corresponding increase in memory and thinking capacity—was proved to be correct for the age groups he investigated.

The question of the increase of intelligence was much discussed at the time. Edward Thorndike was the first to set up a growth curve of intelligence (1926), which showed that the average person reaches the high point of his intelligence at about sixteen years of age. This sounds absurd if not interpreted correctly. What it means is that at this point one's mechanical *memory* has reached its climax and that the *capacity to think* is fully developed. If after this period people build up a tremendous body of knowledge, they do so by means of a variety of intellectual functions, which have been at their disposal since puberty.

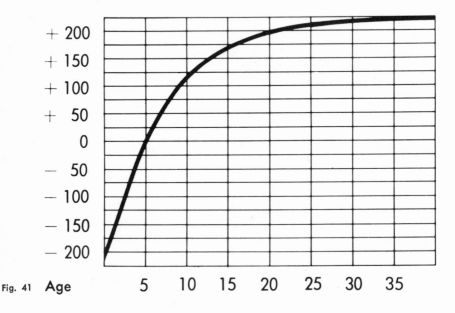

Fig. 41 **Age**   5   10   15   20   25   30   35

Changes in intelligence with age, as shown by three studies: Miles and Miles, 1932; Jones and Conrad, 1933; Wechsler, 1944 (from Pennington and Berg, eds., *An Introduction to Clinical Psychology*, New York: Ronald, 1948, by permission of the publisher).

Henry Goddard was the first to adapt the Binet-Simon method for testing mentally retarded children in the United States. Somewhat later, Stern and Kuhlmann developed the view that the tests could also be used for determining *intellectual precocity* and *late maturity*. This thought was picked up by Lewis Terman, who in 1916 published the well-known *Stanford Revision of the Binet-Simon Tests*. He improved the test series, standardized them by administering them to an extraordinarily large number of people, and added to the method of finding of *mental age* a technique for determining *intelligence quotient* (I.Q.)

The I.Q. is a quotient by which the relationship of *mental age* to *chronological age* is expressed. A subject's mental age is determined by the chronological age at which the statistically average child scores the same as the subject does. The I.Q. in normal intelligence is equal to 1 (since the relation of mental age to chronological age equals 1); in above-average subjects it is more than 1, in under-average subjects less than 1. The intelligence quotient is expressed in values; 100 means normal intelligence; superior intelligences reach values over 120; mental retardation corresponds to an I.Q. of between 50 and 75.

With this new technique an admirable instrument was created. Today we can no longer exclude tests from our educational programs, to say nothing of their clinical use, even though it is generally admitted that interpretation of test results must be made with care. By this we mean that there must be a recognition of those factors that cannot be thought of in purely quantitative terms. Among these are the level of maturity, the motivational structure of the personality, and physical, emotional, and environmental conditions.

These factors, the evaluation of which requires *clinical techniques,* are today considered as important as the quantitative test results. In the United States there has been a lessening of interest in test results as such and an increasing interest in clinical studies incorporating the test results. However, in evaluating school performances, tests are indispensable.

Among the most important test procedures are *maturity tests, intelligence tests, performance tests, tests for special gifts and talents,* and *adaptability tests.*

The difference between intelligence tests and maturity tests lies in the fact that the former aims at determining learning and thinking performance while the latter tests *behavior* with respect to its *appropriateness for a particular age.*

For example, in a maturity test in the Bühler-Hetzer Infant Test Series a four-year-old is expected to complete the task of building a three-dimensional structure, and in a test in Arnold Gesell's series a baby of nine months is expected to hold his bottle by himself.

Infants' maturity tests are frequently criticized as unreliable. To administer them adequately, the investigator should have a good deal of experience with infants and should combine careful observation of behavior with the quantitative procedure.

An example of a valid test result is the case of Sven, whom an American couple was eager to adopt. Sven was already eleven months old, beyond the age at which American adoption agencies generally like to give a child to new parents.

Sven, however, was so harmoniously developed in all respects that those in charge prophesied a good adaptation to his new life. It was recommended that the adoptive parents spend a great deal of time with him, for he was somewhat shy; it was apparent that up to this point not enough attention had been given him. Physically, Sven was unusually skillful; he showed very good coordination in handling his toys.

Sven's adoptive parents devoted themselves to him with a great deal of love and understanding. Once a year they report the progress of Sven's development. In all respects, Sven continues to do exceptionally well. He is good at sports, does well in school, and has a great many interests. He plays a number of musical instruments, among them the saxophone, the oboe, and the guitar. He raises chickens and pigeons, a lamb, a cat, a dog, and turtles, in addition to two horses that he is particularly fond of. He also has two snakes, because he thinks he may want to become a research scientist working with reptiles. He is very popular among his peers and has a warm, close relationship with his parents.

Psychology in Vocational Guidance

The first vocational guidance center was established in 1909 in New York at the suggestion of Frank Parsons, who saw vocational guidance as a problem that could be approached scientifically.

Despite this early understanding of the significance of vocational counseling, there is still no unanimous and comprehensive theory incorporating psychology into the process of choosing a vocation.

Instead, the procedure used in most vocational guidance systems is purely pragmatic. Vocational guidance counselors simply try to match the character, aptitudes, and interests of the individual with the demands that a particular job will make. In addition, there is practical counseling, which deals with the kind of employment available on the labor market.

Beginning early in this century, vocational guidance was the earliest systematically developed form of counseling. In *Principles and Techniques for Guidance,* Lefever, Turrell, and Weitzel report that at the beginning "counseling" and "guidance" were synonymous with "vocational guidance." Although today vocational guidance is but one among many forms of counseling, it maintains an important and special place alongside family, marriage, geriatric, and educational counseling. Below are several points that must be borne in mind when examining the field of vocational guidance.

1. The criteria by which *vocational maturity, vocational aptitude,* and chances for *vocational success* are judged differ not only in various countries and educational systems, but also with individual research workers and officials. There is still no unanimity in this respect.

2. Most counselors consider four principal factors as the basis for diagnosis in the choice of a vocation: *performance, interests, character,* and *personality.* General *maturity* and *attitude toward life* must also be taken into consideration.

3. No sensible counselor will fail to pay attention to the demonstrated *performance* and *abilities* of an applicant. But if he makes them the only, or even the most important, criteria he will often be disappointed. Every clinician sees countless cases in which people who were capable and talented in school and later training, and who scored high on their aptitude tests, failed in their careers.

E. L. Thorndike and E. Hagen made a broad, comprehensive group study of more than 10,000 employees in the American aviation industry to investigate the connection between performance ability and *vocational success.* The group had been selected as statistically representative of a much larger group of 75,000 persons.

These men, who were between the ages of nineteen and twenty-one when they took the test, were examined twenty years later as to their vocational success. The results showed that tests of ability to perform, even when they were substantiated by certain biographical data, proved invalid as a basis for prediction of eventual vocational success. From this the authors drew the conclusion that predictions of vocational success on the basis of performance tests are to be viewed with great skepticism.

4. *Investigations of interests* are today generally regarded as important in vocational guidance. The measurement of interests, however, can no more be considered the sole basis for vocational guidance than can performance tests and aptitude tests.

5. Over and beyond these specialized investigations an *understanding of the whole person* is of great importance. Three different procedures are used.

The first procedure tries to understand the person as a whole by investigating his *character.* Franziska Baumgarten's well-known work, *Character Testing in Vocational Guidance,* reports on this approach. Character tests used to be recommended by those who wanted to know the moral qualities (in the narrow sense of the term) of a prospective employee.

As was shown in Chapter 4, those who are skeptical about our ability to understand character and who are not inclined to consider character as definite prefer the second procedure, *personality studies.* In these, depth-analysis methods (which will be discussed in the next chapter) are primarily used. Personality descriptions are more concerned with statements about maturity, self-control, goal-directedness, emotionality, and the like than with moral values, about which we still do not know enough.

The third method for understanding the whole person is generally considered the most promising. This is the procedure worked out by Donald Super and his co-workers at Columbia University. Super attempts to determine vocational maturity and vocational aptitude in the broader framework of a *theory of vocational behavior* and of the *life maturity* of an individual.

As the theoretical basis for his studies, Super selected the author's theory of life phases, the applicability of which had already been shown by Paul Lazarsfeld. In this theory, which was discussed in Chapter 5, life is divided into various phases of *self-determination.* The preliminary stages toward self-determination in childhood and adolescence normally progress to a definitive, realistic phase of self-determination in the adult. The next period of critical evaluation of the results of life, in which the individual tries to correct failures and to reach his goals, is sooner or later followed by a period of deterioration.

In addition to these phases of self-determination, Super considers many further factors, including performance ability, interests, personality, and vocational demands. The results of the comprehensive tests undertaken by him are presented in "maturity profiles." Of the nineteen factors studied (they turned out to be relatively independent of one another) the highest correlation with vocational maturity is the ability to *plan* a career realistically after procuring adequate *information* and with a serious *interest* in the choice as well as with a *sense of responsibility* for this. Interest, information, plans, and responsibility are especially undeveloped in vocationally immature adolescents.

Super's researches bode well for the vocational guidance of the future, for, instead of working only with isolated abilities, performances, or other individual qualities, he sees the development, success, and satisfaction of a vocation as part of life performance and life development.

CHAPTER II

THE HELPING PROFESSIONS

The Helping Professions Today

"Helping profession" is an expression used in the United States to describe three vocations, *social work, psychology,* and *psychiatry.* Social workers, psychologists, and psychiatrists frequently work together as a team in educational guidance as well as in other guidance centers and clinics. There is no longer a strictly defined line between the social worker's comprehension of a case in its social and economic aspects, the psychologist's psychodiagnostic view, and, the psychiatrist's view toward possible mental disturbance that may require psychotherapy. And there is no longer a strict separation of functions. Of course, the social worker is still the specialist in the examination and possible welfare guidance to improve an individual's social and economic conditions. The psychologist is the specialist in psychodiagnosis. The psychiatrist is the specialist in the treatment of mental illnesses and brain diseases. Many cases require the services of all three professions.

Of the enormous number of tasks facing psychology in the helping professions, we will discuss only its role in *guidance, diagnosis,* and *therapy.* Countless men and women are disturbed and anxiety ridden because of their *life problems.* These are the people who go to pieces because they cannot cope with their tasks as parents or marriage partners or with the demands of their vocations. They are the people whose sexuality, handicaps, or unfortunate relationships with other people drive them into emotional breakdowns, psychosomatic illnesses, alcoholism, misuse of pills, drug addiction, and crime. Today there are *guidance clinics* where professional helpers are prepared to look after the welfare, diagnostic, therapeutic, clinical, and other aspects of their problems. This great mass of

261

human beings is increasingly seeking professional help. Added to these life problems are still other conditions of our times which cause an increasing number of persons to find their way to counselors and therapists.

A great many people are asking: Why do we suddenly need this counseling and psychotherapy? Has not mankind up to now found its way through life without these aids?

To begin with the second question, the answer is that at no time has mankind found its way without help. Jerome D. Frank showed in *Persuasion and Healing* the connections of earlier and recent approaches to mental healing. From time immemorial and in all cultures men have sought and procured spiritual helpers. In primitive cultures these helpers combine the functions of magician, healer, soothsayer, and priest. They were particularly esteemed because of their ability to help physical, mental, and spiritual difficulties. In more advanced cultures, the functions of physician and mental healer are separate. With increasing specialization and advances in mental healing, the treatment of mental disturbances has been differentiated from spiritual care in the religious sense. Of course, spiritual care and mental care often go hand in hand. In many places religious counseling is conducted simultaneously with psychotherapeutic care.

Now we must discover why the need for this kind of help has grown so extraordinarily, and why it continues to grow. Why also do many of those people who formerly solved their problems by themselves now seek the help of counselors or psychotherapists?

Various answers can be given. First, a great many psychiatrists and psychologists point out that the increasing mechanization of the world makes enormous demands on man's psychic apparatus. In a famous address, the atomic scientist Robert Oppenheimer discussed the inconceivable speed at which man's scientific knowledge and technical mastery of the world has progressed and emphasized how vital it is that spiritual and social mastery keep pace.

Understanding all these tremendous and far-reaching innovations, and learning to live compatibly with them, places an extreme demand on human beings. This is an age when young children use the telephone, are taken along to movies where they don't belong, turn on the television and see pictures flashing madly before their eyes, and go rushing around the world in trains, automobiles, and airplanes. The accelerated pace of today's world requires extraordinary adaptability, psychic as well as mental.

How can man master his psychic life and his relations with his fellows to the same tremendous degree that technical power has developed? The tension that results from the existing discrepancy, under which we all live, increases the *anxiety feelings* suffered by so many.

A second point is the extraordinary *insecurity* of man's existence today.

Millions of people have been uprooted and have had to begin a new life in a completely new situation. The earlier continuity of life security, which is so significant for childhood development and therefore for the way people turn out, has been lost. Lost, too, is the faith that there can be any such thing as "security" in this world. This enormous skepticism seems particularly tragic when voiced by the young, who in other times were bold and daring, adventurous and full of high hopes.

While talking with a therapy group of sixteen- to nineteen-year-olds, the author found it extremely depressing to hear security proclaimed as the principal life goal. Most of the six boys and girls came from well-to-do, highly respected families; all had the opportunity to go to college at their parents' expense. Yet the majority agreed that security was the only goal they earnestly sought.

But are increased pressure, anxiety, and insecurity the real reasons why an increasing number of people go to advisers and therapists? The author does not think so. We must not forget that we all have internal regulators that can help make us flexible. Our capacity for adaptation is probably equal to the complications we create for ourselves.

No, it is not increasing complications and rising insecurity that drive people into psychotherapy. Human beings have always been insecure in one way or another. These objective difficulties in and of themselves seldom cause people to make the important and frequently difficult decision to enter therapy.

Is it perhaps that the favorable experiences friends and acquaintances have had with therapy win new converts to this type of help? It seems certain that the dissemination of these experiences does play a role. Undoubtedly many new cases can be explained by the fact that psychotherapy is increasingly being recognized as the most adequate method for solving life problems.

But this alone does not seem sufficient to explain the widespread reliance on psychotherapy. Perhaps the most important reason lies elsewhere. A concrete example may explain this.

Let us recall Victor, whose vocational and marriage problems were discussed in Chapter 2. Victor's life problems were not so insurmountable that this intelligent and basically mentally healthy man could not have solved them by himself. It was not the difficulty of his problem as such that brought him into counseling. Rather, it was his quest for the "right" solution for him—"right" not in the sense of "good" or "bad" but in the sense of the most adequate life for him in his particular circumstances.

The question of what makes life adequate in the sense of fulfillment of one's potentialities, in the sense of one's "destiny," touches upon the meaning of human existence.

The anxiety that arises out of the feeling of "having been hurled into life," which first Kierkegaard and later Heidegger called the "existential anxiety," and the consciousness of in some way being guilty and of having missed doing the right thing strike a responsive chord in many people. In a calm, sober person like Victor, they take the form of a feeling of uneasiness; in others they deepen into a wail of despair that no one seems to hear or heed.

People have always sought to give meaning to their existence; today they seek more adequate reasons than those offered by past authorities and traditions. What are the really true values of human existence? It is not mere chance that existentialism arose out of the ruins of a culture that has been destroyed?

But why should it be the psychologist and the psychiatrist who teach mankind the values of life? The answer is, they do not teach them; they light the way for men by making them capable of seeing themselves as they are and of thinking through their life problems in an objective way, without being led astray by love and hate, by prejudices and authorities. Thereby they restore the inner freedom that had been lost in emotional entanglements and point out the ways of using that freedom for a meaningful determination of what one's life should be. This is what draws men to the psychologist in increasing anticipation and hope, even though they are not always aware of the reason.

Clinical History Taking

Clinical history taking and diagnostic proceedings are part of the preliminary work in psychotherapy. Here our presentation will assume that the particular case being considered has had a recent medical examination and that the psychologist is aware of the findings.

Everything necessary for proper and successful psychological treatment goes into the clinical-psychological history taking. According to the particular problem and to the means at one's disposal, the history taking may be comprehensive or limited.

Even the most limited history includes the determination of the complaints. The life history is practically always ascertained; this is called the "anamnesis" and may be more or less thorough.

In hospitals, more frequently than in private practice, it is often customary to have a social worker investigate the life history of the individual and his family, for knowledge of the socioeconomic and cultural background of a case is essential to the psychiatrist.

A volume edited by Roy Grinker shows the new development of the psychiatric social worker, who is trained to take part in the psychotherapy or even, under supervision, to perform it himself. Social workers today are therefore, like psychologists and psychiatrists, active both in counseling and in treatment.

Diagnostic Problems and Procedures

A diagnosis is the identification of an illness made on the basis of its symptoms and the determinations as to its origin and course. A diagnosis usually appears in the form of a classification, in which the illness is identified by a definite name. Earlier reference was made, for example, to the word "schizophrenia," which is used to designate a specific type of mental illness.

Signs of a Healthy Personality

Diagnostic problems arise as soon as we enter that border territory populated by people with life problems. Many of these people are indignant if they are designated "neurotic" or "sick." One psychiatrist, Thomas Szasz, has actively maintained that people who have life problems should not be called "sick." Yet these people are not really healthy.

Just what is "sick"? Mental illness can be defined, but to define mental health is much more difficult. For a long while it was thought that health was simply the absence of sickness. It was finally recognized that mental health would have to be defined by means of its own positive signs.

Among the various studies that have taken up the question of the definition of mental health, the best known is that of Marie Jahoda. She concludes that a great number of different criteria have to be taken into consideration and that there are primarily six indications emphasized by various authors, as follows:

1. The mentally healthy person has an adequate attitude toward himself. He sees himself realistically the way he is; he can look at himself critically without losing self-esteem.

2. He is interested in his adequate internal development and self-realization. He wants to bring out his best potentialities.

3. He makes an effort to achieve internal unity or integration of his strivings. He does not allow himself to be worried by strivings that are irreconcilable, but makes an attempt to solve his inner conflicts.

4. He is autonomous; he makes his own decisions and does not depend on other people.

5. He has an adequate perception of reality; he does not allow himself to be influenced by wishes and fears in his grasp of the external world.

6. He is capable of coping with the circumstances of his life. This includes the capacity to love, adequacy in love, work and play, adequacy in interpersonal relationships, the ability to handle the demands of given situations, the ability to adapt, and competence in solving problems.

To these main criteria we must add another, which is of great importance to psychotherapy—the capacity of the healthy person to look at his life in its continuity. The neurotic more or less forgets whole sections of his life.

Now, how does the diagnostic understanding of mental health and mental illness proceed?

Diagnostic Procedure

Like the history taking, the diagnostic examination can be more or less comprehensive. It may be limited to obtaining information by interviews, or it may include tests and systematic observations.

After the detailed history taking, physiological and psychological tests are given. In addition to tests that are quantitatively and qualitatively evaluated, children are studied in a free-play situation.

The diagnosis then follows in two stages: descriptive and classificatory. In the descriptive part, the procedure follows certain generally determined steps. On the basis of statements concerning the general impression that the subject makes, detailed findings are assembled on bodily functions and habits, on movements, emotions, perception of the environment, on his thinking, speech, fantasy, self-conception, and on his relationships to people and to his physical environment.

The classificatory diagnosis distinguishes between psychogenic disturbances, that is, those that are psychically caused, mental retardation, and so-called organically conditioned behavior disturbances that can be traced to diseases of the brain and nervous system.

Today, psychodiagnostic tests are used almost everywhere, and the psychologist is the appropriate professional to make them. The tests consist of problems, and the way in which a person approaches and solves them sheds light on his mental and psychic life. Only standardized series of problems are used, that is, only those that have been tested in a representative group and have been made statistically dependable.

The understanding of the personality, which is the primary concern of psychological diagnosis, can proceed by means of verbal and nonverbal methods.

Verbal Tests

Questionnaires and other questioning techniques are a part of the verbal method of gaining information about the test subject or patient. The verbal test most widely used in the United States is the Minnesota Multiphasic Inventory, developed by Starke Hathaway and J. C. McKinley. It consists of 566 questions which are to be checked True or False. Examples are:

I have a good appetite.	True	False
I am sure I got a raw deal from life.	True	False
A large number of people are guilty of bad sexual conduct.	True	False
I have nightmares every few nights.	True	False

The results of this test have been standardized for the diagnosis of various mental diseases that are established on a quantitative basis.

Projective Methods

The nonverbal methods proceed from the belief that the person questioned will naturally strive to hide his weaknesses and that he is not conscious of his deepest strivings. If, as happens in a nonverbal test, the material placed before the test subject causes an unconscious emotional reaction, then the examiner may be able to delve more deeply into the emotional world and true motives of that person. Here we rely on the mechanism called *projection.* This means the patient's reaction to the material presented to him will express what he feels and thinks; he will project this into the material.

As an example of the many excellent projective methods, as these tests are called, a few of the best known will be mentioned.

The Rorschach Test

The most frequently used projective method is the test invented by Hermann Rorschach popularly known as the inkblot test. Ten cards with inkblots on them are shown to the subject with the request that he describe what he sees. This is something like looking at clouds and seeing objects or happenings in them.

Glenn, a young man of twenty-five whose case will be discussed later, gives the following comments on Card No. 2:

1. I see two people who are having an argument while playing a game of clapping hands with each other. They are wearing red hats and long black cloaks of some heavy material.

2. When I turn the card over, I see a dog that has a red sock in his mouth that he is shaking playfully. He is standing in front of a mirror while he does this.

3. Two people are fighting about something they have between them in their hands. It is a symbol of power that they are fighting about. We see them from the back.

4. On the reverse side, a rocket space ship is about to blast off. It is white; behind, the fire comes out.

Anyone not familiar with these tests will ask what in the world we can deduce from such answers. The feelings expressed and the experiences hinted at in the answers can be deciphered only through interpretation. This leads us to an important factor, so fundamental in modern psychology: *interpretation.*

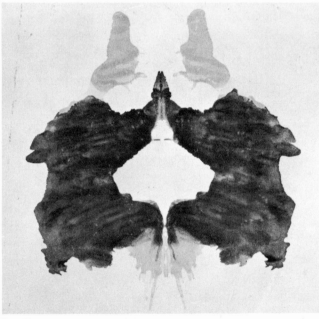

Fig. 42

Card No. 2 of the ten cards of the Rorschach Test. In the original the light parts are red.

As is well known, interpretation means explanation and explication. Interpretations must be applied when something is expressed only indirectly.

Interpretations of conscious concealments are easily understood by everyone, and most people are capable of recognizing intuitions and feelings that are not directly expressed. But interpretation is difficult and not generally understood when *unconscious* material is involved. A considerable knowledge of human psychic life is required. Freud discovered that people often use indirect indications and picture-like concealments when an experience is unacceptable or unbearable to them.

The psychologist must be well trained in the methods of interpreting hidden meanings. Sometimes several interpretations of an experience are possible. This is because human experiences are complex and various things can be asserted about them. Therefore, one interpretation may not be less correct than another; it may merely put forward another aspect or connection of the experience from deeper or shallower layers of the personality.

Two different methods are used in the interpretation of the Rorschach Test. The interpretation of the contents of the answers represents only one, and for many people not the most valuable, part of the evaluation of the test. Interpretation cannot be standardized; it appears different to psychologists of different theoretical orientation.

The author concludes that Glenn has inner conflicts and arguments, in which questions of play and power play a part. This is actually the case, as we shall see.

The Rorschach primarily aids the psychologist in comprehending the patient's personality structure. This results from a quantitative process, by means of which formal aspects of the reactions are determined and assembled. This is the second evaluation technique of the test.

In the quantitative presentation of the so-called Rorschach profile, Glenn appears as a personality in a severe conflict between great frustration and a strong need to adapt to demands made of him. His hypersensitivity and inner insecurity contribute to his anxiety and excessive tension. He has a great deal of fantasy and appears to be a talented person who does not realize his capacities. He thinks in stereotypes and travels in a rut. A strong inner protest against this situation seems to lead to nothing. He is full of aggression and explosiveness, yet accomplishes nothing thereby. He is sexually immature and is perhaps troubled by homosexual tendencies.

All in all, he presents the picture of a personality that is immature and somewhat emotionally disturbed.

The therapy that was undertaken following the diagnostic study proved the correctness of the Rorschach interpretation. The test's usefulness lay in the fact that it provided a quick insight into the type and degree of Glenn's disturbance and prepared the therapist for what was to be expected.

The TAT Test

A second widely used test, which in certain respects supplements the Rorschach, is the Thematic Apperception Test (TAT) created by Henry A. Murray. Here the subject is shown a number of pictures, generally ten or twelve and told to tell a story about them. The ingenuity of this test is that the situations shown in the pictures are subject to various explanations and will therefore be explained by different people in different ways. The subject's explanation reveals his projection. Here is an example:

Fig. 43

One of the pictures from the Thematic Apperception Test. The subject must tell a story about the picture (from H. A. Murray, *TAT Test*).

In the illustration, an older woman and a young man are shown in a situation intimating some sort of tension between them.

One of the most frequent stories told about this card is that of a conflict between a mother and son. Generally the son is conceived of as the bearer of unpleasant news: perhaps he plans to marry a girl his mother does not accept; perhaps he has decided to leave home and take a job overseas.

If the test subject wants to avoid conflict, he sees the son bringing sad news: he must go into the army; he has just learned that his brother has died in a foreign country. In this case there is no conflict between the two, but a common sorrow.

If, however, the subject feels an inner distance between himself and his mother, then he will not see the picture as a mother and son.

That is the way it was with Glenn. He visualizes the bearer of news as a friend of the son's. Added to this distance, a certain cruelty toward the mother is demonstrated when he reports that the friend brings news of the son's death. In this way he unknowingly reveals his hostile attitude toward his mother. Like many children who wish themselves dead in order to see their parents mourning for them, he would enjoy his mother's mourning at his death and her regret for what she has done to him. All these revelations are, naturally, unconscious as far as the subject is concerned.

In the TAT as in the Rorschach, different interpretations are given by different interpreters. Here, too, however, they serve the therapist mainly as signals of what is to be expected.

Whatever the interpretation, the TAT is generally used for an understanding of the relationship of the patient to his family and to himself.

Test Methods for Children

Both projective tests and certain play techniques are used with children. Diagnostic play with dolls or other toys is used in many analytically oriented clinics to interpret emotional happenings and family relationships. The World Game, introduced by Margaret Löwenfeld and standardized by the author with the help of M. van Wylick, G. Kelly, and others as the World Test, consists of miniature real-life objects—houses, trees, fences, people, animals, wagons, and the like—and is frequently used for diagnostic purposes. It helps to reveal the child's feelings about his environment: does he see himself hemmed in by fences (prohibitions); does he see life as chaotic and confusing or as well ordered; does he enjoy many people, or does he avoid people because he is afraid of them; does he conceive of the world as full of dangers; does his world reflect an inner emptiness?

The World Test, developed from the World Game, is used internationally today.

Fig. 44

The dangerous world of a 17-year-old English girl.

Fig. 45

The rich, full world of a 5-year-old Viennese.

Fig. 46

A mentally retarded American boy sees the world lined up in series.

Fig. 47

The rigidly fenced-in world of an American 8-year-old girl.

Fig. 48

The empty world of a 9-year-old English boy.

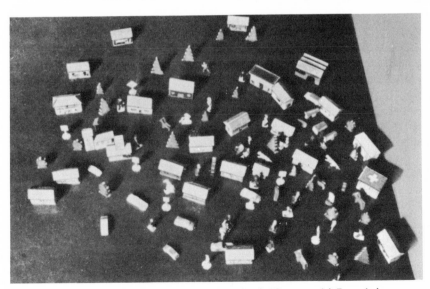

Fig. 49

The chaotic world of a seriously disturbed 13-year-old French boy.

The Test Battery

In the majority of cases, the psychodiagnostic studies made by clinical psychologists rest not on a single test but on a number of tests. The expression used is "test battery." Depending on the subject's problems, a battery may comprise a large number of tests that supplement one another or only two or three tests. Today three tests are generally considered the classical basis of an adequate battery: the Rorschach, the TAT, and the Wechsler Intelligence Test.

The Wechsler Test is the modern intelligence test that has extensively taken the place of the Stanford-Binet Test; it consists of only ten problems and has proved to be productive clinically. The Wechsler Test combines five purely verbal tests with five tests of practical activities. One may thus compare the verbal test results of memory and thinking with practical performances based mainly on perception and motor ability.

This comparison proved to be particularly helpful in cases of partial disturbances of brain functions.

The Wechsler Test has standardized forms for adults and for children and has been found suitable for both America and European countries.

The Differential Diagnosis

With the help of an integrative reworking of the Rorschach, TAT, and Wechsler tests, a differential diagnosis of the patient's illness can be given. Dr. Rogers H. Wright, a psychologist in private practice in Los Angeles, has kindly put an example of such a diagnosis at the author's disposal. This somewhat shortened differential diagnosis deals with the differentiation of organic-neurologically and functional-psychologically conditioned causes of a learning disability.

The patient, S. Y., a young man of twenty-three, went to a psychiatrist because of his marriage problems and his great anxieties and tensions. During the interview, he mentioned that he had a "psychological block" in reading and that since the age of eleven he has been in and out of counselors' and psychotherapists' offices. The psychiatrist considered this strange and sent him to Dr. Wright for a thorough examination.

First, Dr. Wright wanted to determine once and for all just how much the patient was able to read. Full of shame, the serious young man admitted that he could not read at all and that he could write only his name and a few words. Asked how he had been able to get through high school, the patient reported that he had learned by heart everything that was said in the classroom, that friends read their textbooks and notebooks to him, and that, because of his "block," sympathetic teachers gave him oral examinations instead of written work.

Dr. Wright undertook a comprehensive test examination of the patient. The test battery consisted of the Wechsler-Bellevue, the Bender-Gestalt, the House-Tree-Person, and the Rorschach tests.

The intelligence test showed that S. Y. had a high intellectual capacity— an I.Q. of 130—but with great fluctuations.

The patient's performance revealed particularly what K. Goldstein called "concrete thinking," which indicated an incapacity to grasp abstractions. This incapacity is a symptom of certain types of brain damage. The presence of brain damage became clearly recognizable in several tests based on perception differentiations. The patient was aware of this incapacity and often said, "I know that has got to be done, but somehow I can't do it." He solved many problems in a roundabout way by means of peculiar deliberations.

Finally, he showed an unusually great falling off in performance as a result of fatigue.

In the Rorschach Test, all the signs that characteristically point to brain damage appeared with particular clarity.

From the test material as a whole it became apparent that the patient was suffering from an unusual form of organic damage that revealed itself in his incapacity to comprehend symbols such as those used in reading and writing. It was an aphasia-like disturbance, that is, a phenomenon related to organically conditioned speech disturbances.

The patient reacted to his heretofore-undiagnosed defect as if it were an inferiority and had a destructive, contemptuous attitude toward himself. He saw his defect as a hopeless disability. A number of his Rorschach answers indicated that he also doubted his virility and compensated for this by aggressive behavior.

Dr. Wright concluded that the patient should be given complete insight into the nature of his defect and suggested that he take a course in practical perception and the formation of concepts such as those given to children with brain damage. The patient took the course and continued his psychotherapeutic treatment. Thanks to his high intelligence and the help of these new methods, he learned to read and write in a very short time. His acceptance of his defect and the psychotherapy contributed to his greatly improved self-confidence.

Psychological Counseling

Although counseling and therapy cannot be strictly separated, and indeed often merge into each other, there are differences in counseling and in therapeutic procedures, and the same therapist may make use of both.

A clear presentation of the differences can be found in *Therapeutic Psychology* by L. M. Brammer and E. L. Shostrom, two psychologists, one of whom is primarily active in counseling, the other in therapeutic practice.

Brammer and Shostrom emphasize that counseling concerns itself essentially with the conscious problems conditioned by certain life situations that the patient wants to learn how to cope with better. In the process he receives extensive help and emotional support from the counselor.

Therapy, on the other hand—and this holds true regardless of the specific system the therapist uses—is directed at the unconscious conflicts of a person affected by more serious emotional disturbances. Support from the therapist is limited to certain aspects of the case. The main emphasis is on depth therapy, and the goal is the complete or partial restructuring of the personality.

This can be made clear by citing an example.

Mr. and Mrs. Brown came for counseling because they are having trouble with their fourteen-year-old daughter, Jo Anne, the older of two sisters. For the past two years she has been rebellious and difficult to handle. Jo Anne no longer attends to her schoolwork and her duties at home. Instead, she goes out with her girl friends, talks for hours on end on the telephone, or sits in front of the mirror. She is much more interested in having fun than in anything serious. She is "crazy about" two boys who take her to the movies, yet she refuses to go to church with her family because at the moment she is full of doubts. She has almost given up her piano playing; her music teacher is as disappointed about this as her parents.

In a typical case of educational counseling like this, the psychologist will first try to determine just how serious the situation is. Just what is the matter here? Is it one of those difficulties that so frequently develop between parents and children at the beginning of puberty? Are we perhaps witnessing pedantic and duty-oriented parents with a daughter who has suddenly discovered that there are more amusing things to do than wash dishes, iron blouses, and do homework? Has she finally realized that she has a will of her own and doesn't always have to do what is asked of her? Or are there deeper problems at the bottom of this?

When we use the word "deep," we are referring to the motivations and emotions peculiar to certain experiences. Since the time of Freud, we speak of depth layers as those inner realms inaccessible to consciousness in which preconscious and repressed experiences are stored. As already described, experiences are repressed when they are unacceptable and carry with them a sense of guilt too great to be borne.

In the case of the Brown family, "deeper" problems might consist of various things: the parents might not want to admit to themselves that they are making absurdly high demands on their children; or perhaps by their strictness they want to prove their authority or their firm conservative principles. It is possible that the father and the mother have different reasons; perhaps the father is tyrannical and the mother helpless in dealing with her children.

Jo Anne, on the other hand, may have deserted her former amiability for deeper reasons. Perhaps she has been building up resentments, and now she has let them out. Perhaps—as appeared in the counseling—she had always adored her father and gradually developed a strong jealousy of her mother.

It is pretty certain, however, that we are not dealing with extremely deep entanglements such as hatred between children and parents. On the other hand, there appears to be more in the situation than the ordinary puberty difficulties.

Jo Anne told the counselor in the interview that she loves her parents and adores her father, but that both parents have completely old-fashioned ideas and her father tends to be tyrannical to the members of his family, even to his wife. He is vain and always wants to be acknowledged as right and to be admired. Jo Anne says that her mother never did understand her, although she has good intentions. Besides, her mother is somewhat jealous that Jo Anne has so much fun, whereas she herself had a serious and unhappy childhood.

Jo Anne believes that she is no different from her girl friends. In time she would regain her pleasure in doing her work. She explains "the church bit" by saying she doesn't want to be a hypocrite and right now she is unable to believe in anything. Anyway, her father, who made such a fuss the other day when she finally did go to church, fell asleep the minute the sermon began. So she questions how honest his religious devotion is. And as for playing the piano, she hasn't any talent and doesn't want to play. As far as she's concerned, the whole thing's a waste of time.

According to all this, Jo Anne does not seem to hold any deep resentments. But the situation requires further working through in order to give the parents more understanding of her need to express independence at this age. Jo Anne needs to delve more deeply into the reasons for her rebellious behavior and must achieve a better understanding of herself.

The bringing about of self-understanding is one of the main goals of counseling and therapy, and the growing realization of its importance for a satisfactory life has brought ever growing expansion to the profession. Today, in addition to counseling branches already mentioned, there are counseling centers for education, family problems, sex, marriage, and divorce problems, for the problems of the aging, the problems of alcoholics and drug addicts and their families, and many others.

Except for educational counseling, marriage counseling is probably the most widespread. Below is a relatively uncomplicated example taken from a compendium on marriage counseling edited by E. H. Mudd, M. J. Karpf, A. Stone, and F. Nelson for the American Association of Marriage Counselors.

The problem concerns twenty-five-year-old Miss Winston and her thirty-year-old fiancé, Mr. Evans. The young woman was assailed by doubts and anxieties with regard to her marriage, which her fiancé did not want to postpone any longer. Her fears were indefinite; she insisted that they loved each other very much. Nevertheless, the counseling psychologist got the impression that she wanted to see the marriage plans postponed or perhaps even given up.

Her main reasons were that she and her fiancé could not communicate well enough with each other and that she did not want to move away from her family to a big city. Furthermore, she was worried that their sexual relations might not be satisfactory, as neither of them had had any experience.

On the basis of findings obtained in interviews the counselor diagnosed the problem not as a deeply founded neurotic one, but as an acute problem conditioned by the situation. He thought the case could be suitably treated without therapy.

Miss W. and Mr. E. both came from conservative middle-class families and had excellent educations, but both of them had gone to non-coeducational colleges. Therefore they had had less than average experience in associating with members of the opposite sex. Mr. E. was an engineer, Miss W. had studied journalism and was one of the editors of the women's page of her local newspaper. She was prepared to give up her career for marriage and a family, which seemed more important to her, but for that very reason she wanted to be certain that her marriage would be a success.

The counselor found that Miss W., despite her vocational independence, was much too dependent on her family, especially on her father. She was bound to him by a relationship of mutual understanding, which explained her worries about getting along with her somewhat stiff and socially inexperienced fiancé.

In the interviews, at first held separately and later together, the counselor succeeded in leading the young people to a clear self-understanding and understanding of the other partner, and effected mutual self-expression, which then did lead to a happy marriage.

The case given here in abbreviated form was chosen because it is an example of a case that is eminently suitable for counseling.

Just as the case of Jo Anne essentially represents an adolescent problem, so this case shows an acute problem brought about by the decision of two emotionally immature partners, both inexperienced with the other sex, to marry.

A third case, kindly provided by Maurice J. Karpf from his extensive practice in marriage counseling, shows us how the counselor can aid a chronically involved situation.

Mrs. A., the daughter of a businessman, had been marrried six years. As her husband devoted more and more time to his business, he gradually caused the marriage, which at first seemed happy, to become strained. As the result of his competence he became his father-in-law's partner, but in his devotion to his work he neglected his wife and child, his social life, and, as a result of increasing fatigue, his sex life, which had been satisfactory.

During the marriage counseling sessions, which he finally declared himself ready to seek, Mr. A. for quite a long time refused to admit the error in his way of life. The counselor formed the impression that this was a matter not of neurotic compulsiveness, but of zealousness and an immaturity. His discussion of these aspects was aided by the fact that the father-in-law was ready to place more help at his son-in-law's disposal, thereby giving Mr. A. more leisure time.

The situation had become complicated by the fact that the young wife in the meantime had gotten involved in an affair, which came to mean more to her than she had at first thought possible. She was not clear in her own mind how hard it would be for her from now on to devote herself to her marriage.

An external event facilitated a happy solution. Mrs. A. suddenly became fearful that her lover had made her pregnant. She finally admitted that she, too, had been immature and had not given any thought to the possible consequences of her actions. Her frightened awakening to reality caused her to break off her relationship with her lover immediately and return wholeheartedly to her marriage, which was actually what she wanted and which now made both partners happy.

Psychotherapy

From the standpoint of what modern psychology is able to give man for the betterment of his life, two themes in this book are of special significance: the presentation of the structure of the healthy person's course of life, as described earlier, and the pointing out of the fundamental role of psychotherapy in self-education and development.

What Is Psychotherapy?

Psychotherapy is a process designed to heighten a person's well-being. During systematically organized meetings an experienced, accredited therapist helps brings about certain positive changes in the feelings, ideas, and behavior of the patient.

Does the therapist accomplish these changes? And what exactly are the changes?

Unfortunately, there is no basic agreement in the answers to these fundamental questions.

However, there is general acceptance that the following are the most important factors in psychotherapy: the relationship between the therapist and the patient; the patient's talking things out; the interventions of the therapist; the goal of the process; the result of the process.

For simplicity's sake, reference will be to T. for the therapist and to P. for the patient.

The Relationship Between T. and P.

The relationship between T. and P. is considered by all therapists to be of the utmost importance; however, it is conceived of differently by different therapists. Freud's theory stated that a *transference* neurosis is of decisive significance for successful treatment. This means that the patient must go through a period in which he transfers to his therapist all the feelings of love and hate he once had for one of his parents. Freud considered this to be requisite for the release of all the feelings that prevented the patient from having a healthy development. Freud saw the inner demands made by such feelings as the basis for neuroses.

The transference method is, for the most part, used only by psychoanalysts. The fact that a person's past relations with his parents plays a part in the present and makes itself felt in the relationship of patient to therapist is widely recognized, but it is not considered the decisive dynamic factor by all therapists, or else it is not always treated by means of a transference relationship.

Carl Rogers, a renowned therapist, represents the extreme opposite of Freud in this respect. He emphasizes that the *helping relationship,* as he calls it, becomes effective more through the attitudes and feelings of the therapist than through the particular techniques and methodology he employs. He states that the relationship rests on the fact that T. is experienced by P. as trustworthy, sympathetic, kind, helpfully loving, interested, secure in his own person, understanding of hidden feelings, and sensitive; he does not criticize or judge.

Thus, Rogers sees the effectiveness of the therapeutic relationship as arising from the personality of the therapist and his ability to identify with the patient. Freud, on the other hand, sees its effectiveness in the fact that the therapist understands how to let the patient transfer the parent role to him.

Rogers' theory of the most effective relationship between T. and P. continues a tradition that began with Ferenczi, Rank, and Sullivan. Otto Rank, one of the most important of Freud's followers, enjoys increasing recognition because he, in tune with today's thinking, emphasizes the release of creative powers through therapy.

A transference relationship or a "helping relationship" will evolve for anyone in psychotherapy. Indeed, there are still other types of dynamically effective relationships, as will be illustrated in cases contributed by Dr. Hedda Bolgar and Dr. Franz Alexander. The capacity of the therapist to set up the most effective personal relationship with his patient is decisive.

The Patient's Talking Out

Who is the patient? Why does he enter psychotherapy and what does he talk about?

Suppose we stop here for a moment and ask the question: Who ought to seek psychotherapy? In a charming article in the Los Angeles *Times,* William Menninger, one of the founders of the famous Menninger Clinic in Kansas, described what he as a psychiatrist likes to know about a person.

Menninger says that, like him, many people believe in the necessity of regular examinations by their physician. But he also believes in periodic examination of the emotions: that, perhaps once a year, everyone should take the time to make clear to himself where he is going, what is important to him, what his intentions are, and what his goals are.

Menninger is very much in favor of a person's believing in and taking a stand on what he looks upon as his *calling.* But it is just as important for emotional health to take a vacation from work and to have hobbies, for they enrich life.

In his examinations of emotional health, Menninger likes to know about the personal relationships of the patient: What kind are they? How lasting are they? Whom does he like and why? How does the person behave in a serious situation? Does he become angry or anxious? In what way does he master reality? How much does he enjoy expending himself constructively and creatively with respect to people, ideas, things? How well is the person able to accept frustrations, and how free of anxiety and tension is he?

Menninger says that everyone naturally has periods of anxiety and tension, but a person who is never free of them is sick. Finally, he likes to know if the person has the courage to see himself as he really is. This is naturally the most difficult, as difficult as admitting to oneself that one needs help.

It is also very difficult, and very necessary, to be able to recognize whether or not one is inwardly free.

The author believes that it is the general experience of all therapists that the people who are least inwardly free always insist how healthy they are and how they are really not in need of therapeutic help. However, the author believes that everyone can at some time in his life make use of modern therapeutic help, if only as a guide to seeing himself realistically.

Thus the patient we will discern here is not a person who has broken down completely. He is someone looking for advice and help with respect to life problems he is unable to solve adequately. However, he is a person prevented by deep unconscious conflicts from carrying out the rational solutions presented to him as possibilities. Something holds him back; this hindrance can be of any depth and extent.

This person's first need is to talk things out. This talking out, in sessions that may continue for days, months, or even years, is the essence of therapy. Now, of course, everyone knows the healthy effect of talking things out, even without therapy. Nothing is more restful to an excited spirit than to be able to talk about hardships or disappointments to an understanding friend or marriage partner.

The Catholic Church, which understands the healing value of talking things out in the confessional, also sees regret, penance, and the freeing of man from guilt as significant for man's comfort and for regaining his inner freedom.

For some time Freud saw free expression as the most important part of the therapeutic process. But he soon came to the realization that its goal, *catharsis*—the inner process of cleansing—as such does not bring about healing.

He then began to practice the so-called *free association* techniques. He had his patients talk about anything that occurred to them. He thus introduced a technique that is much more complicated than just talking oneself out; in the patient's spontaneous and disconnected thoughts Freud could recognize indications of deep problems and determine paths to their solution. Therefore, what takes place is far more than listening with understanding; by *interpreting* disorganized material the therapist participates actively.

At this point, however, it should be noted that there are analysts, as well as other therapists, who for the most part limit themselves to listening and who are of the opinion that the patient himself gradually works his own way to a deeper understanding of his problems.

This technique was championed by Carl Rogers. In his procedure, originally called the *nondirective method,* Rogers held that, as a result of inborn needs to grow and to be well, every person is capable of independently working out his own problems and of finding himself. He believed that the patient needs no help other than the sympathetic, kindly disposed, considerate listening of the therapist.

Rogers was the first therapist to tape-record all verbal communications during the therapy sessions. He thereby gave his colleagues an opportunity to study a procedure that up to then had been inaccessible. This courageous scientific procedure ushered in an entirely new phase in psychotherapy, which had previously been a sort of secret science. Thanks to the Rogers method, therapists today have empirical examples with which to compare various techniques.

Rogers himself, however, learned from his experiments that only under particularly favorable conditions does the patient press forward to adequate self-understanding without help from the therapist. Today, in his "helping relationships" he interposes questions that further the patient's awareness, that is: he too makes use of the principles of intervention.

The Therapist's Intervention

Intervention by the therapist can come about in very different ways, depending on his experience, conviction, and personality. The type of intervention constitutes the main difference among the various therapeutic possibilities.

First, intervention is obviously an active process, in contrast to the purely passive process of listening. Basically this activity of clarifying serves to clear up past and present problems in the patient's life, or it can set new directions and goals for the patient's future.

Analytical Exploration

The most important technique of intervention is interpretation, which was introduced by Freud. Today, however, it is no longer handled exactly as Freud conceived it.

As was said in the discussion of projective tests (pp. 267–70), the interpretations applied in psychology consist of explanations of actions and experiences. The therapist is especially interested in the motives and feelings that his patients do not reveal to him directly.

Why do interpretations actually produce a deep, far-reaching change in a person, and how does this change come about?

The short answer to this vital question is that the suffering human being, robbed of his freedom by anxieties, guilt feelings, compulsions, and wrong attitudes, is able to experience a change when he is able to use the therapist's interpretations to dig down into the emotional origins of his suffering. This can happen suddenly and in a single session, or, as is more frequently the case, gradually and step by step. It can be illustrated by an example.

Glenn, the young man of twenty-five discussed earlier in this chapter, finds himself in difficulties and is very rebellious about problems at work. He feels there is no justification for the pressure under which the company places the individual. The compulsory work hours at the plant and the prescribed examinations at the university he attends as a working student enrage him. He feels he should have the right to develop his talents as a painter without being constantly criticized, hearing that everyone has got to earn money, and passing the prescribed examinations. All this pressure angered him even in high school; now he is in such a state of rebellion that he is ready to run off to some South Sea island.

When asked why he didn't do that instead of seeking therapy, he answered that he thought something must be the matter with him because most of his acquaintances don't share his opinion.

Within a few weeks, Glenn became aware that he now reacts against authority in the company exactly as he reacted against his mother's authority. The one seemed to him just as unjustified as the other. He burst out passionately about the unjustified and senseless way his mother exerted her authority. With a sense of outrage, he reported that she heaped punishment when as a child he didn't carry out his duties the way she wanted him to: didn't hang up his clothes, didn't keep his things in order, didn't do his homework, or didn't help dry the dishes. As punishment she kept him indoors, and he was not allowed to play with his friends. When he stuck stubbornly to his opposition, she raised the punishment hours "to astronomical figures," as he expressed it. She carried over from week to week the punishments that had not been completed, and apparently did not realize that her method only caused her son to become more and more stubborn.

And what did Glenn's father do in the meantime? Oh, his father had an entirely different view of life. Always friendly and happy, he took things easy. He was usually not at home when Glenn's mother had her arguments with her son. But when he was present, he declared that Glenn would have to obey his mother. He did not enter into questions of upbringing and punishment.

Glenn said bitterly, "Well, the result of all this discipline is that today I am a completely undisciplined person."

"But," replied the therapist, "it would seem that somehow this doesn't suit you."

"Yes, that's what's so strange. Although I rebel against the company just the way I did against my mother when she exerted her discipline over me, I do think that one ought to have some sort of discipline."

In the course of several months, Glenn discovered what was troubling him. It made him angry, it weighed on him, and it depressed him. He began to feel that he really was not able to do anything he could respect and admire as an accomplishment.

What a senseless way to live! Surely there must be something he could really accomplish. And he owed it to himself to make the best of himself. Waiting and hoping for the proof of his talent was a self-deception; if he did possess any talent, surely by now it would have shown itself. Because of his identification with his father, he had wanted to develop his artistic hobby further; he wanted to achieve success and fame, but there was really no basis for this ambition.

When Glenn had reached this point, the therapist asked him whether this still was connected with his mother. He suddenly saw clearly that the desire to make the most of himself was his *own* wish, the task that *he* had set for himself. It no longer had anything to do with authority figures. He saw that his identification of performance with the demands of authorities had barred him from setting up his own goals. He had remained fixated in his childhood situation, in his dependence on his mother, and in his rebellion against her. Now he felt himself free. This inner freedom enabled him to see clearly how and why the company for which he worked had a right to his cooperation and a suitable degree of adaptation.

Setting aside for the moment the father-son relationship, which will be discussed later, we shall now examine what took place here. Glenn's realization is the type that builds slowly to an "Aha! experience" called *insight*. His case presents a relatively simple problem structure. It was chosen to give the reader some idea of what is involved in therapy without having to introduce various technical complications. Many cases are much more complicated, and progress toward decisive insights is drawn out and difficult. It is important that these insights be experienced not only intellectually; they should not come about as the result of conscious decisions. They must be experienced emotionally and in depth.

Freud found that in many cases the dreams of his patients aided this process. His discovery of the meaningful content of dream symbolism is believed by many to be his most brilliant accomplishment.

Interpretation of Dreams

Freud interpreted the happenings in dreams as experience of fulfillment of secret wishes that the dreamer in his waking state would not dare admit to himself; such experiences are forbidden and are rejected by the conscience, the superego.

Thomas French recently showed convincingly that the dream represents much more; that it represents deep thought work. The dreamer attempts to see the conflicts in which he is involved and to bring them to some sort of solution. These conflicts may be partly conscious and partly unconscious. The solutions can then, in certain conditions, be wish fulfillments; but they can also be rational realizations of actual situations.

For example, at the time Glenn overcame his dependence on his mother and his rebellion against her, he dreamed that he was riding away from home on the bicycle he had owned as a young boy. He saw himself, however, as an adult. Attached to his arm was a strong rope, which kept pulling him back. He got off the bicycle, looked at the rope, and discovered that it was just one of his mother's washlines. He rolled it up, stuck it into his bag, and rode off.

What had appeared to him as the tremendously strong influence of his mother pulling him back proved on closer examination to be only a light bond he could carry away.

Two other dreams will serve to show a solution that had been found and a wished-for solution.

Beatrice, a woman of thirty, has just been divorced for the second time. Her therapist pointed out the parallels between her two marriages. Both husbands were very charming, sexually satisfying men who, however, later proved to be dubious characters and had placed her in dangerous situations. The first had almost choked her in an attack of jealousy, and she discovered that the second had committed a number of serious thefts. She divorced him shortly before he was arrested for frauds involving large sums of money.

While she was thinking over the reasons for her attraction to this type of man, she dreamed the following:

"I saw myself walking into the huge wide-open jaws of a whale. Inside everything was brightly lit, and the walls were a shimmering pink. I went farther along his spine to the end, which appeared to be a pleasant and comfortable place. Someone said, 'Get out of here, fast!' But I thought, I like it here for the time being, so I'll stay."

In other words, she recognized that she enjoyed her comfortable and glamorous circumstances and did not want to admit danger.

Philip is a sixteen-year-old who does not want to admit to himself that his problems arise from his relationship with his father, whom he hates. Philip was a war baby, who did not know his father until one morning, when he was three, he found him in his mother's bed. "Get out of Mummy's bed," he yelled.

From this traumatic beginning of his relationship with his father and up to the frictions of puberty there was always tension between them. Philip denied the depth of his resentment. While he was finally bringing this out into the open in therapy, he dreamed that:

"My father and I drove up a hill. We parked the car and went up to the precipice. Looking down we saw a truck full of hay. My father said, 'Let's jump down on the hay and get the car.' I said, 'It is much too far down, don't do it.' He answered, 'You are lying, it isn't so far down.' He jumped and fell down miles and miles and was dead when he reached bottom. I had the feeling that I had killed him."

Once he was able to put it into words, the conflict that Philip is experiencing comes clearly to the fore in the dream. While he wants to prove to his sarcastic and know-it-all father that his judgment of the situation is terribly mistaken, so mistaken that he will die because of it, he immediately regrets the act he has wished for, and feels guilty.

The technique of interpretation was shown here because it is a cardinal part of the psychoanalytical process. But even outside the therapeutic situation there is, as the result of analysis, an understanding of human dealings based on interpretation. This was shown in the example of the mothers in Chapter 2. In the last chapter of this book we shall once more have occasion to discuss the role of understanding and self-understanding based on interpretation.

Interpretation represents, however, only one form of intervention: *analytical exploration,* in which faulty personality development is analyzed. But there are other processes designed to contribute to the building-up of a new personality.

Constructive Exploration

Carl Jung was the first to emphasize that an analytical treatment had to be followed by a *synthetic* treatment. However, there is still no unanimity with respect to this constructive process.

Many therapists, especially those oriented to Freud's teachings, believe that therapy makes it possible for the patient to find his new way by himself. For this and other reasons they reject any interference in the new life development and self-development of the patient.

Those who conclude that many people need help in developing their future more favorably than their past may have different ideas as to the extent or type of direction they should give the patient. Their views vary from authoritarian *precepts,* to *advice* and *expressions of opinion,* to *questions* and *discussions.*

Just what is at stake in these interventions that aim to guide the patient? Obviously, the patient who is emerging from his neurosis is now for the first time in a position to choose his goals freely. And in this new choice of goals, so much depends on the patient's setting up for himself more appropriate *values* than he had before.

The independent adoption of new values is extremely difficult, especially in a time such as the present, when there is great insecurity concerning values and attitudes toward values. The person seeking new values today has more difficult decisions than, for example, the decision to be more dutiful, to have more loving understanding, to have more realistic goals, or to be more honest toward himself. He is often bothered by the question: What is the meaning of all this, and what can I believe in?

Martin Grotjahn, who introduced into psychoanalysis the treatment of whole families, uses the technique of direct advice. For example, he tells the mother of a young girl he is treating: "Of course you have got to give your daughter a car; otherwise how can she get around in a city that was built for cars rather than for human beings?" Grotjahn is of the opinion that his request to the mother allows the general advice—"Give your daughter more freedom"—to be glimpsed and that this advice, as well as the value of this orientation, can be interpreted by the mother herself.

Other psychologists hold that the patient's right to determine his own values must be preserved and that the therapist should intervene only in the sense of *constructive exploration,* as the author calls it. Here the influencing is more *indirect,* and the therapist appeals to the capacity for choice by the patient, who under certain conditions is made aware of alternative *value possibilities.*

Glenn's case may serve as an example of a relatively independent choice of values. Glenn, who began his therapy with statements about his rebellion against society, had very confused ideas as to values. He believed that nobody had the right to make rules for any other person and that society did not have the right to put individuals under pressure. He declared that a person should be able to continue the development of his talents, although he did admit that one could scarcely expect society to finance this. When Glenn was asked what sort of values his parents recognized, he said that his mother did not really have any values, only nebulous, abstract ideas, although she did have certain rules: it was right to do this and wrong to do that.

It was his father who always stood before him as a model, although he, too, had not pointed out any clear direction. "My father," Glenn said, "was easy-going, and did everything without any trouble. He was a technical draftsman for various firms, but as he had some money of his own, he did not work regularly. In his leisure hours, he painted."

"Did he sell his pictures?" the therapist asked.

"No, I don't think so. He did it more for his own pleasure. He also taught us children how to draw and in general took more interest in us, much more than our mother did. So we all loved him very much."

"Did you admire the way he lived?"

"Yes, at that time it seemed wonderful. But today I'm beginning to have my doubts. What did he really live for?"

"Do you believe one ought to live for something?"

"Well, at least one ought to know in what direction one is going. My father really had quite a disorganized life. At that time, I thought his way of working, which came so easy to him, was ideal—today I begin to find that maybe it wasn't so good."

Glenn developed these viewpoints some eight months after starting therapy. After these beginnings of reorientation he frequently examined the question, "Where am I going?" In his search he discovered that he did not have any self-confidence because he had not received any real training and had not accomplished anything, and that his impetus had been weak. Gradually the idea that one should make the most of oneself became the leitmotiv for Glenn. The therapist's questions were planned in such a way that they guided him in this direction, but left him free to declare himself against the idea of a life meaning if this was not convincing to him.

Remembering what has been said about human motivation, if one now asked what Glenn had accomplished for himself through therapy, the reply might be this:

When Glenn came into therapy, he was wholly dissatisfied with himself and his life. His distress, which because of space limitations was here shown only in his work, was no less great in social and sexual life. Here, too, he was immature and motivated neither by sufficiently strong drives nor by strong social needs. All his relationships were vague and superficial—with the exception of his great, unconscious dependence on his family. Sexual needs had led to a few short affairs with female partners, without any deeper relationships having developed. Occasionally, in addition to heterosexual fantasies, he also had had homosexual ones.

In essence, Glenn was immature and unfulfilled in every respect, a person who visualized only vaguely the ideals of need satisfaction and creative expansion. He rebelled against self-limiting adaptation and possessed no sort of inner order. Therapy made him overcome his rebellion. He gave up the idea that need satisfaction is the exclusive goal. He set up new values for the first time in inner freedom, proceeding from the growing insight of the social meaningfulness of his work. He adapted himself to the given possibilities and established an inner order based on these reorientations. To sum up, by a newly acquired *dynamic equilibrium and integration of all basic tendencies,* Glenn found himself on the way to a fulfillment of life.

Three years after he had discontinued therapy, he reported continuing success. In a letter to his therapist he described the satisfaction that he got out of his studies and the happiness he has experienced in his recent marriage to a girl who was also working toward her degree and who shares his interests and convictions. He wrote that he valued what he had learned in psychology and thought of it often.

The Goal of Therapy

The goal of therapy varies according to the case and according to the therapeutic school to which the therapist belongs. The goal may be *support* of a personality that requires support, partial *personality changes,* or complete *restructuring of the personality* by depth treatments.

Glenn's case represented a fairly extensive restructuring of personality, culminating in the setting of entirely new values. This has been discussed only with regard to his professional activity, and not with respect to his social and sexual personality.

Since analytically oriented psychotherapy is often attacked because it requires so much time, two *brief therapies* by two analysts are given below, with emphasis on the goals sought for and attained.

Dr. Hedda Bolgar, a psychoanalytically trained psychologist, put at my disposal a case of brief therapy, applied in a case of *crisis,* in which, in five interviews, she arrived at a remarkable partial restructuring. Her analytic knowledge of psychodynamics was applied in her carefully planned strategy.

Mrs. R., a woman of forty-five, had been referred by her physician, to whom she had complained in great agitation about her nervousness, her insomnia, her inability to look after her household, her deep depression, and her weariness with life. Since there was acute danger of suicide, Dr. Bolgar received the patient at once.

Mrs. R. reported a whole succession of difficulties and annoyances that had accumulated during the previous few months to such an extent that they now overwhelmed her. It began when her husband accepted a position across the country and left it to her to break up the household, drive to Los Angeles from New York, and find a new home for the family. What made everything more difficult was that, not long before the move, she had broken her leg; during the drive it was still in a cast. Added to this, the relatives in the West did not welcome her; the children, aged eleven and thirteen, had trouble adapting to the new conditions and new schools; and her husband had disagreeable working hours. There was a good deal more unpleasantness.

She appeared restless and very agitated, and her face was tear-streaked. Her restless hands kept wringing her damp handkerchief; her mouth trembled; and often she could scarcely speak. One might have thought that Mrs. R.'s breakdown was brought on by the present situation, but her report of her life history revealed that her problems were only the climax of a life that had been unhappy for a long time and that had reached the breaking point.

Mrs. R. was the only child of a strict, unloving father and a mother who was wholly self-involved because of many illnesses. Her good middle-class family gave her security and an excellent university education, but made great demands on her capacity to perform and expected her to be perfect in every respect. The atmosphere of the home was unfriendly, serious, and strictly religious.

Mrs. R. had met her future husband at college. He came from a simpler family, which she somewhat looked down on but whose cordiality and friendliness she enjoyed. Her husband did not finish his education, but took an unstimulating management job.

As a result of his passivity, a certain effeminacy, and his sexual inexperience, he left much to be desired as a sexual partner, but Mrs. R. loved him for his goodness and understanding. The children, too, loved him— more than they did her, for she was far too strict. She probably got what she deserved, she said in the midst of her tears.

From Mrs. R.'s tale it became evident that she had suffered many emotional frustrations and had got little pleasure out of her relations with others. Although she continually criticized herself, she was obviously as full of hostility as she was of guilt feelings.

Dr. Bolgar says: "At the end of the first interview, I had to come to a decision as to the immediate handling of the case. My diagnostic impression was that Mrs. R. was in the serious state of an agitated depression and was close to a psychotic breakdown."

Dr. Bolgar considered three possibilities: commitment to a hospital; referral to a clinic for prolonged outpatient psychotherapeutic treatment; or brief, intensive, exceptionally supportive psychotherapy. Dr. Bolgar decided upon the third course. She asked the help of Mrs. R.'s father, to whom she entrusted full care of the patient.

The reasons for her decision were as follows: commitment to a hospital would have severely damaged the family life and perhaps destroyed it; it would have undermined the self-esteem of the woman, and would have confirmed her fears that she was very sick mentally. The therapist also took into consideration that, despite all her problems, Mrs. R. had always managed to get along up to this time and that she was an intelligent woman whose cooperation could be counted on.

Dr. Bolgar explained her proposed treatment to her patient and planned a few interviews, giving careful consideration to the psychodynamics of depression. Dr. Bolgar states: "I decided to accomplish three things: First I was of the opinion that Mrs. R. most urgently needed *support, warmth, and recognition.* I decided to give her as much of this nourishment as possible. I talked a great deal, I emphasized her strength, I complimented her on her accomplishments and on her capability. I let her participate in my feelings and my experiences, and suggested an identification with me by pointing out parallels between our respective life courses. Wherever I could, I put myself on her side, and indicated that I liked her and that I admired her for the way in which she had coped with her many difficulties in the past. I also showed great concern for her physical well-being during the sessions and in between."

As a second important point, Dr. Bolgar considered the treatment of Mrs. R.'s hostility. She tried to show the patient that anger and resentment are normal human reactions, that she had the right to express such reactions toward her family, and that this need not have the destructive effects that Mrs. R. feared.

Third, Dr. Bolgar took up Mrs. R.'s tendency toward *self-punishment.* "It was clear to me," she said, "that her pathologically strict—that is, sadistic—conscience, in response to the satisfactions that I provided her with and to my encouraging her to express her hostile feelings, would have to react so that later it would make her punish herself. I tried to work against this development by concentrating her guilt feelings on something else. I criticized her for her exaggerated demands on herself; I told her she was arrogant for believing herself to be the only person in the world who could get along without fulfillment of her needs and without any pleasures. I blamed her for not wanting to be like other people, and for not making any attempt to make her life more pleasant. In other words, I gave her a sense of guilt for not permitting herself to have normal needs and wishes."

Fortunately, the patient reacted splendidly to the whole procedure, and in the five hours of her therapy went through a change that passed through all the desirable phases. At the end of the sessions she discussed plans for the future with Dr. Bolgar, she showed a hopeful, constructive attitude that, as was later demonstrated, actually bore fruit.

In her discussion of this brief therapy, Dr. Bolgar explains what her *goal* was, for of course she did not look on the improvement as a "cure" or as a thorough change of personality. Her goal was to break through the vicious circle of the depression, which consisted of longing, hate, and self-destructive guilt feelings.

The goal here was inner reorientation, and its attainment sufficed to put an end to the immediate dangerous situation. But the treatment represented only a first step, which would have to be followed by many others in order to remove the neurosis completely.

Of interest is the character of the *therapeutic relationship* favorable for this type of supportive treatment. It was planned that the patient identify very strongly with the therapist. Thereby, the detour over transference relationships could be avoided.

A different sort of reorientation was sought by Franz Alexander, a former co-worker of Freud's and one of his most prominent disciples, in his work toward a *corrective emotional* experience.

The case we shall discuss here was published as "Case A" in the pioneering book *Psychoanalytic Therapy* by Alexander, T. M. French, and others. Dr. Alexander was kind enough to add some remarks to my report.

Mr. A., a forty-two-year-old businessman, had been referred to psychotherapy by a neurologist because of epileptic symptoms on a hysterical basis. He suffered from cramps, was irritable, intolerant, and domineering; and for some months had been impotent. The treatment consisted of twenty-six interviews extending over ten weeks. After the sixth week the symptoms disappeared.

The patient had spent all his life in the shadow of his domineering father, a self-made man with a stormy temper and unlimited self-confidence who tyrannized his family and business subordinates. The mother, who loved and protected the child, died when he was nine. Twice in his life Mr. A. attempted to stand up to his father. After the second time, when he had married against his father's wishes, the father remained unreconciled until shortly before his death.

When Mr. A., at the age of thirty, took over the management of the family business after the death of his father, his principal wish was to prove that he was a better businessman than his father had been. With stubborn determination he succeeded.

Business, however, was his only success. He failed in all his personal relationships; everywhere he went he made enemies. His wife divorced him, and, although she had remarried him, she was now ready to divorce him a second time.

In the therapy, Mr. A. immediately made an attempt to present the father-son relationship as he knew it, by transferring to the analyst the role of the father, whom he faced rebelliously, but with subservient admiration. The analyst, however, was determined not to allow any transference neurosis to ensue, and worked against a substitute father-son relationship.

He accomplished this by displaying an unusual *tolerance* and allowing the patient to make many of his own decisions with regard to the therapy; for example, how often he wished to come, whether he wanted to sit, lie on the couch, or walk about, and that sort of thing. Further, in contrast to the critical attitude that the father had shown, the analyst repeatedly expressed admiration for many of the patient's qualities.

The patient, who had needed a tyrannical father figure in order to be aggressive and rebellious in his own way, was confused and somehow dissatisfied. When he expressed his irritation in new aggressions, the analyst was able to show him that these were not reactions to a domineering father figure, but obviously corresponded to his own need.

After initial resistance, Mr. A. gradually accepted these interpretations. The first success came when he began to be as gentle in his relations with his own son as the analyst was being toward him.

Three dreams mirrored the change experienced during this period. In the first, Mr. A. saw the analyst, full of anger, breaking some glassware that he, the patient, had made in his factory. He reported that this reminded him of a scene with his father when the father smashed a whole set of glassware because he did not like the pattern the son had designed.

After these remarks the analyst asked the patient to describe his work. The patient did so with enthusiasm, in a didactic, condescending manner. As a result of this session, in which he had been able to prove himself to the analyst as someone who knew his field and, in fact, as an authority on it, he regained his sexual potency.

In the twentieth interview, Mr. A. reported a dream in which he saw himself as a student who had come home with a rapier that he had broken while fencing. His father gave it back to him repaired. Here he thanked his father for having given him back his rapier—that is, his virility—while in a previous dream he had seen himself humbled by his analyst instead of by his father.

Working slowly through this confusion into a clearer state of mind, he found himself in the next dream on a new plane. He saw himself as the presiding judge in a court, with a famous Chicago judge by his side. The case he was judging was a divorce suit, and he succeeded in reconciling the couple.

Here he identified the analyst with a colleague who had helped him rescue his marriage. Analyst and patient were no longer father and son, but colleagues.

In his comments on this case, Dr. Alexander emphasized that the experience of a new father-son relationship helps the patient attain the corrective emotional experience that forms the basis of his recovery. Here again, brief therapy is not so valuable as a full analysis, but it is sufficient to substitute a healthy basic attitude for a neurotic one.

The writer asked Dr. Alexander on the basis of what findings had he decided to use "brief psychoanalysis" in this particular case. He replied with the following statement, which is quoted with his permission.

"In my therapeutic work I make no sharp distinction between brief and extended psychoanalysis, nor between real psychoanalysis and psychoanalytically oriented psychotherapy. I do not decide in advance whether the treatment is to be long or short, whether the patient is to lie on the couch or to sit across the desk from me. I feel my way and make the details of the method correspond to the steadily changing psychodynamic situations of the patient.

"I consider it the task of the therapist to help the ego of the patient so that it can exercise its integrative function and finally can free the patient to regain his spontaneous potential. In this respect I am strictly Hippocratic and believe that the essential healing power consists in the *integrative capacity* of the patient, which became blocked through faulty interpersonal adaptive processes. In some cases a single breakthrough, which comes about through *corrective emotional experiences* during the treatment, may open up the way for the further spontaneous healing.

"In the personality as a whole, all forms of emotional happenings— all impressions left by early experiences—are connected with one another. A definite change in one of the central fields unavoidably has an effect on the entire personality. The early emotional development of the patient as well as his inborn and acquired integrative capacity decide how many such corrective emotional experiences are necessary until the ego of the patient can find his future way along the right path without the help of the therapist. Continuation of treatment beyond this optimal point may delay rather than expedite an improvement.

"In the present state of our knowledge it is impossible to decide theoretically when one has reached the point at which further therapy is not necessary or, possibly, holds up the improvement. Therefore, I use the technique of *repeated shorter or longer interruptions* in the treatment.

During the interruptions the patient is left to his own devices and has the task of coping with his problems himself. When the treatment is taken up again, it soon becomes clear what still has to be accomplished. Treatments uninterrupted for too long a time indulge the patient's tendencies toward delay.

"My technique was erroneously called 'brief analysis.' The entire time span of my flexible procedure is often no shorter than that of a long, drawn-out, uninterrupted standard analysis. In my experience, however, the total number of interviews is appreciably lessened.

"My main technical principle consists of a flexible adaptation to all aspects of the treatment, including the frequency of interviews and the course of the therapeutic process, which can vary from patient to patient and which, in the present state of knowledge of psychodynamics, are unpredictable.

"Consequently, I take patients not with a previous agreement that the treatment will be long or short, or that it will more or less assume the form of a standard analysis, but I arrive at this decision during the course of the treatment. I take my patients into a kind of treatment that is based on psychoanalytic principle, but not for a specific type of technique. I regard the therapeutic process as a highly complicated transaction process between therapist and patient, the course of which depends on a great number of known and unknown variables and which therefore cannot be forced into any kind of preconceived technical plan. The technical details have got to develop empirically in the course of the process. The only firm frame of reference is the application of fundamental psychodynamic principles that stem from psychonanalytical theory and practice."

Through the examples of the two brief therapies the reader has become familiar with a procedure that penetrates through a neurotically conditioned way of life and opens a path for release from *compulsion* and *suffering*.

The goal of prolonged psychotherapy, as was indicated in Glenn's case, is the *bringing about of a new attitude with respect to values* that make possible a deeper life fulfillment.

The Success of Psychotherapy

The *success* of psychotherapy depends on what is understood by "success." In a study by Werner Wolff carried out with forty-three representatives from different therapy schools, the analyst Sandor Lorand said: "Every therapy does good. The question is, to what extent? Much depends on the material with which you are working." He then declared how in some cases he considers small improvements to be a success, whereas in other cases he expects extensive changes before he speaks of success. The same view was expressed by other therapists.

Of particular interest is a book by Carl Rogers and co-workers that, on the basis of carefully defined criteria, examines *personality changes* as a result of psychotherapy. Statements about patients' behavior, attitudes toward others, and personality integration were obtained from a high percentage of those engaged in prolonged counseling. Rogers uses a control group of individuals who were not in therapy, but who were tested and retested with the same techniques over the same period. The maturity of those in therapy at the end of the period proved to be much further advanced than that of the control group.

Rogers considers the capacity for realistic self-perception—seeing oneself as one really is—as the most important criterion for maturity. This can also be expressed in this way: psychotherapy educates toward greater inner *honesty*.

E. Gendlin emphasizes that it is not *insight* as such that guarantees major personality change, but a new, intensive feeling process that takes place in the individual during a continuing personal relationship with the therapist.

Rogers calls his procedure "counseling," since he does not engage in any deep interpretive therapy. What is the difference with respect to success?

The controversial question here is how far inner honesty is a guarantee that a person, over and beyond self-understanding, will be able to set up new life goals and actually pursue them. *Self-knowledge* is one thing, *self-formation* another.

As the author tried to show in *Values in Psychotherapy*, deeper restructuring methods are required, methods that will delve deep into the unconscious to replace old value settings with new ones. Furthermore, procedures to generate effective impulses toward new goal direction are required; today they are only in the process of development.

For the present, there is no satisfactory method for understanding these restructurings adequately. They can be described case by case, and it can be shown when they are reached and when they are not reached. One of the most important research tasks of the immediate future is probing into the secret of the processes by which personality can be formed and actually re-formed. This research is of great significance, not only for psychotherapy but also for the education and training of young people.

SPECIAL METHODS IN PSYCHOTHERAPY

Psychotherapy with Children

Psychotherapy with children, by and large, uses the same principles as psychotherapy with adults. However, the techniques are different.

Generally, child psychotherapy is built up on *play situations*. By means of toys, as well as such unstructured materials as sand, clay, and water, the child is given an opportunity to express his feelings. Furthermore, many therapists encourage children to draw, paint, and engage in other artistic occupations.

The play activities and productions of the child serve a double purpose in child therapy. First, the child can give almost unlimited rein to his feelings. Second, the play and games, as well as the products that are produced or destroyed by the child, provide an opportunity for the therapist to *understand* the problems disturbing the child and, in certain circumstances and depending on the theoretical attitude of the therapist, to *interpret* them to the child.

It was early discovered that the free expression of feelings in play is *cathartic* in the same way and to the same degree that talking out is in adults. David Levy made extensive use of this method to free children from deep anxiety, especially after such traumatic experiences as accidents, a surgical operation, or the divorce of the parents. Some therapists permit the child a free hand in his play, while others direct the play activity in a definite way.

A type of play therapy based mainly on free activity is demonstrated by Clark E. Moustakas. However, verbal expression is suggested in addition to the activity, and the therapist tries to establish a positive relationship with the child. Moustakas' book, which originated from his work at the Merrill-Palmer School in Detroit, provides a good survey of the various situations and procedures in the treatment of children.

The use of *artistic activity* in the course of child therapy was particularly recommended by Lauretta Bender. From her many years of activity at Bellevue Hospital in New York City there emerged a book with instructive examples of the diagnostic and therapeutic significance of children's art creations in diverse media.

The use of *interpretation* in child therapy is controversial. Many professionals are opposed to making children conscious of their feelings in words. Others are of the opinion that the therapist should give the child insight into his problems in the same way he would the adult, though in language appropriate to the child. Those who try to explain the child's motivations and reactions to him are generally aware of the difficulty of, as well the responsibility for, what they are doing.

Thus Rudolf Ekstein, an experienced and sensitive child analyst, has concerned himself intensively with the question of the *right* interpretation. When there is a lack of verbal communication, the therapist cannot always be absolutely sure that he is interpreting the child's unconscious processes correctly. The following case is cited as an example of an interpretation sensitive to the limited contact possible for a disturbed child.

Ted, a ten-year-old borderline case—he was considered almost schizophrenic—was in treatment with one of Ekstein's co-workers, Judith Wallerstein. Both reported the following game which Ted repeatedly initiated.

The therapist had to stand in the middle of the school courtyard and was not allowed to move while Ted ran at high speed from one end of the courtyard to the other. Ted gave her the task of guessing in that fraction of a second while he passed by her the particular secret fantasy he was having (which he designated as the "secret zone"). The rule for this game, which was to be strictly followed, was that Ted would drop the ball he was holding if the therapist guessed correctly. If she didn't, he would continue running and each time he passed her would give her one single chance—a single hint, a single second to guess the secret.

In those rare instances when the therapist succeeded in guessing the secret, the child was visibly relieved.

The game gives a picture of Ted's almost complete inability to set up a relationship with another person. He could be helped only by a magical intervention somewhat like the sort we know from movies, where at the last moment, through some miracle, the heroine is rescued.

Melanie Klein recently published a book on the successful analysis of a ten-year-old boy, Richard, to whom, in the very first hour, she explained his fear of a nightly intruder on his mother as his fear that his father might do harm to his mother during the night. Further, she explained that he was perhaps afraid that something might be happening to his parents' genitalia in bed whereby his mother might be harmed. She reports that at first Richard reacted with fear to this as well as to other interpretations but that later he seemed to accept them.

In contrast to this, other therapists either give no interpretations at all or they give very careful, and very few, interpretations. As an example, we may take a case that was successfully handled by Phyllis Blanchard in a child guidance clinic under the direction of Frederick Allen. Nine-year-old Henry was referred to the clinic because of a speech disturbance and difficulties in his relations with other children.

Not until the tenth interview did Dr. Blanchard offer the interpretation that perhaps Henry wanted to be superman, so that he could do something to those he hated. In further interpretations she pointed out that he was behaving well in the session because he was afraid she might get angry with him; that he felt the other children did not like him; that he was thinking that really nobody could like him, perhaps not even his therapist, because he was bad. She assured him that he need not be afraid of this.

Parallel with Henry's treatment there was, as often happens, counseling with his mother. It was explained to her how she was contributing to her son's difficulties and how she might help him.

It is extremely important that parents be aware of the possible development of unconscious anxieties in their children and become familiar with modern child psychology and child therapy. Furthermore, group therapy is now often used with children and even more with adolescents.

Hypnosis

Hypnosis is one of the oldest methods of psychotherapy. By "hypnosis" (from the Greek word "sleep") is meant a sleeplike state induced by suggestion. There is self-hypnosis as well as hypnosis by others.

Today hypnosis is an accepted technique for bringing about relaxation and recovery. It is being used more and more by dentists, gynecologists, and other physicians to eliminate the pain of dental operations, births, burns, and other traumas.

Psychiatrists and psychologists often use hypnosis in combination with psychotherapy to help patients recall early childhood experiences or to bring about complete relaxation. The purpose is to help the patient in the uncovering and working-through processes.

There are different theories as to what actually takes place in hypnosis. According to Erika Fromm, "the field of perception is narrowed. Outside stimuli are largely shut out. The range of interaction with external reality is reduced. The subject sharply funnels his attention on his inner-world reality. As the breadth of attention is decreased, its qualitative intensity seems to increase.

"There is a freer expression of affects and ideas; motility becomes available to repressed impulses; there may be changes in body feeling, depersonalization. . . .

"The patient in psychoanalysis has to learn introspection, which can be defined as the skill to separate the observing ego from the experiencing ego. In hypnosis this separation occurs naturally and spontaneously (particularly in subjects who participate as interested students in experiments).

The experiencing ego 'regresses in the service of the (observing) ego'; the observing ego remains on its mature level of functioning.

"In hypnosis, the observing ego can be so totally separated from the experiencing ego that pain is observed, but not felt.

"For example, a woman in labor who wishes to be free from pain is hypnotized. She is asked to relax and to imagine herself being driven to the hospital by her husband, entering the building, signing in. Then these two ego functions are separated. She is told to imagine herself walking down the hospital corridor. Now the hypnotist says: 'Let that woman who looks like you get ahead of you a few steps. She is dressed like you, and soon she is going to have a baby. That woman is being brought up to a pre-delivery room, put to bed . . . and you sit down in a comfortable chair beside her, watching her and talking to her. Then that woman is wheeled into the delivery room and you are allowed to come along. You sit on a chair in a corner of the delivery room and watch that woman having a baby.'

"Here we have dissociated and detached the observing from the body ego. Ego cathexis remains with the observing ego ('*you* watch . . . *you* sit'), while the body is de-egotized and has become an object—'that woman.' The patient does not feel labor pain since the outside, observing ego cannot experience the sensations of 'that woman over there.' Just before the baby is born, the observing and the experiencing ego must be reunited and reintegrated, so that the patient can fully participate in the moment of birth and feel the baby is really her own."

In the case described, hypnosis was used to dissociate the patient from an acute experience. In psychotherapy it is used to help the patient uncover his past. Through hypnosis he is enabled to remember forgotten incidents and to work through their significance and emotional impact in his life. For this purpose, hypnosis is best used at irregular intervals depending on what kind of experiences the patent needs to work through.

Psychopharmacology and Shock Therapy

While hypnosis techniques are frequently used by psychologists, shock therapies and pharmacological therapies are exclusively the concern of the physician. However, in a great many hospitals, as well as in private practice, physicians and psychologists can be found working together. The physician takes over the medical treatment of a case and the psychologist the psychotherapeutic treatment.

In *shock therapy* either *insulin* or cardiozol is given in large doses, or electric currents are allowed to enter the brain (electroshock). *Pharma-*

cological therapy is the use of medication and is termed *psychopharma-cology.*

The use of such drug treatments in mental illness is still controversial. Opinion depends in great measure on the theoretical conception of how mental illness comes about. Definitely opposed to one another are the experts who are convinced of the pre-eminent role of *heredity* and those who give *psychogenic causes* pre-eminence.

The real question is: What are the actual effects of such drugs? In 1957, F. Bello said in his study *Tranquilizers* that "nervously the United States is entering into a new era, into an era of the change of human personality by chemical means." In *Drugs and Behavior,* edited by Uhr and Miller, a number of researchers examine the effects achieved by drugs. This comprehensive work on psychopharmacology describes the vast increase in the use of drugs that has occurred in the relatively short time of twenty years.

Medications with a calming and relaxing effect are sometimes called Ataractica. These drugs are used primarily in the treatment of serious mental and emotional disturbances. Certain Ataractica are helpful in relieving the anxiety and tension states to which both neurotic and healthy people are prone. Many patients, however, prefer to get by without "crutches" of this kind.

Group Therapy

Group therapy is one of the most successful and popular of the special methods. It is developing to such an extent into a principal method that many therapists use it simultaneously with individual therapy or even use it exclusively.

Group therapy is the process by which therapy is undertaken *in* a group and, for the most part, *by* a group.

The latter statement may seem absurd. How can patients treat each other? Naturally, they can do this only within certain limits and within groups that are working together constructively. That is why leadership by a trained professional is a prerequisite for a systematic, deep penetration into the problems of the individual members of the group. In many places—for example, Alcoholics Anonymous and Synanon—groups of alcoholics, drug addicts, and others who have joined together for self-help report favorable results. However, it is still to be proved how well the individuals can function away from the special community that sheltered them.

The typical group, working under a psychologist or psychiatrist, consists of from six to twelve members, who sit together and discuss problems with frank self-expression. Some therapists prefer to work with small groups of three or four patients; others, with groups of as many as sixty patients. Most participants in large groups are also in private therapy with the same therapist.

The selection of members for a particular group, or for participation in group therapy at all, is based on the severity and type of problems of the patients and their ages and jobs.

The discussion, which for the most part is initiated by the members, develops easily. The direction varies with the theoretical orientation as well as with the personality of the therapist. Analysts and nonanalysts can influence what takes place in their groups in various ways, usually corresponding to the principles they use in individual therapy.

By their nature, groups are best suited for the working through of problems concerning *interpersonal relationships.* In contrast to individual therapy, in which the patient can only report on his relationship to others, the group offers the therapist an opportunity to see his social personality in action. The frank and open discussion and the reactions of each individual to the group bring to light social and frequently sexual attitudes in a way that is possible in no other situation. Mutual tolerance prevails among the group members because everyone knows that he too has faults, and the respecting of the members' secrets, which is guaranteed by the fact that each member is equally interested in discretion, makes the group a unique instrument for mutual help.

A few examples will provide a sense of what takes place in group therapy.

The first group opens with Allen, the industrious and overconscientious young engineer who has been mentioned several times in this book. He is about to take his Ph.D. examinations.

Allen: I have a problem. I'm always terribly worried. I'm a regular worry-bug. I don't know when and how it began. But right now it's becoming unbearable. It's wearing me out. I've always worried, in school and at college. But it's worse now than it ever was before. I'm so excessively worried that I won't be able to prepare properly for my exam.

John: Are you working for perfection?

Allen: Yes, I always do.

Grace: Do you feel that you're accomplishing less than would correspond to your abilities?

Allen: Yes. At all events, I keep criticizing myself and I tell myself that I really could do better.

John: Is your family poking at you?

Allen: No, it's my own pressure. Perhaps the reason is that I'm expecting and hoping to find myself through my performance.

Mark: You just expect too much of yourself. Or maybe you're in the wrong field?

Allen: No, I don't think so. I wouldn't fit into any other profession. I'm also worried all the time about other things. For example, my car. And about money matters. And about social problems.

Barbara: What do you worry about in your social life?

Allen: I'm really not fit for any social life at all. I've simply shoved all that aside.

Phyllis: Are you afraid that girls don't want to have dates with you?

Allen: I have dates sometimes. But I don't feel at ease when I go out. Before my therapy, I never went out at all. Now I do it, but I'm always afraid I'm going to be rejected.

At this session, which is mostly devoted to Allen, most of the group members participate. Later, the intervention of the therapist leads Allen to the connection of his continual worry with his relationship to his mother, which he has already reported. His earlier decision "never to make a mistake" is making his life increasingly unbearable. The question of getting over this perfectionism is discussed.

The following example is taken from a group session led by George Bach and reported in his *Intensive Group Psychotherapy*.

The occasion was the departure of the mother of one of the woman members of the group. Her hostile attitude toward her mother with a simultaneous guilt feeling with regard to her departure led to a discussion about the attitudes of the various other group members toward their mothers. (F. are female participants, M. are masculine ones; Th. is the therapist.)

H-F: I can't understand E.-F.

B-M: What can't you understand?

G-M: That she's upset by her mother?

H-F: That she doesn't want her mother with her.

E-F: I think that's why H-F can't ever understand . . .

H-F: That you don't want her with you?

E-F: She thinks this is a horrible rejection of her mother.

Th: If you had your mother alive, would you want her with you?

H-F: Yes.

E-F: She would not be with you. You have your sister, but you don't want her. It's a comparable situation.

Th: H-F's attitude interests you quite a bit?

E-F: Yes, it interests me intensely.

Th: What within yourself?

E-F: She and I have exactly the same problem. And I have the same solution to it, my mother's solution. And there's nothing I can do about it.

G-M: Why don't you want your mother with you?

E-F: Well, I don't get along well with her.

G-M: What exactly don't you like?

E-F: Well, she tries to tell me what to do.

A-M: Well, that's the same situation I'm in, and the situation anybody
who has a mother close by is in. They never wean themselves from us!

In the working through of acute or chronic problems, the members of
a group help one another to a better self-understanding, to better solutions, or at least to more relieved feelings about their worries.

Group Therapy Session

In some cases, groups may be critical of a person who tries to set himself up in a special way. The following is an example of how a group
helped a girl accept her role in reality.

Ned: Before we get into anything else, I'd like to ask Josie something.
You know, every week, *every single* week, Josie comes in after all the
rest of us are seated here waiting for you, Dr. Bühler. She's never
really late, but just late enough to "make an entrance," you might say.
I was just wondering if Josie has any idea why she does this so consistently.

Josie: Well, I think you're blowing up something very insignificant. Monday nights, Monday night is my only night in town and I have dinner
with a couple of friends. They don't get off work until 6:30 so we don't
have much time to eat. I hate to just rush away and . . .

Margaret: But isn't your first responsibility here . . . I mean, why can't
you leave just a couple minutes earlier each time?

Ned: Yes, it's the consistency that made me aware of what you were
doing . . .

Josie: What do you mean, "what I was doing"?

Ned: All right, let me be perfectly frank, if you're going to spar with me,
don't you "plan" that entrance as a way of getting attention, of setting
yourself up as apart from the rest of us?

Josie: That's absolutely ridiculous. It's purely coincidental. If I'm apart
from the group, it's because of the group, not me. I've tried ever since
I came here to feel that I belonged. I'm not doing the rejecting, you are.

Betty Jean: Who . . . specifically . . . how do we reject you?

Josie: Well, just by being exclusive. I mean, you don't really want to hear about me, I represent some indefinable . . . some weird misfit-type or something, I don't know. You just set me apart.

Betty Jean: But you started that, Josie, from the first minute you talked to us—the story you told, of always having older or younger friends, of . . .

Josie: Yes, that was the reason Dr. Buhler put me in this group, so that I would be with my peers, because all my life I've been "pushed ahead."

Ned: But you don't really feel we're "peers," do you? Don't you consider yourself intellectually superior to anyone here and . . . more important, uniquely better by virtue of the fact you're a writer, a "creative artist"? *Pause*.

Margaret: You know you do, Josie. How many times, for instance, have you mentioned that the only thing you were ever certain of in childhood and adolescence was your intellectual "status" at school? And you even mentioned having a "genius I.Q." You've let us know more than once that you're better than any of us and it really bothers me.

Josie: Of course, I mentioned those things, they were part of my past, and so, part of the person I am today. But if you had listened, you would have heard me say that the intelligence didn't make me feel superior. Other things were more important. That's what I mean, you didn't really want me to . . . want to know about me. All I did was state some facts.

Ned: Facts which produce in you certain *feelings* . . .

Josie: In the midst of your attack, Ned, you might consider that you've always felt in competition with me . . . I think that leads you to misinterpret a great deal of what I say. And I think you resent the fact that I don't feel hostility toward you.

Ned: You certainly *sound* hostile.

Josie: That's not directed against you personally . . . not at all. It's just this . . . situation, of not having any of you understand who I *am*, of . . . If you listened, you would know I feel *in*ferior, not *su*perior.

Dr. B.: You can feel *both*, you know, Josie.

Josie: Well, I *don't*, not superior . . .

Dr. B.: Not in any area? Haven't you always felt you loved harder, felt more than others, were more . . . sensitive? *Pause*.

Margaret: Oh, come on, Josie, you've said so in almost those precise words.

Josie: I've only said I had experienced more at a younger age and that . . . that . . .

Ned: That you felt those experiences more deeply. Don't you believe that?

Josie: Aren't you projecting again?

Margaret: If you could hear yourself, Josie, your whole tone has changed. You're protecting yourself with defensiveness—why not just admit what you feel? You won't be punished for it.

Josie: (*Laughs.*) Won't I? Your Catholic sense of sin is so blatant that you'd pounce on me with an "I told you so" the minute it was out of my mouth.

Margaret: Try me.

Pause.

Dr. B.: I'm wondering how the rest of you feel about this? Mike, Jenny, Alex?

Alex: I don't feel I've been here long enough to really know Josie, but from what I've seen I don't think you're right, at least not altogether. She's more . . . she seems to reach out more than any of the rest . . . she's been warmer to *me*. But then sometimes I wonder . . . oh, I suppose that's silly . . .

Dr. B.: What, Alex?

Alex: Well, I . . . a couple of times it's occurred to me that Josie believes that she *should* care for anybody . . . yes, that's it, that any . . . well, *anybody* deserves to be cared for . . . shown attention . . .

Ned: She thinks that, all right.

Josie: How do *you* know what I think? What gives you the right to put words into my mouth?

Margaret: *Who's* being hostile? You won't admit to anything that puts you in a bad light. You can't drop your phony image even for a minute.

Josie: If you can even slam my interest in people . . . you really don't know me at all, not at all.

Ned: Nobody likes *every*body, Josie. And there's nothing wrong with that. Isn't your desire to identify with everyone, especially those of the empty-shell variety, another indication to the world that you're *more* feeling, *more* "with it"? Or maybe even a symbol of your own desire to be cared for, I don't know . . . But just look at the facts of your life now . . . it's organized to express sensitivity . . . you take great pride in acting out the hermit life of the writer-artist, holed up alone with wine and a typewriter . . . the essence of Romanticism . . . And the drinking itself, do you really like it, or isn't that another way of proving how different you are and securing a license to escape . . . you talk so much about drinking to excess, for example. Aren't you trying, in every possible way, to cast a bright spot on *you,* on *your* life, the only focus on an otherwise . . . empty stage?

Josie: My drinking? That's another *fact*. I told you about it because we're supposed to be honest . . . to share things as they happen. Why would I be proud of it?

Betty Jean: Excuse me, Josie, but you've told us about it quite frequently. We *know* about it, so what are you reinforcing? I think Ned has something.

Josie: You're all twisting things . . . You're, well, the "hermit writer" thing, for example . . . the artist *is* alone—in this capitalistic society, a poem is worth nothing on the open market. He has to compromise in order to survive even on the most basic subsistence level. He isn't a part . . .

Pause.

Dr. B.: This could lead us into an extensive discussion, but, one point, is it the artist who is alone, Josie, or man in society . . . just the very fact of one man struggling with the human condition . . .

Josie: I didn't say others *weren't* alone, I only said . . .

Ned: That's true, Josie. You didn't say . . . anything about the *others,* but you did and do glorify, worship your own singularity, whenever, wherever you can find it. You don't let yourself be one of us . . . we're all in the shabby position of the late twenties . . .

Josie: Oh, drop the cute phrase-making.

Ned: Well, we're not settled yet, we're in a transition between . . . ideals and reality. *You* say, "I'll never accept reality and that makes me different." You haven't been willing to compromise . . . and you want to be rewarded with adulation for "hanging on."

Josie: An artistic person probably has his greatest development in that transition period . . . he . . .

Ned: An "artistic person"? And what is that? Is that *you*? I am sick, really sick of your sensitive artist pose, and I am sick of your denying that you have that pose. You have gotten succulence and sustenance from it, financially and emotionally, ever since you were a kid, out of being a special person. What on *earth* gives you the right to set yourself apart . . .

Josie: I don't make that distinction at all. But, as far as *I* go, I don't care to spend my life in coffeeklatches after the kids go to nursery school . . . talking over "the pill" or the PTA fun-fest or some grocery-store sale on canned goods.

Margaret: Those things aren't *valuable,* right? Their *little* problems of those people don't measure up to *your* big ones.

Josie: They allow themselves to get involved in, to magnify the mundane because they're bored, because every day is a routine . . . They want to give their lives more essence, so they drag out a one-sentence fact to a fifteen-minute deliberation.

Dr. B.: But, Josie, you didn't really answer Margaret. Or have you answered her? Do you really think their problems are trivial compared to yours?

Josie: No . . . mine are just *different,* that's all.

Betty Jean: And if your problems are different, then you too are different, isn't that so?

Pause.

Dr. B.: Josie, if you *do* feel this way, can you tell us about it . . . can you remember when it started?

Pause.

Josie: From the very beginning, I was . . . well, I was raised with adults . . . being the only child and . . . at school, I was pushed ahead two grades right away so . . . But you *know* these things . . . and you can see it was done *to* me . . . Then, there were years when the other kids were playing dolls or something and I . . . I just preferred to stay in my bedroom and read books . . .

Betty Jean: Why?

Josie: Because the people in the books were . . . Oh, I don't know.

Ned: Special, dramatic? . . . Like you felt yourself to be?

Josie: Well, yes, they were more like me.

Dr. B.: People from another world, Josie?

Josie: Well, I wanted to, I *had* to believe there was a better world. This one is so . . . people are hypocrites, they are not trustworthy. They keep checking to see if their wallets are still in their pockets. It's all . . . *twisted.*

Betty Jean: And so from the books and dreams you created a "better world" . . . the fantasy life you've talked about? So you *did* isolate yourself?

Josie: I *was* isolated, I don't see that I *did* it.

Pause.

Jenny: I haven't said anything previously because it's very difficult for me to challenge Josie in any way. I suppose, well, in a sense, I'd like to be like her . . . to be creative, you know . . . and . . .

Dr. B.: Aren't you confusing being "creative" with being an "artist," Jenny? Maybe you too are glorifying.

Jenny: Well, you don't deny that Josie is creative, do you?

Dr. B.: No, but I believe that you too are creative, in your own unique way—the sewing, for instance, of most of your wardrobe. I think this may be what we're all driving at here . . . that Josie puts a greater value on being the "unique artist" than just being unique by virtue of her being human.

Ned: Yes, yes, we're *all* unique, but, in some sense, that struggle you were talking about, we're all in it . . . fighting it in whatever way fits our individual personalities . . .

Dr. B.: You wanted to say something, Mike?

Mike: Well, I don't quite know how to say . . . I mean, I've always known that Josie thought of me as a . . . well, an "ordinary person."

Margaret: She's thought of all of us that way, Mike, and I've resented her from the first minute because of it.

Ned: And she projects her attitude toward us into a situation where "*we* deny *her.*"

Betty Jean: The best, the very best we can do, Josie, is to accept you for yourself, without requiring you to present your "sensitive writer's badge." That just isn't the most important thing here. Why are you looking at your feet? Just look at us, do you really read rejection in our faces?

Pause.

Margaret: Well, Josie?

Josie: I . . . I guess . . . you seem interested.

Ned: "Guess . . . seem." Can't you use more definite words? Or are you afraid to commit yourself to us?

Pause.

Jenny: I like you very much, Josie, especially in those few moments you've allowed me to really see you . . . without the *labels* you use so often. You don't need them, I wish you knew that. What are you laughing at?

Josie: It just occurred to me that this was pretty ironic, that all of you won't *let* me pull away . . . I guess, well you must care. I can't help but see that, because you're refusing to let me withdraw and almost commanding me to stay here with you.

Dr. B.: I don't think it's a "command," Josie. They are trying to help you away from your fantasy life into reality.

Josie: You're *right* . . . I never saw myself as being a part of reality . . . and everyone else *was*. But I *am here*, sitting in a circle, making up part of that circle. Yes, *I am here.*

Many therapists have *continuing* groups that go on for years; those who have completed their therapy drop out, and new members are accepted in their place. Sometimes a group is begun exclusively with new participants. In some instances there is often restraint or hesitancy at the beginning, and the skillful therapist, through interpretations, will allude to anxieties of the members for the benefit of the process. A good example is given by Raymond Corsini in *Methods of Group Psychotherapy.*

At the beginning, the therapist explains the goal of group therapy and how it works. Then he calls on the group, consisting of three women and three men, to begin the discussion.

T.: Well, who will begin?

A.: I guess no one wants to start.

T.: Of course, it is difficult to begin. I am sure all of you feel, "I hope somebody else begins." This may be our first lesson; that we are all alike in being afraid of a new situation. The fact that you, Mr. A., spoke first is probably no accident. What do you think it may mean?

A.: I am a somewhat impulsive person, and it is typical of me that I take the initiative. As a matter of fact, this is a problem for me. I want to learn to allow others to have their way as I tend to be too bossy, too impulsive. If I can learn greater control from this group I will appreciate it. I think people resent my being so aggressive.

X.: However, it seems to me that you did react appropriately. No one wanted to say anything, and the fact that you spoke up made me feel better. At least you broke the ice.

A.: But an icebreaker suffers a lot of damage, and sometimes he gets stuck in the ice.

The therapist's remark is so worded that one of the participants immediately gets an opportunity for self-observation. This, of course is only one of the techniques the therapist can choose. In this case we are dealing with a very *active* therapist.

Up to this point, only the *discussion form* of group therapy has been mentioned. *Psychodrama* is a second form; it is interwoven into the discussion by some therapists, and others use it as the sole method.

Psychodrama, also called "role playing," consists of having group members play certain scenes in which they act out their problems. J. Moreno, who introduced the form, built his own theater in New York for psychodrama therapy. He uses assistants whom he calls "alter egos" (the other "I") and who are trained to bring out hidden facets of the patients' egos. Experience shows that the emotions are more strongly aroused in these role-playings than in mere discussion and that things become clear which were earlier not clear to anyone.

For example, in one of the author's groups, a young man complained of rejection by girls who had dated him once or twice. When the scenes were acted out in the group, the reason became clear: he never bothered himself with the girl's preferences; he himself decided on everything that they were to do, where they were to eat, and so on.

Psychodrama is particularly well adapted to *children and adolescents,* whose treatment in groups has proved extremely successful.

Dr. Zelda Wolpe, an experienced child psychologist, kindly provided the following dramatic scene enacted by a group between twelve and sixteen years of age.

Serena, one of the oldest members of the group, spoke of the way in which her father often makes her unhappy. She states she loves her father and considers him a fine man, but when he comes home from the office in a bad mood and lets out his frustrations on the family then she does not love him.

Th.: Suppose we act out the scene. Serena will play herself, Joan the mother, Bruce the father. (The three withdraw for a moment to discuss the scene.)

"Father": Serena, you left the paper lying on the grass. That doesn't look good, right there in front of the house. If I see that once more, I'll be very angry. Perhaps you think that too much is expected of you?

Serena: Well, that's another of your friendly remarks. I too like to have things look nice, and I don't think too much is expected of me. Why do you always have to say such unpleasant things? — And then he throws the paper in my face. — That's the way it always is, I tell you, I can't even talk to you.

"Father": Be quiet!

Serena: I can never say a thing. It's as if I were nothing at all.

"Mother": Really, Greg, you shouldn't come home and let out your anger on your daughter.

Serena: Well then I start to cry and go off to my own room . . . I cry about how helpless I am against such tyranny.

Chrissie: That's just the way my father is, except that he doesn't throw things in my face. He makes fun of me, and he gets sarcastic. Sometimes I could kill him!

Serena: I yell: "I hate you." And yet I understand why he behaves the way he does—just at the moment he's got a lot of problems.

Group therapy was originally recommended because it makes the participation in therapy economically easier for a large number of people. Quite apart from economic considerations, however, group therapy is of irreplaceable value. The method is spreading in various areas. It is used in marriage and family counseling, for employees and management, in hospitals, prisons, and other institutions. In the United States today, some 20,000 patients participate in therapy groups and 1,500 group therapists belong to professional organizations. The movement is also international, with proponents in the most diverse psychological schools.

CHAPTER 12

BUSINESS PSYCHOLOGY

Industrial Psychology

In the beginning, technology won such strong support that it was believed it could solve all economic, social, and human problems.

Early in this century, the psychology applied in industry was mainly psychotechnology. The theory and practice of that period were heavily influenced by a movement known as "Taylorism," named for the American engineer Frederick W. Taylor, or as "Scientific Management." Its objective was the analysis of jobs into their components, and the discovery of sequences of actions that workers should follow in order to attain the best possible, most efficient performance. Taylor, whose principal publications appeared in 1903 and 1911, failed to take into account the complexity of the social aspects of man's work. Performance and the satisfactions resulting from it were seen by him without full consideration of basic human motives.

The social problems of industrialization were for a long time regarded as questions of social-political welfare and benevolence. Only gradually did people come to realize that the relations of the worker with his co-workers and the management of the plant in which he works are extremely important. The findings of the well-known Hawthorne studies made at the Western Electric Company in Chicago were interpreted by Elton Mayo, Roethlisberger, and others. They showed that the most decisive factor for good work behavior is the *interpersonal* relationships in "formal" and, even more, in "informal" groups. Whereas man's ability to perform has grown steadily for 200 years, Mayo found that the capacity for working together diminished during the same period.

313

These and other researches drew the attention of psychologists to the *plant's social structure,* in which the most important factors are the work group and plant management.

Small, *informal work groups* represent "human islands" in the formal structure of any industrial plant. The Hawthorne studies and subsequent investigations showed that the informal work group has great influence on work morale, productivity, and individual satisfaction. Behavior norms and work practices also depend on the type and degree of cooperation in these groups.

The observations originally based on industrial plants are today recognized as equally valid for offices.

Work groups are an important but not the only factor of value for favorable working conditions. The influence of the management of a plant is important, and the *leadership* given is of great consequence.

Some historians have suggested that in early days "spontaneous cooperation" was sufficient to meet the demands of industrial organization. Today *management* has taken its place. Koontz and O'Donnell list the responsibilities of management as organization, staffing, direction, planning, and control.

In the personnel organization, as well as in work groups, there are various types of *leaders.* In experiments, comparisons were made between "democratic" and "work-oriented" leaders, and "authoritarian" and "production-oriented" leaders. The first-named were found to be more successful. Particularly satisfactory was the management method called "joint leadership," in which the workers are given the right to participate.

In the development of management in this country, special consideration is given to personal relationships between executives and workers. Many plant managers are trained in *social sensitivity* through psychology courses. In these, often in the form of psychodrama, the effect of a manager's personality is studied and the results are analyzed so that the most effective type of leadership can be shown in practice.

Work psychology strives to introduce better working conditions and working methods as well as to help the individual choose a vocation that will be satisfying.

Comprehensive studies in work psychology investigate the working conditions, the work location, climate, a person's suitability for the job, choice of vocation, vocational training, and other factors.

What do these extensive researches mean to modern man? Today's business psychology sees and studies work in two main aspects: its meaning for the individual's *personal development* and for his *social role.* Increasing knowledge allows us to do greater justice to individual enthusiasm for work. We are better able to judge capacities for certain activities and what the best conditions are for them, and we can evaluate the factors of social satisfaction as well as of social pressure. The increasing use of clinical psychology to resolve the problems and conflicts of working individuals and groups constitutes further progress. Thus, with the continuing development of industrial psychology, we can hope that work will be made into a positive experience and a constructive life factor for the dissatisfied masses.

Vocational Personality Imprinting in the Business World

Among the most interesting psychological studies are those on the subject of personality structuring or "imprinting" in which an individual's reactions to occupational activity are studied.

The concept of *imprinting* has already been mentioned (p. 14) in connection with the subject of human development. H. Thoma regards imprinting primarily as a natural learning process by which the individual gradually settles down to certain modes of behavior.

In *vocational studies* it has been shown that persons at work—including those who work in industrial organizations and management, as well as those who work creatively on their own—are imprinted or significantly influenced by the conditions and demands of their jobs. The need for investigations in this field was recognized when the problem of the *factory worker* arose. The monotony of much of his work and his apparent unimportance in the overall production process were regarded as giving rise to conditions of chronic dissatisfaction and alienation.

While in American industry even factory jobs vary significantly in challenging the worker's creative capacities, one may consider Chris Argyris' observation to the effect that often the worker has little control over his work environment, and that his opportunities for planning his future may be limited by lack of relevant information. Argyris explains that these circumstances may hinder the development of personality in such a way as to lead to varying degrees of passivity and short time-perspective—all of which are characteristics of immaturity.

Mention has already been made of the various programs in modern plants that attempt to combat these factors by encouraging meetings of small informal groups and participation in plant management. Some research workers regard the capable foreman as the most important factor to the worker on the assembly line under the speed-up system. By establishing a rapport with his men, he can change an anonymous and impersonal work situation into an individual one.

Nevertheless, factory work hinders rather than furthers the personality development of the individual.

Bureaucratic organizations were studied by Robert K. Merton and also by Arthur K. Davis with regard to the way they influence the personality development of workers. Merton emphasizes how pressure that aims at methodical, disciplined, politically cautious behavior stamps its impression on certain personalities and creates *bureaucrats*. The obeying of rules, says Merton, that were originally set up to ensure reliability, discretion, and the like gradually becomes an end in itself. Added to this is a certain depersonalization.

In the case of the *executive,* whose vocational life Davis describes, the extreme formality of his business relationships makes him stiff and impersonal even in social life. Davis cites the imprinting effect that the strict protocol of naval life has on the naval officer.

Many studies are concerned with the personality structure of *top executives.* The image of the young executive striving upward from division head to department head fascinates many people. In a study on cultural values, Donald A. Bloch expounds the idea of the sympathetic, self-controlled, moderate personality of the successful junior executive as the ideal for the American middle class. In many instances, he says, it seems also to be the ideal that therapists envisage for their patients.

Other investigations show the pressure under which a top executive has to function. William E. Henry discusses the demands he has to meet: he has to live according to the norms of the executive world and belong to the right clubs, political party, and other groups; he has to be continually industrious, for he lives in fear of being surpassed or pushed aside; he may not make mistakes, and can never know complete security.

A study by William F. Whyte on the personality structure in a *service job,* namely that of a waitress, seems of special interest. Whyte's work is part of an extensive investigation of the hotel industry from the point of view of industrial psychology.

In this vocational category the main requisite is compliance to the requests of the customers, without any possibility of refusal. The pressure can be exceptionally great.

In an interview with Whyte one waitress said: "The worst thing is when the guests are unpleasant and you can't defend yourself and say what you think. You've got to swallow everything. That's what makes the work so nerve-wracking. It would be much easier for us if we could give them an answer."

Another said: "I could have screamed, but since I couldn't do that, I ran out of the room and burst into tears."

Whyte concluded that the quantity of tears shed is in direct relation to the length of time the waitress has had experience in her work. To have to swallow insults, not to receive the praise one had hoped for, and not to be able to defend oneself against unjust criticism all make this job a psychologically difficult one. The waitress must have great self-control, inner equilibrium, and self-confidence.

Further investigations are devoted to the personality structure of the physician, the trained nurse, the telephone operator, the railroad worker, and others. These studies mark the beginning of a *new kind of understanding of personality*. The new method, a clinically oriented interview technique, enables a deeper penetration than was possible under former methods of observation.

Producer and Consumer in Market Psychology

The science of market psychology originally served to find out how buyers behave, mainly in the interests of the businessman who wanted to sell his products. Today, as Paul Lazarsfeld, one of the first market psychologists, states, *market psychology* is a part of sociology.

Lazarsfeld goes back to Max Weber in his theoretical discussion of buying and selling as systematized interactions. Weber examined the "market situation" and its regulation from the viewpoint of sociology. The market is a situation of buying and selling. There is an *exchange* of goods, in which each participant gives something and gets something. The acquisition of *property* of some sort is the goal of these activities.

Ideally, the giving and acquiring consists of the exchange of equivalent property. The buyer needs the goods; the seller needs the money. The transaction represents an advantage for both, for they increase their possessions. However, it represents a loss for one party if the other, over and above *honest* profit, makes an excessive gain.

As Max Weber shows with his analysis of capitalism, a gain that exceeds a recognized profit margin represents an exploitation of one's partner in the marketing process.

Along with actual exploitation, many people desire to gain an *advantage*. On this principle of apparent advantage for the buyer rests the tremendous success of sales "at reduced prices" and of stores that give trading stamps.

In the author's opinion, this desire for gaining an advantage encourages trade, but the commercialism of the process is frowned upon by many sociologists and accounts for their lack of interest in working in market psychology.

The early market researches were carried out to determine advantages to the seller. In one investigation of the shoe business it was found how favorable it was for the seller to take off the customer's shoes as soon as the customer sat down, thereby "landing" him.

For many people, modern *advertising* is very irritating. The consumer feels himself helpless in the face of it. Even when he tries to ignore advertising, it pressures him and makes him prey to the "hidden persuaders." Surrounded on every side by advertising, the consumer often feels as though he were the victim of a conspiracy. He frequently cannot resist buying some new product that has been sophisticatedly recommended.

"And that is how we know that we are right," says Martin Mayer, as the introductory remark to his amusing, informative, somewhat frightening book, *Madison Avenue, USA.* Mayer discusses advertising that is unfailingly effective. However, it must be admitted that today the techniques of advertising are much more geared to success by pointing out the *legitimate advantages* of a product.

"What's new in Colgate's? What's missing—missing—missing in every other toothpaste?" This advertisement, which caused Colgate to triple its sales, prompted Rosser Reeves, the head of the advertising agency that had accomplished this success for Colgate, to make the following remarks.

"First," says Reeves, "we have a good product. We can sell a product only if it is good, and even then we use a unique USP."

His advertising follows the principle of the "unique selling proposition" (USP). There are three rules for this: a unique quality must be pointed out; a specific gain or value must be promised; and the product must be of superior quality.

Reeves reports that the slogan "Comes out like a ribbon, lies flat on your brush" was not successful because nobody cared if the toothpaste lay flat. But when the slogan became "Colgate cleans your breath while it cleans your teeth," consumption rose enormously.

Actually, he says, every good toothpaste combines these two advantages, but up to that time no firm had used the point in its advertising.

This story demonstrates an important, positive function of good advertising: it informs the public about qualities of which they were ignorant and advises them of new products.

But, as the economist Wesley Clair Mitchell noted more than fifty years ago, "No one can be expected to possess expert knowledge of the qualities and prices of such varied wares . . . The single family can no more secure the advantages of such division of labor in caring for its wants as consumers than the frontier family could develop division of labor in production."

People experience different feelings in their role of consumer. To women, the role of shopper is compatible with their feminine role, especially where purchases of groceries and household goods are concerned. The male shopper, on the other hand, may feel ill at ease in shopping for foodstuffs, while the purchaser of an automobile fits in more readily with his concept of the male role.

Advertisements may, as in the Colgate example just cited, call attention to the *usefulness* of an article or they may emphasize the pleasure it gives. They may point out how *everybody* is interested in the product, or they may flatter the buyer by implying he is exceptionally bright.

Voting in Politics and Business

In a study made in 1948 by Lazarsfeld, Berelson, and Gaudet, the voting pattern of a district of Ohio was analyzed, psychologically. The investigators studied the *reasons* why people make their choice and the *influences* that affect the election. It was the election of 1940, in which Franklin D. Roosevelt, the Democratic candidate, and Wendell Willkie, the Republican candidate, were the opponents. Socioeconomic, ideological, and personal factors were the three aspects involved in the study.

The social and economic nature were shown by the fact that certain social groups and certain income groups rallied to one or the other party. The majority of the well-to-do, who had business interests and who belonged to the upper vocational groups, were Republicans; most of the poor and those in the lower job categories voted Democratic. For reasons that Lazarsfeld regards as partly conditioned locally, the majority of Catholics voted Democratic, while Protestants were more inclined to vote Republican. The young members of both religious groups were less apt to vote Republican than the older ones.

As Lazarsfeld says, young people are inclined toward progressive democratic ideology. This means that age plays a part in the party choice.

The ideological difference in party preference is shown by the fact that the Democratic voters emphasized that they wanted a President with experience in government and the Republicans wanted a President with experience in the business world.

If these results are interpreted further, it becomes evident that *progressive ideas* are more favored by those who have not yet "arrived," unless their social and economic situation is such that their economic future is assured. Those who have arrived are usually *conservative*.

One of the most interesting findings of Lazarsfeld and his co-workers is that the public is *notably little influenced by electioneering propaganda*. The majority of the electorate have already made up their minds for whom they will vote. They use campaign propaganda primarily to strengthen their own arguments.

This seems to be the case whenever people have preconceived opinions. In a book on the effects of mass communication, Joseph T. Klapper comes to the conclusion that *changes of opinion* occur under two conditions: when a new subject is introduced and the person who offers it does not encounter preconceived opinions and when a viewpoint is offered by someone known *personally* to the voter.

The second point was one of the main discoveries of Lazarsfeld's study. Personal influence was often of great importance among those who were not a part of any existing group and who were still undecided. In this connection friends and relatives were frequently mentioned. Often they belonged to a circle in which some *opinion holder* was at work. Through these, there is what Lazarsfeld calls the "two-step movement" of communications: the opinion holder disseminates certain information from newspapers, magazines, radio, and the like and then announces his opinion to his circle.

Here small groups prove to be as influential as those among workers in plants and factories. An opinion may be formed by personal contact in the small group without any leader appearing: "Some of the men in the factory said . . ." or "In the office my husband heard them talking . . ." or a waitress says, "Lots of the guests were against Willkie."

Family groups are very important. A woman says: "I was always a Democrat, and I think Roosevelt was good. But my whole family is for Willkie. They say he would make the best President, and they put so much pressure on me that finally I did vote for Willkie." And a young man declared, "My grandfather would skin me alive if I didn't vote for Roosevelt."

These studies show that, in political elections, people are influenced by their group. Even those who vote independently are unconsciously subject to the influences of certain groups.

In political activity that is understandable because of the complexity of these matters. It is almost impossible for the individual to form an opinion of his own. He has got to rely on those whose judgment he values.

But what influences a consumer's choice when a purchase has to be made?

For the past thirty years the procedure of *buying* has been the subject of psychological studies. Paul Lazarsfeld recently published a study that provided fascinating details. However, the standards by which buyers choose one or another item are only partly understood and are much more complicated than one would expect.

Here, too, however, group influences make themselves felt. These processes were mentioned in Chapter 7 in connection with fashion. Here the tyranny of those groups who prescribe the current vogue is enormous.

Taste is generally influenced by groups, for example, the taste for certain styles in art, music, books and plays; for certain brands of cars, of food and drink, for certain types of houses and furnishings; for the kind of life one leads, the things that one wants to own, the look that one wants to achieve.

We are still living in the age of "gentlemen prefer blondes but they marry brunettes." The looks of women follow different ideal concepts according to cultures and subcultures. These in their turn affect choices in business. In the last analysis, the psychological interpretation of choices in business, like business activity in general, brings us back once more to questions of cultural psychology and basic motivations of human beings.

CHAPTER 13

PSYCHOLOGY AND PHILOSOPHY OF LIFE

The basic thesis of this book has been that modern psychology can be of great help in people's lives. Now, in a final comprehensive review, let us inquire how psychology can provide us with insight deeper than the mere recognition of life's blows and joys.

First, some limitations have to be set. Psychology and philosophy are naturally not the same, and psychologists do not feel it their role to suggest a philosophy of life to all mankind. All they can do is direct attention to those findings of modern psychology from which certain benefits can be drawn and orient man toward a better life.

To clarify these concepts briefly, a *philosophy of life* may be defined as an integrated system of *guidelines* for man's practical life. *Weltanschauung* is a philosophy that attempts to explain the happenings in the universe and their possible meaning and purpose.

Throughout the centuries *religions and philosophies* have been concerned with the meaning of life and have set up various tenets and dogmas as a basis for understanding the universe and have made use of cosmological concepts to provide basic principles for human activities.

The majority of people believe in a specific religion and accept its teachings regarding creation and the order of the universe. Others try to develop theories that seem compatible with scientific data. Still others hold the view that we should not attempt to understand the universe. They reason that we are unable to cope with this task with the mental tools at our disposal.

As a result of these unresolved questions a large number of people believe that ethical behavior is more relevant than religious dogmas and philosophical theories.

Immanuel Kant offers the premise that "common sense" has to be distinguished from knowledge, a point of view attracting more and more adherents.

Widely read and many times reprinted is the speech made by the famous physicist and Nobel Prize winner Max Planck, *Physics in the Battle for Weltanschauung.* Like Kant 200 years earlier, Planck reached the conclusion that guidelines for human action cannot be arrived at scientifically but that "purity of heart and good will" assure the pursuit of the right path.

Perhaps pure motives and good will do bring about subjective assurance. But unfortunately, psychology, psychiatry, and sociology have shown that pure motives and good will alone are not sufficient to bring about an adequate improvement in human existence. Besides honesty and good intentions *knowledge* and *insight* are essential to show us *how* good will can be translated into truly *constructive activity.*

In *The Trend of Human Development,* Ashley Montagu points out that, in order to know *for what* man was born, he must first know *as what* he was born.

That is precisely the purpose of this book. All the knowledge and insight at our disposal in modern psychology have been presented so that we may derive from them possible guidelines for *constructive behavior,* that is, the most beneficial paths for the well-being and fulfillment of the individual.

Just what have we learned that we can use constructively to achieve fulfillment?

What is most important is that the *goal* should be clear. The people who come closest to fulfillment are those who find *self-realization in creative dedication* to others. In the life of Anna Sethne, presented in the first section of this book, we saw life fulfillment developing before our eyes. "Every day is wonderful because of my work, only no day is long enough. I have been a happy woman," said Anna Sethne toward the end of her long, successful life.

Fulfillment is obviously not attained without difficulties and struggles. We are faced with the task of repeatedly controlling impulses that pull in various directions. In repeatedly renewed efforts we must choose between need satisfaction, self-limiting adaptation, creative expansion, and maintenance of inner order. The balancing of these tendencies has to be maintained by strong self-discipline.

To achieve self-realization in creative dedication, we need to *release our best potentialities.* Here we are partly dependent on our inherited qualities and partly on our environment, both of which continually condition us. Under the pressure of all these influences we often lose our peace of mind and develop neurotic handicaps.

Especially damaging are certain early conditions such as lack of *love* and stern *discipline*. The tremendous importance of love, of communication between parents and children, and democratic principles in education have been demonstrated in modern psychology.

We have gained insight of great significance by our understanding of the social and cultural conditions of our time.

Peaceful co-existence among the various groups and peoples can be attained only by the understanding and worth of individuals.

This brings us to the last and most important point, the idea of a psychologically oriented educational system. The author's thought is primarily of group therapy, but it would perhaps be more realistic and beneficial to conduct clinically oriented group discussions in the upper grades of high schools under the direction of trained teachers. One could also try to introduce *encounter group-like* exchanges of feelings, as early as in the "sharing" classes of school beginners. In fact, experiments in these directions are already now being made in various places. They are also being extended to college students, teachers, and administrative groups. In some of this work, Carl Rogers has become a leader and instigator.

The greatest need is training in *methodical thinking*. Although we learn countless facts inside and outside school, we acquire little understanding. Fifty years after Freud introduced them, understanding and self-knowledge have still not been incorporated into practical methods of teaching. Our system of education at home and in school should include these studies so that the young will learn to think with insight about themselves, their fellows, and the world.

And now the final question: How can we attain the happiness for which we all strive?

Man can achieve *happiness,* says R. M. MacIver, an English philosopher of our time, if he is unselfish and forgets the search for it and looks outside himself—that is, creative dedication to others is the principal condition for life fulfillment. Everything else proves to be short-lived.

One last remark concerns *belief,* which has been repeatedly mentioned in connection with values.

In order for us to defend our standards and dedicate ourselves, we must believe in something. For the person with religious beliefs, this is no problem. The well-known biologist Julian Huxley says: "It is necessary to believe in something, for if we did not believe in anything, we would not act at all." Rollo May, a psychologist of our time who has studied this subject, says: "The degree of inner strength and integrity of an individual depends on how much he himself believes in the values by which he is guided."

To build up a thoughtful existence, a person needs deeper convictions than belief in specific values. He must, like Huxley, Montagu, MacIver, and many others, believe in working for the better psychological development of mankind.

For many people it is also necessary to believe in a universe permeated by a constructively creative, meaningful, and goal-directed force into which they can integrate themselves.

INDEX

164